The Photographic History of The Civil War

In Ten Volumes

THE CARTOON OF BRADY BY NAST

MANY CELEBRITIES OF THE CIVIL WAR PERIOD WERE CARICA-
TURED BY THOMAS NAST, DEAN OF AMERICAN CARTOONISTS. BRADY,
MAKER OF FASHIONABLE PORTRAITS, THEN PIONEER PHOTOGRAPHER
OF SOLDIERS AND ARMY LIFE, WAS FAIR GAME FOR NAST'S TELL-
ING YET KINDLY PENCIL AS THIS REPRODUCTION ILLUSTRATES.

JOHN C. BABCOCK
A SECRET SERVICE MAN FROM '61 TO '65
PHOTOGRAPHED IN 1862 WITH HIS FLEET HORSE "GIMLET"

"Avoid the camera" is the rule of the twentieth century secret-service man. But on that sunny day of October, 1862, the dashing young scout was guilty of no impropriety in standing for his portrait: direct "half-tone" reproductions were yet unknown, photography itself under the limits of its first pioneer years, and the photographer was Alexander Gardner, himself a trusted secret-service employee. It was correspondence about this very photograph which, forty-eight years later, brought the editors of the PHOTOGRAPHIC HISTORY into touch with Babcock himself. He had enlisted in the Sturges Rifle Corps, of Chicago, but was soon detailed to McClellan's secret service with Pinkerton. He remained after the latter left, did most of the scouting and news gathering under Burnside, and continued in the bureau, as reorganized by Colonel Sharpe, until the end of the war. No small part of his success was due to "my horse 'Gimlet,' that I rode in the Secret Service from 1861 to 1865." "Gimlet" looks an ideal mount for the man who had to be "the eyes of the army"—alert, nervous, eager to be off, bearing the news that would influence the fortunes and lives of thousands.

[4]

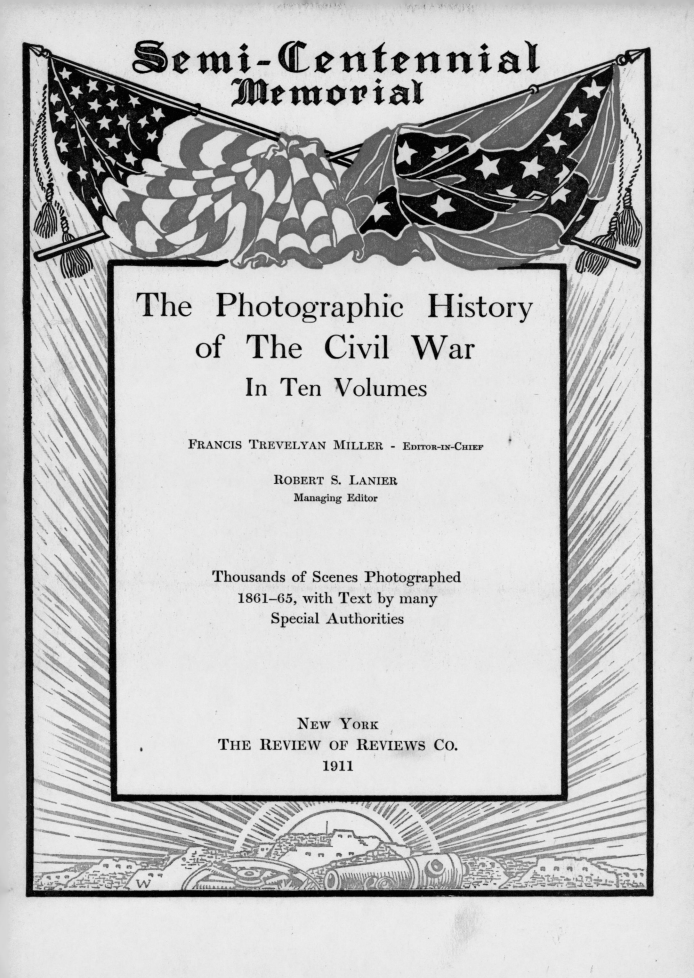

Semi-Centennial Memorial

The Photographic History of The Civil War
In Ten Volumes

FRANCIS TREVELYAN MILLER - EDITOR-IN-CHIEF

ROBERT S. LANIER
Managing Editor

Thousands of Scenes Photographed
1861–65, with Text by many
Special Authorities

NEW YORK
THE REVIEW OF REVIEWS CO.
1911

The Photographic History of The Civil War

In Ten Volumes

Volume Eight
Soldier Life
Secret Service

Contributors

CHARLES KING
Brigadier-General, U. S. V.

RANDOLPH H. McKIM
Army of Northern Virginia, C. S. A.

ALLEN C. REDWOOD
Army of Northern Virginia, C. S. A.

JOHN W. HEADLEY
Captain, C. S. A.

WILLIAM B. SHAW

A. W. GREELY
Major-General, U. S. A.

T. S. C. LOWE
Balloon Corps, Army of the Potomac

FENWICK Y. HEDLEY
Brevet-Captain, U. S. V.

L. R. STEGMAN
Late Colonel 102d New York, U. S. V.

GEORGE H. CASAMAJOR

ROY MASON

New York
The Review of Reviews Co.
1911

CONTENTS

Introduction

PAGE

THE TWO PRACTICAL PROBLEMS OF THE GENERAL 13
  Charles King

Part I—Soldier Life

THE BUSINESS SIDE OF WAR-MAKING 37
  William B. Shaw

MARSHALING THE FEDERAL VOLUNTEERS 57
  Charles King

GLIMPSES OF THE CONFEDERATE ARMY 105
  Randolph H. McKim

THE CONFEDERATE OF '61 137
  Allen C. Redwood

THE CONFEDERATE IN THE FIELD 155
  Allen C. Redwood

THE SCHOOL OF THE SOLDIER 179
  Fenwick Y. Hedley

BOYS WHO MADE GOOD SOLDIERS 189
  Charles King

MARCHES OF THE FEDERAL ARMIES 197
  Fenwick Y. Hedley

WITH THE VETERAN ARMIES 221
  Charles King

Part II—Military Information

THE SECRET SERVICE OF THE FEDERAL ARMIES 261
  George H. Casamajor

THE SECRET SERVICE OF THE CONFEDERACY 285
  John W. Headley

THE SIGNAL SERVICE 305
  A. W. Greely

[9]

Contents

PAGE

TELEGRAPHING FOR THE ARMIES 341
   A. W. Greely

BALLOONS WITH THE ARMY OF THE POTOMAC 369
   T. S. C. Lowe

PHOTOGRAPHIC DESCRIPTIONS THROUGHOUT THE VOLUME
   Roy Mason
   Louis R. Stegman

PREFACE

IN General King's " Introduction," the reader steps behind the scenes of warfare, where the machinery is found to be very different from the popular notion. It is soon plain that the most brilliant and profound calculations of strategy will amount to little unless there are leaders in the field with the faculty for gathering news and other military information against obstacles which might dumfound the ablest newspaper editor—coupled with the ability to distribute supplies and transport men on a scale more immense than the grandest engineering construction operations of the twentieth century. These two practical functions of the general are properly treated in one volume under the heads of " Secret Service " and " Soldier Life."

The obtaining of military information through scouts and spies is of little use unless there are available the clothing, food, and transportation whereby soldiers are made " fit." An understanding of these problems uncovers the human realities behind military phrases otherwise burdensome. How the grandest moves on the campaign chess-board can be thwarted by the blunder of a credulous scout, or the mud from a few days' rain, is made clear in General King's preface and the pages that follow.

THE STATES AND THEIR QUOTAS

As Illustrated and Described in This Volume

The index below refers the reader to pages of this volume upon which appear photographs showing representatives of every State engaged on either side in the Civil War, with some account of the volunteers in '61:

Union — *Pages*

California........102
Connecticut...... 62
Delaware........102
Illinois.........258, 259
Indiana 197, 281, 299
Iowa............251
Kansas.........102
Maine..........59
Massachusetts 63, 100, 101, 183
Michigan........71, 73, 75, 77, 255
Minnesota 79
Missouri........102
New Hampshire...102
New Jersey.......85
New York.......67, 69, 87, 89, 91, 93, 95, 97, 99, 179, 181, 183, 200, 203, 229, 233, 243, 257, 258, 259, 293
Ohio............249
Pennsylvania.....189, 224, 225

Union — *Pages*

Rhode Island.....60, 61
West Virginia....102
Wisconsin 248
Vermont.........64, 65
U. S. Regulars....222, 223

Confederate

Alabama 161
Arkansas........103
Florida..........103, 105, 106, 107, 156, 157, 159
Georgia.........139, 141, 145
Kentucky........103
Louisiana........119, 121, 125, 127, 143, 169
Maryland........103
Mississippi.......149, 151
North Carolina....103
South Carolina....115, 117, 131, 147, 153, 163, 167, 313
Tennessee........103, 171
Texas...........129
Virginia 109, 111, 113

The matter above referred to appears in this volume merely as illustrating the respective chapters. It is entirely independent of the extensive charts, tables, and statistics covering State activities, as well as those of the armies, corps, famous brigades and regiments, which will be found in the volume devoted to biography.

INTRODUCTION

THE TWO PRACTICAL PROBLEMS
OF THE GENERAL

READING THE DISTANT MESSAGE

AN OFFICER OF THE FEDERAL SIGNAL CORPS

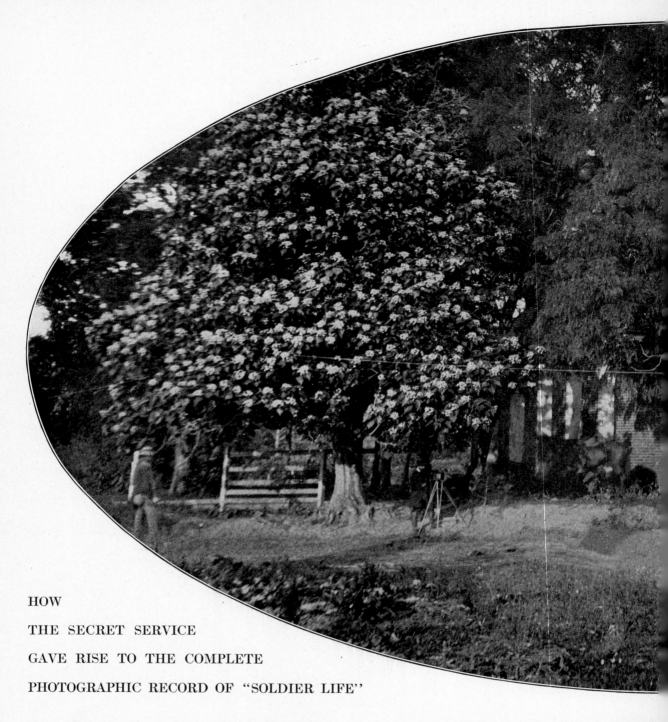

HOW
THE SECRET SERVICE
GAVE RISE TO THE COMPLETE
PHOTOGRAPHIC RECORD OF "SOLDIER LIFE"

It is quite astonishing to discover that the immense collection of photographs reflecting the "soldier life" of 1861–65 so intimately and vividly had its rise in secret-service work.   It is literally true, however, that Alexander Gardner's privileges of photographing at headquarters and within the Federal lines, at a thousand historic spots and moments, resulted entirely from the desire of the authorities to insure the strictest secrecy for their movements.   Obviously, any commander was pretty much at the mercy of the individual who copied the maps, charts, and the like for his secret service.   Through an untrustworthy or careless employee the most zealously guarded secrets of contemplated destinations or routes might reach the adversary.   The work of preparing these maps, therefore, was confided to Alexander Gardner, the brilliant Scotchman

[14]

PHOTOGRAPHER

AND SOLDIER, 1862,

AS THE ARMIES PAUSED

AFTER McCLELLAN'S ATTEMPT ON RICHMOND

brought to America and instructed in the photographic art by Brady himself. He proved so trustworthy that he was permitted in his spare time to indulge his hobby of photographing the soldiers themselves— a useless hobby it seemed then, since there was no way of reproducing the pictures direct on the printed page. But Gardner, first and last an artist, worked so patiently and indefatigably that, before the campaign was over, he had secured thousands of outdoor views which, with the many that Brady took in '61 and part of '62, and later in the path of Grant's final campaign from the Wilderness to Richmond, form the nucleus of the collection presented herewith. Needless to say, Gardner did not break faith with his employers or pass any of these photographs to Southern sympathizers, or through the Confederate lines.

MATTHEW B. BRADY UNDER FIRE IN THE WORKS BEFORE PETERSBURG

Shells were flying above the entrenchments before Petersburg at the time the photograph above was taken
—June 21, 1864—but so inured to this war-music have the veterans become that only one or two of them
to the right are squatting or lying down.   The calmness is shared even by Brady, the indomitable little
photographer.   He stands (at the left of the right-hand section above) quietly gazing from beneath the
brim of his straw hat—conspicuous among the dark forage caps and felts of the soldiers—in the same direction in which the officer is peering so eagerly through his field-glass.   Brady appears twice again in the

[Brady]

THREE OF THE "BRADY" PHOTOGRAPHS TAKEN IN GRANT'S LAST CAMPAIGN

two lower photographs of the same locality and time. "I knew Mr. Brady during that time," writes William A. Pinkerton, the son of Allan Pinkerton, who was in charge of the secret-service department throughout the war, "but had no intimate acquaintanceship with him, he being a man and I being a boy, but I recollect his face and build as vividly to-day as I did then: a slim build, a man, I should judge, about five feet seven inches tall, dark complexion, dark moustache, and dark hair inclined to curl; wore glasses, was quick and nervous. You can verify by me that I saw a number of these negatives made myself."

[Brady]

MILITARY INFORMATION AND SUPPLY

By Charles King

Brigadier-General, United States Volunteers

ONE of the gravest difficulties with which the Union generals had to contend throughout the war was that of obtaining reliable information as to the strength and position of the foe. Except for Lee's two invasions, Bragg's advance into Kentucky, and an occasional minor essay, such as Morgan's raids in Indiana, Kentucky, and Ohio, and Early's dash at Washington, in 1864, the seat of war was on Southern ground, where the populace was hostile, and the only inhabitants, as a rule, who would furnish information were deserters or else the so-called "intelligent contrabands," whose reports were in many cases utterly unreliable.

Renegade or "refugee" natives many a time came into the Northern lines cocked, primed, and paid to tell fabulous tales of the numbers and movements of the Southern armies, all to the end that the Union leaders were often utterly misled and bewildered. It may have been the fact that they were fooled once too often that made some of these generals so skeptical they would not believe their own officers, eye-witnesses to the presence of the foe in force, as when Jackson circled Pope and dashed upon his communications at Manassas; when Longstreet loomed up against his left at Second Bull Run, and when Jackson again circled Hooker and Howard and crushed the exposed right flank at Chancellorsville. Be that as it may, there is no doubt that from the very dawn of the war until its lurid and dramatic close, the Southern leaders had infinitely the advantage in the matter of information.

The Southern people were practically united, devoted to

SCOUTS AND GUIDES OF THE ARMY OF THE POTOMAC, 1862

The scouts and guides of the Army of the Potomac were attached to the secret-service department conducted by Major A. Pinkerton. It was more than difficult for the Union generals to obtain reliable information as to the strength and position of the enemy. The Southern people were practically united, devoted to their cause and all that it comprised. The only inhabitants, as a rule, who would furnish information were deserters or else the so-called "intelligent contrabands," whose reports were in many cases utterly untrustworthy. Therefore it became necessary for these men of indomitable courage to brave the halter in order to obtain information. During the campaign of the army in front of Fredericksburg, they proved of incalculable value. Each man was provided with a pass from the commanding general, written with a chemical preparation that became visible only when exposed to solar rays. On the back was penciled some unimportant memoranda, to deceive the adversaries, should the scout fall into their hands. If captured, he could drop this paper, apparently by accident, without exciting suspicion; and if successful in his expedition, the pass, after a moment's exposure to the heat, enabled the bearer to re-enter his own lines and proceed without delay to headquarters. The scouts generally passed as foragers within their own lines, always coming in with vegetables, poultry, and the like, to preserve their *incognito* their cause and all that it comprised. The North was filled with spies, special correspondents, paid agents, Southern sympathizers by the score, "copperheads" innumerable, and among the border States and in Louisiana and Mississippi, whither Union armies had penetrated in force, the blue lines enclosed hundreds of homesteads of Southern families whose men were with their regiments in Virginia or Tennessee, leaving the women and the faithful blacks, the household servants, to look after what was left of their once fertile and productive fields and the hospitable old mansions of their forefathers.

It followed that the South often knew pretty much everything worth knowing of the disposition and preparations of the Union forces—often, indeed, of their carefully guarded plans. It followed that, on the other hand, the Northern generals had as often to guess at the opposing conditions, since so very much of the information paid for proved utterly worthless.

With an overwhelming force at his back, well organized and equipped, better disciplined than were the Southern troops late in 1861, and their equal at least in experience, McClellan's splendid divisions, fully one hundred and forty thousand strong, were held up in front of Washington by not more than forty-seven thousand Confederates, all because agents induced the overcautious commander to believe he was confronted by fully two hundred thousand men. Again, on the Peninsula, when McClellan could have smashed through to Richmond by simple weight of numbers—such had been the casualties of battle in the Southern lines—the specter of Southern superiority in numbers unnerved the young leader, and the story of thousands of Southern reenforcements drove him to the change of base and the shelter of the gunboats on the James. A few weeks later and the same tactics told on Pope and his subordinates. "Old Jack" was at their heels or on their flanks, with sixty thousand men—"the flower of the Southern infantry," said prisoners who had ridden, apparently accidentally, into the Federal lines.

[20]

GUARDING
FEDERAL
ARMY SUPPLIES

AT
FORT FISHER
NORTH CAROLINA

AT   AT
NASHVILLE CITY POINT

European history abounds in illustrations of all that is scientific and systematic as clockwork in the logistics of warfare—all made possible because of their military roads.   But in the Civil War it was almost impossible to calculate with any great degree of certainty the movement of a single regiment for more than a few miles, much less the movement of a cumbrous wagon-train.   The way of the armies lay through seas of mud, through swamp, morass, and tangled wildwood, and over roads that would seem impossible to a European army.   From the mountains to the sea, the quartermaster's easiest route lay along the great open waterways.   The upper photograph shows a quartermaster's sentry at Fort Fisher, N. C., on the Atlantic seaboard.   In the lower one to the left stands a sentry guarding the quartermaster's stores at Nashville, Tenn., on the Cumberland, while the sentry on the right is at City Point, Va., on the James.

Again, after Antietam, what tremendous tales of Southern strength must have held McClellan an entire month along the north bank of the Potomac, while Stuart, with less than two thousand troopers, rode jauntily round about him unscathed. It was not until well along in 1863, when the Federals began to wake up to the use of cavalry, that fairy tales gave way to facts, and Hooker and Meade could estimate the actual force to be encountered, so that by the time Grant came to the Army of the Potomac in 1864, he well knew that whatsoever advantage Lee might have in fighting on his own ground, and along interior lines, and with the most devoted and brilliantly led army at his back, the Union legions far outnumbered him. Then, with Grant's grim, invincible determination, there were no more footsteps backward.

Yet even Grant had very much to contend with in this very matter. Southern families abounded in Washington; Southern messengers of both sexes rode the Maryland lanes to Port Tobacco; Southern skiffs ferried Southern missives in the black hours of midnight under the very muzzles of the anchored guns in the broad reaches of the Potomac; Virginia farm boys, or girls—born riders all—bore all manner of messages from river to river and so to the Southern lines southeast of Fredericksburg, and thus around to Gordonsville and the Confederate army.

The Northern newspapers, under the inspiration of professional rivalry, kept the Southern cabinet remarkably well informed of everything going on within the Union lines, and not infrequently prepared the Confederate generals for the next move of the Union army. It was this that finally led the vehement Sherman to seek to eliminate the newspaper men from his military bailiwick, about as hopeless a task as the very worst assigned to Hercules. Grant, with his accustomed stoicism, accepted their presence in his army as something inseparable from American methods of warfare, adding to the problems and perplexities of the generals commanding,

MAP
PHOTO-
GRAPHING
FOR THE ARMY
IN THE FIELD

THE
PROCESS
THAT TOOK
GARDNER INTO
THE SECRET SERVICE

Alexander Gardner's usefulness to the secret service lay in the copying of maps by the methods shown above—and keeping quiet about it. A great admirer of Gardner's was young William A. Pinkerton, son of Allan Pinkerton, then head of the secret service. Forty-seven years later Mr. Pinkerton furnished for the PHOTOGRAPHIC HISTORY some reminiscences of Gardner's work: "It was during the winter of '61–'62 that Gardner became attached to the Secret Service Corps, then under my father. I was then a boy, ranging from seventeen to twenty-one years of age, during all of which time I was in intimate contact with Gardner, as he was at our headquarters and was utilized by the Government for photographing maps and other articles of that kind which were prepared by the secret service. I have quite a number of his views which were made at that time." These negatives, more than a thousand in number, are among the collection so long buried in obscurity before becoming represented in these volumes. Mr. Pinkerton adds: "I used to travel around with Gardner a good deal while he was taking these views and saw many of them made."

heralding their movements, as did the Virginia maids and matrons, and impeding them, as did the Virginia mud.

Other writers have described the " Intelligence Bureau " of the rank and file, by means of which the troops seemed well supplied with tidings of every Union move of consequence— tidings only too quickly carried by daring and devoted sons of the South, who courted instant death by accepting duty in the secret service, and lived the lonely life, and in many an instance died the lonely, unhallowed death of the spy. Men who sought that calling must have had illimitable love for and faith in the cause for which they accepted the ignominy that, justly or unjustly, attaches to the name. Men like Major André and Nathan Hale had succeeded in throwing about their hapless fate the glamour of romance and martyrdom, but such halos seem to have hovered over the head of few, if any, who, in either army during the bitter four years' war, were condemned to die, by the felon's rope, the death of the spy.

The Old Capitol Prison in Washington was long the abiding place of men and women confined by order of our " Iron Secretary " on well-founded suspicion of being connected with the Southern system, and in the camp of the Army of the Cumberland, two sons of the Confederacy, men with gentle blood in their veins and reckless daring in their hearts, were stripped of the uniforms of officers of the Union cavalry, in which they had been masquerading for who can say what purpose, tried by court martial, and summarily executed.

Secret service at best was a perilous and ill-requited duty. In spite of high pay it was held in low estimation, first on general principles, and later because it was soon suspected, and presently known, that many men most useful as purveyors of information had been shrewd enough to gain the confidence, accept the pay, and become the informants of both sides. Even Secretary Stanton was sometimes hoodwinked, as in the case of the " confidential adviser " he recommended to Sheridan in the fall of 1864.

THE PHOTOGRAPHERS WHO FOLLOWED THE ARMY

In the early years of the war the soldiers were so mystified by the peculiar-looking wagon in which Brady kept his traveling dark-room that they nicknamed it the "What-is-it?" wagon, a name which clung to the photographer's outfit all through the war. The upper photograph, with the two bashful-looking horses huddling together before the camera, shows Brady's outfit going to the front, in 1861. The lowest photograph demonstrates that even the busy photographer occasionally slept in his camp with the army. The left-

hand of the three center pictures shows the "What-is-it?" again, on the Bull Run battlefield; in the next appears the developing tent of Barnard, Colonel O. M. Poe's engineer-corps photographer, before one of the captured Atlanta forts, in September, 1864; and in the last stands Cooley, photographer to the Army of the Tennessee, with his camera, on the battered parapet of Sumter in 1865. In spite of these elaborate preparations of the enterprising photographers, among the million men in the field few knew that any photographs were being taken. These volumes will be the first introduction of many a veteran to the photography of fifty years before.

Sheridan had the born soldier's contempt for such characters, and though setting the man to work, as suggested, he had him watched by soldier scouts who had been organized under Colonel Young of Rhode Island, and when later there was brought to him at midnight, in complete disguise, a young Southerner, dark, slender, handsome, soft-voiced, and fascinating in manner—a man who "had had a tiff with Mosby," they said, and now wished to be of service to the Union and act in concert with Stanton's earlier emissary, "Mr. Lomas of Maryland," Sheridan's suspicions were redoubled. The newcomer gave the name of Renfrew—that under which the Prince of Wales (Baron Renfrew) had visited the States in the summer of 1860—and was an artist in the matter of make-up and disguise. Sheridan kept his own counsel, had the pair "shadowed," and speedily found they were sending far more information to the foe than they were bringing to him. They were arrested and ordered to Fort Warren, but in most mysterious fashion they escaped at Baltimore. A few weeks later and Stanton found reason to believe that his friend Lomas was closely allied with the conspirators later hanged for the assassination of Abraham Lincoln, and then it dawned upon Sheridan that Renfrew was probably none other than John Wilkes Booth.

At best, therefore, the information derived from such sources could never be relied upon, at least by Union generals, and Sheridan's scout system was probably the most successful of all those essayed during the war. It was also most daring and hazardous, for the men took their lives in their hands, and the chance of immediate and ignominious death when they donned, as they had to, the Confederate uniform and penetrated the Confederate lines. There, if suspected and arrested, their fate was sealed. Yet it was one of these who successfully bore to General Grant, Sheridan's urgent "I wish you were here," when, on the 5th of April, 1865, the latter saw slipping away the chance of penning Lee's harassed and panting army

THE ARMY PHOTOGRAPHER AHEAD OF THE WRECKING–TRAIN

When the Confederate cavalry made life a burden for the United States Military Railroad Construction Corps in the vicinity of Washington, the enterprising photographers on their part were not idle.   This photograph shows the engine "Commodore" derailed and lying on its side.   Even before the wrecking crew could be rushed to the scene, the photographer had arrived, as is attested by the bottle of chemicals, the developing tray, and the negative rack in the right foreground, as well as the photograph itself.   Every negative had to be developed within five minutes after the exposure, a fact which makes all the more marvellous the brilliant work that was accomplished.   In the buggy and wagon shown in the lower picture, Brady safely transported glass plates wherever an army could march.

THE BÊTE NOIR OF THE SECRET SERVICE

At the headquarters of the New York *Herald* in the field, August, 1863, sit some of the men who had just conveyed to the breathless nation the tidings of the great battle as it surged to and fro for three days on the field of Gettysburg. No Union general could object to dissemination of such news as this; but wide protest was made against the correspondents' activity at other times, their shrewd guesses at the armies' future movements, that kept the Southern Cabinet so remarkably well-informed of everything going on within the Union lines, and not infrequently prepared the Confederate generals for the next move. "Of course," wrote General Sherman to his wife, in a letter from camp in front of Vicksburg, dated April 10, 1863, "the newspaper correspondents, encouraged by the political generals, and even President Lincoln, having full swing in this and all camps, report all news, secret and otherwise . . . All persons who don't have to fight must be kept out of camp, else secrecy, a great element of military success, is an impossibility . . . Can you feel astonished that I should grow angry at the toleration of such suicidal weakness, that we strong, intelligent men must bend to a silly proclivity for early news that should advise our enemy days in advance?" The newspaper correspondents pitched their tents in the wake of the army, but they themselves were more than likely to be found with the advance-guard. Not a few of the plucky newspaper men fell on the field of battle, while others, like Richardson of the *Tribune*, endured imprisonment.

at Amelia Court House. The courier had to ride southward across a dozen miles of dubious country. It was nip and tuck whether " Yank " or " Reb " first laid hands on him, and when he finally reached the wearied leader, and, rousing to the occasion, Grant decided to ride at once through the darkness to Sheridan's side, and set forth with only a little escort and the scout as guide, two staff-officers, thoroughly suspicious, strapped the latter to his saddle, linked his horse with theirs, and cocked their revolvers at his back. That scout rode those long miles back to Jetersville with these words occasionally murmured into his ears, " At the first sight or sound of treachery, you die." Not until they reached Sheridan at midnight were they sure it was not a device of the desperate foe. Volumes could be written of the secret service of the Union armies—what it cost and what it was really worth—but the South, it is believed, could more than match every exploit.

Serious as was this problem, there were others beyond that of the strategy of a campaign of even greater moment— problems the Union generals, especially in the West, were compelled to study and consider with the utmost care. Napoleon said, " An army crawls upon its belly." Soldiers to march and fight their best must be well fed. Given sound food and shoe leather, and the average army can outdo one far above the average, unfed and unshod. East and West, the armies of the Union suffered at the start at the hands of the contractors, because of " shoddy " coats and blankets and " pasteboard " shoes, but in the matter of supplies the Army of the Potomac had generally the advantage of the armies of the West—it was never far removed from its base.

From the farms, granaries, mills, and manufactories of the Eastern and Middle States, in vast quantities, bacon, flour, coffee, sugar, and hardtack for the inner man; blankets, caps, coats, shirts, socks, shoes, and trousers for his outer self were shipped by canal and river to the sea and then floated up the Potomac to the great depots of Aquia and Washington, and

THE HARPER'S WEEKLY ARTIST SKETCHING THE GETTYSBURG BATTLEFIELD, 1863

Photo-engraving was unknown in the days of 1861 to 1865, and it remained for the next generation to make possible the reproduction in book form of the many valuable photographs taken by Matthew B. Brady and Alexander Gardner in the North, and George S. Cook, J. D. Edwards, A. D. Lytle, and others in the South. The public had to be content with wood-cuts, after sketches and drawings made by the correspondents in the field. On this page appears A. R. Waud, an active staff artist, in war and peace, for *Harper's Weekly*.

WAUD AT HEADQUARTERS, 1864,

later in the war up the James to City Point, thence by mule wagon or military railway to the neighboring camps. The entire army could always be freshly clothed and newly shod before it set forth on a campaign, to the end that the wagon train had little to carry but food and ammunition.

The seasoned soldier bore with him none of the white tentage that looked so picturesque among the green hills around Washington. The little *tente d'abri* of the French service, speedily dubbed the " pup tent " by our soldier humorists, was all he needed in the field, and generally all he had. So, too, with his kitchen and its appliances. The huge pots, pans, kettles, and coffee-boilers seen about the winter cantonments were left behind when the army took the field, and " every man his own cook " became the rule. Each man had speedily learned how to prepare his own coffee in his own battered tin mug, season it with brown sugar, and swallow it hot. Each man knew the practical use of a bayonet or ramrod as bread or bacon toaster. It was only in the matter of beans that community of cooking became necessary, and the old plains-bred regulars could teach the volunteers—ready pupils that they were—famous devices for reducing these stubborn but most sustaining pellets to digestible form. There never was a time when the Eastern army, after the first few months, was not well fed and warmly, if clumsily, clothed.

But in the West it was far different, far more difficult. Almost from the start the armies of the Ohio, the Cumberland, the Tennessee, and the forces beyond the Mississippi, setting forth from such bases as Louisville, Cairo, and St. Louis, pushed far southward through hostile territory, spinning behind them, spiderlike, a thin thread of steel, along which, box by box, car by car, were to roll to them the vast quantities of supplies without which no army can exist. The men of Grant and Buell, trudging on to Shiloh, had the Tennessee for a barge and steamboat route, and so fared well upon their hostile mission; but the men who later marched with " Old

MAIL AND NEWSPAPERS AT "A. OF P." HEADQUARTERS

It was important for the people at home to receive news of the armies that their enthusiasm might be kept high and their purses wide open; but it was also desirable that the soldier boys should receive their news. Whether in swamp, morass, or on a mountain-top, the men in camp rushed to read their newspapers, and yearned to know what was going on at home. They wanted to know what the people thought of them, how they were describing the situation of the armies, what they told of their battles, and were voracious readers of all and every class of publications, magazines as well as newspapers. In 1864, the post-office at the headquarters of the Army of the Potomac was a leading institution. Thousands of letters passed through it every week, and so systematically was this department conducted under the supervision of Army Postmaster William B. Haslett, with a mail-pouch for every corps and detached command, that their distribution was seldom delayed when the army was not on the march. Shrewd merchants, men who were willing to take chances to earn an honest dollar, followed the army with wagons or little trucks, selling to the men every sort of publication, but especially the journals of the day. In the lower photograph is shown quite an elaborate outfit then for the sale of Philadelphia, New York, and Baltimore newspapers.

Rosey " to Tullahoma and then beyond the Tennessee, well-nigh starved to death in their Bragg-beleaguered camps about Chattanooga, until Hooker came to their relief and established the famous " cracker line " beyond reach of shot and shell.

Then came long weeks in which, day by day, the freight trains, squirming slowly down that long, sinuous, single-track road from the Ohio River, reached the wide supply camps at Chattanooga, dumped their huge crates of bacon and hard-tack, or the big boxes of clothing, accouterments, and ammunition, and went rumbling and whistling back, laden with sick or wounded soldiery, creeping to the sidings every thirty miles or so to give the troop and " cracker " trains right of way. Nearly four long months it took Sherman, newly commanding in the West, to accumulate the vast supplies he would need for his big army of one hundred thousand men, ere again he started forth another two hundred miles into the bowels of the land, and every mile he marched took his men further from the bakeries, the butcher-shops, the commissary and quarter-master's stores from which the " boys " had received their daily bread or monthly socks, shoes, and tobacco. Another long, sinuous, slender thread of railway, guarded at every bridge, siding, and trestle, was reeled off as fast as Sherman fought on southward, until at last he reached the prize and paused again to draw breath, rations, and clothing at Atlanta before determining the next move.

And then, as in the Eastern armies, there loomed up still another factor in the problems of the campaign—a factor that European writers and critics seem rarely to take into account. From the days of the Roman Empire, Italy, France, Switzerland, and even England were seamed with admirable highways. The campaigns of Turenne, of Frederick the Great, of Napoleon were planned and marched over the best of roads, firm and hard, high and dry. The campaigns of Grant, Lee, Sherman, Johnston, Sheridan, Stuart, Thomas, Hood, Hooker, Burnside, and Jackson were ploughed at times

"LETTERS FROM HOME"—THE ARMY MAIL WAGON

HOW THE SOLDIERS GOT THEIR LETTERS FROM HOME

Letters from home were a great factor in keeping up the *morale* of the army. Wheresoever the armies might be located, however far removed from railroads or from the ordinary means of communication, the soldier boy always expected to receive his mails. The carrying of letters from his tent to his beloved ones was also a vital necessity. Each regiment in the field had a special postmaster, generally appointed by the colonel, who received all mail and saw to its proper distribution among the men, also receiving all mail forwarded to the home address. He sold stamps to the men, received their letters, and at stated periods made trips to what would be established as a sort of main post-office. The man designated as the postmaster of the regiment was generally relieved from all other duties. Each regiment in the Army of the Potomac had a post-boy, who carried the letters of his command to the brigade headquarters. There the mails of the different regiments were placed in one pouch and went up to division headquarters, and thence to corps headquarters, where mail-agents received them and delivered them at the principal depot of the army to the agent from general headquarters. At times it was an arduous task for the mail wagons to transport the accumulated mail over bad roads, and several trips might have to be made for the purpose of securing all that was lying at some distant depot.

through seas of mud, through swamp, morass, and tangled wildwood. Southern country roads, except perhaps the limestone pikes of Kentucky and northern Tennessee, were roads only in name, and being soft, undrained, and unpaved, were forever washed out by rains or cut into deep ruts by gun and wagon wheels. Then there were quicksands in which the mule teams stalled and floundered; there were flimsy bridges forever being fired or flooded; scrap-iron railways that could be wrecked in an hour and rebuilt only with infinite pains and labor and vast expenditure of time and money.

Just what Frederick, or Napoleon, or Turenne would have done with the best of armies, but on the worst of roads, with American woods and weather to deal with, is a military problem that would baffle the critics of all Christendom. It is something for the American people to remember that when Grant and Sheridan cut loose from their base for the last week's grapple with the exhausted but indomitable remnant of Lee's gallant gray army, it rained torrents for nearly three entire days, the country was knee-deep in mud and water, the roads were utterly out of sight.

It was the marvelous concentration march of Meade's scattered army corps, however, that made possible the victory of Gettysburg. It was when they struck the hard, white roads of Pennsylvania that the men of the Army of the Potomac trudged unflinchingly their thirty miles or more a day, and matched the records of Napoleon's best. It was " Stonewall " Jackson's unequaled " foot cavalry " that could tramp their twenty-four hours through Virginia mountain trails, cover their forty miles from sun to sun, and be off again for another flank attack while yet their adversary slept. Moltke said the armies of the great Civil War were " two armed mobs," but Moltke failed to realize that in the matters of information and logistics, the Union generals had, from first to last, to deal with problems and conditions the best of his or Frederick's field-marshals never had met nor dreamed of.

[36]

PART I
SOLDIER LIFE

———

THE BUSINESS SIDE
OF THE
WAR DEPARTMENTS

———

EMBARKING TROOPS
NINTH ARMY CORPS
LEAVING ACQUIA CREEK
IN FEBRUARY, 1863

GOVERNMENT BAKERIES AT ALEXANDRIA

COMMISSARY BUILDINGS AT ALEXANDRIA

ONE OF THE GOVERNMENT MESS-HOUSES AT WASHINGTON

GROUPS AT THE QUARTERMASTER-GENERAL'S OFFICE IN WASHINGTON

EMPLOYEES, TRANSPORTATION OFFICE, ASSISTANT QUARTERMASTER'S OFFICE, AND WAREHOUSE NO. 1—WASHINGTON

SUPPLIES ON THE TENNESSEE

BRANDY STATION, VA.

NEW YORK FERRY ON THE POTOMAC

STORES AT STONEMAN'S STATION

COL. J. B. HOWARD, Q. M.

SIBLEY, WALL, AND "A" TENTS

SUPPLIES AT WHITE HOUSE

"ARMY BREAD"

SUPPLIES AT CITY POINT

By water, rail, and horse the busy quartermasters traveled during the war. All kinds of river and sea-going craft were employed as transports for army supplies. In the left-hand corner appears a Tennessee River side-wheel steamer of the type that was said to be able to "run in a heavy dew," so light was its draught! And in the upper right-hand corner of this page a New York ferry-

GRAND REVIEW AT WASHINGTON

boat is seen at the City Point dock, on the James River, in Virginia. Both boats were engaged in bringing food and other supplies to the Federal armies in the field. Sitting on the box above is Captain T. W. Forsythe, provost-marshal. It was fitting that the army wagons, which had played so important a part in all the aggressive movements of the troops, should have a place in the Grand Review.

OFFICE OF U. S. REPAIR SHOPS   GOVERNMENT TRIMMING SHOP   GOVERNMENT PAINT SHOP

OUTSIDE THE REPAIR SHOPS   BLACKSMITH EMPLOYEES   WHEELWRIGHT SHOP

During the progress of the war, repair shops were established by the Federal Government at various points inside its lines, including Washington, Cincinnati, St. Louis, Louisville, Kentucky, and Nashville, Tennessee. The Washington shops above pictured were among the largest of their kind. The huge buildings were used for the purpose of repairing army wagons, artillery wagons, ambulances, caissons, and every kind of vehicle used by the Government for transportation. The materials for prompt repair were always on hand in these immense establishments. The mechanics and artisans were selected from the best the country afforded. All of these repair depots were maintained by the Government at great expense.

GOVERNMENT WHEELWRIGHT SHOP

HORSES AND WAGONS OF FIELD REPAIR-TRAIN IN SEPTEMBER, 1863

FIELD FORGE, PETERSBURG

BUILDING WINTER–QUARTERS

FIELD WHEELWRIGHTS

GOVERNMENT WORKSHOPS, CORRALS, AND RESERVOIR AT CAMP NELSON, KENTUCKY

MULE–CHUTE AT CAMP NELSON

"Wagon busted, axle broken and wheel gone to smash!" was a frequent exclamation that met the repair gangs accompanying the armies. Miry or rocky roads were usually accountable for the disasters to the wheeled vehicles. Even the best of wagons were liable to break under the heavy strain of the poor roads. Hence the above cry, with the usual accompanying direction: "About a mile down the road—have shoved her over into a field." The repair wagons would make for the scene of trouble, and if possible the break would be temporarily patched up. If not, the wagon would be abandoned. The repair department had many other activities at headquarters, and kept excellent workmen of many trades working constantly at fever-heat, especially when the army was engaged in a hard campaign.

UNITED STATES "FRANKLIN SHOP S" AT NASHVILLE, TENNESSEE

THE BUSINESS SIDE OF WAR–MAKING

By William B. Shaw

IT is one of the purposes of this " Photographic History " to show more clearly than has been shown before what the Civil War meant to the common man, on either side of Mason and Dixon's Line, whether volunteer or non-combatant. It must be remembered that thousands of men and women, North and South, rendered loyal service to their respective Governments throughout the four years of strife, without so much as lifting a musket. This series of photographs shows not only how battles were fought, but how the armies were made fit to fight them, how campaigns were conducted, how soldiers were made out of raw recruits, how railroads and bridges were destroyed and rebuilt, how rivers were dammed and their channels deflected, how blockades were maintained and eluded—in short, how the *business* of war went on in America for four full years of three hundred and sixty-five days each, practically without interruption.

Clearly, there would have been no wisdom in recruiting and organizing great armies without making provision for feeding and clothing them. Even more futile would have been an attempt to use such armies in aggressive movements without suitable equipment. The essential requisite to every army's success on the march or on the field of battle is good nourishment; yet so lacking in the picturesque was the machinery for feeding the armies in the Civil War, that historians have given it but slight attention. To equip, clothe, shelter, and transport a million men in arms at once was the task that confronted the Washington Government in the second year of the war. The country's long period of peace had not prepared it

"HOME ON FURLOUGH"—ABOARD THE ARMY TRANSPORT

After McClellan's Peninsula campaign in 1862, thousands of Northern soldiers were debilitated by swamp miasma. It was necessary that all the men who had been attacked by typhoid and various forms of intermittent fever should be taken from the environment of the Virginia camps to their homes in the North for recuperation. The photograph is that of a transport on the River James carrying a number of these furloughed men, most of whom had become convalescent in the hospitals and so were able to make the homeward journey. The lower photograph shows a transport steamer crowded with troops for Grant's concentration of the army at City Point.

for such an undertaking. A wholly new military establishment had to be created. The supply departments of the old army organization were fitted for the work of provisioning and equipping a dozen regiments; they were suddenly called upon to provide for a thousand. The fact that department and bureau chiefs rose to the situation and responded to these new and unprecedented demands is usually regarded quite as a matter of course.

Every American schoolboy knows the names of the men who led the armies, whether to victory or to defeat, but who saw that the soldiers were clothed and fed? Hundreds of faithful officers were engaged in that duty throughout the four weary years of war; without their services the battles that brought enduring fame to victorious generals could never have been fought, much less won. The feats that these men performed were largely unknown to the public and even to the armies themselves. Frequently in the face of appalling difficulties, we are told, a whole army corps was saved from starvation and defeat by the ready resourcefulness of a commissary. More than once the intelligent cooperation of the Quartermaster's Department made possible a rapid movement of troops, crowning with success the brilliant plans of a commander to whom history has awarded all the credit for skilful execution.

At the outbreak of the war the army's two great supply departments were directed by the quartermaster-general and the commissary-general of subsistence, respectively. The Quartermaster's Department was charged with the duty of providing means of transportation, by land and water, for all the troops and all materials of war; it furnished the horses for artillery and cavalry, and for the supply trains; supplied tents, camp and garrison equipage, forage, lumber, and all materials for camps; it built barracks, hospitals, wagons, and ambulances; provided harness, except for artillery and cavalry horses; built or chartered ships and steamships, docks and

TRANSPORT ON THE TENNESSEE

AN OCEAN–LINER TRANSPORT

OCEAN TRANSPORT AT CHARLESTON

THE DECK OF THE "ARAGO"

Army transports represented all types of river craft and sea-going vessels. Steamboats, propellers, tugs, barges, and canal boats were all utilized for this important service. The vessels shown upon this page were used for moving regiments, brigades, divisions, and even entire corps from point to point along the rivers and up and down the Atlantic coast-line. The

TRANSPORT ON THE APPOMATTOX

Arago had been one of the great side-wheel ocean-liners plying between New York and Liverpool in the days preceding the war. She was especially desirable for the transportation of large bodies of troops along the Southern coast. The *Washington Irving* in the lower picture was a North River passenger-boat loaned or leased to the Federal Government.

wharves; constructed and repaired roads, bridges, and even railroads; clothed the soldiers, and supervised the payment of all expenses attending military operations which were not regularly assigned by law or regulation to some other department.

Upon the Subsistence Department fell the duty of securing food for the army. During a great part of the war, the Washington Government was expending approximately one million dollars a day upon the maintenance and equipment of troops, and the prosecution of campaigns. The greater part of this expenditure was made through these two departments, the Quartermaster's and the Subsistence.

The matter of railroad transportation concerned both of these intimately. The total railroad mileage of the United States at the outbreak of the war was 30,635—about one-eighth of what it was in 1910. The railroads of 1861 connected the Mississippi valley with the seaboard, it is true, but they had not yet been welded into systems, and as a means of transportation for either men or materials they were sadly inadequate when judged by twentieth-century standards. Deficient as they were, however, they had reached the Mississippi River some years in advance of the traffic demands of the country, and in the exigencies of war their facilities for moving the wheat and corn of the Mississippi valley were to be taxed to their limit for the first time, although the country's total yield of wheat was less than one-fourth, and of corn less than one-third of the corresponding crops in 1910.

In tapping the rich grain fields of the interior, the Government at Washington had decidedly the advantage over that at Richmond, for the Confederate authorities were served by transportation lines that were even less efficient than those of the North, and, moreover, a large proportion of their tillable land was devoted to cotton growing, and the home-grown food products of the South were unequal to the demands of home consumption. In January, 1862, the Confederate quartermaster-

At Belle Plain, at Centerville, Virginia, and at Baton Rouge appear the omnipresent army wagons, which followed the armies from Washington to the Gulf. The dimensions of the box of these useful vehicles were as follows: Length (inside), 120 inches; width (inside), 43 inches; height, 22 inches. Such a wagon could carry a load weighing about 2536 pounds, or 1500 rations of hard bread, coffee, sugar, and salt. Each wagon was drawn by a team of four horses or six mules.

THE BIVOUAC—WAGON-TRAIN AT CUMBERLAND LANDING, PAMUNKEY RIVER general complained that the railroad lines on which his Government was dependent for transportation, were operating only two trains a day each way, at an average speed of six miles an hour. Before the war, the railroads of the South had been dependent for most of their equipment on the car-shops and locomotive-works of the Northern States. The South had only limited facilities for producing rolling-stock. After communication with the North had ceased, most of the Southern railroads deteriorated rapidly. Quite apart from the ruin caused by the war itself, many of the railroads soon became comparatively useless for lack of equipment and repairs, and the familiar expression "two streaks of rust and a right of way" was applied with peculiar fitness to some of them.

Yet the railroads played an important part in the war from the beginning. This was indeed the first great war in history in which railroads entered, to any important extent, into the plans of campaigns and battles. The Federal quartermaster-general, not being harassed by hostile movements within the territory from which his supplies were drawn, perfected the system of railroad transportation for both troops and supplies, until he had it working with smoothness and a high degree of efficiency. The railroad corporations that remained loyal to the Government at Washington, came together in the early days of the war and agreed on a schedule of rates for army transportation. This was probably the earliest instance of a general railroad agreement in the history of the country. These rates were adhered to throughout the war, and while the prices of almost all commodities rose far above the price-level of 1861, transportation rates, so far as the Government was concerned, remained uniform and constant. The railroads, for the most part, prospered under this arrangement. Never before had their rolling-stock been so steadily employed, and the yearly volume of business, both passenger and freight, was unprecedented. The Government soon found that in the transportation of troops, the two thousand dollars which was paid

WEIGHING BREAD FOR THE UNION ARMY, 1864

The counting of every pound of flour was one of the essentials required of the quartermaster's department. Each pan of baked bread must be weighed. This was systematically done by the commissary-sergeant especially detailed for that purpose. In this photograph the scales stand in front of him, while a colored boy has placed a batch of loaves from the pyramid of bread upon the scales. A soldier is handing out another batch of loaves ready to be weighed. When the Army of the Potomac lay in front of Petersburg in 1864 and 1865, there were a great many inventions brought to the fore for the benefit of the men serving at the front. Among them was the army bake-oven, a regular baker's oven placed on wheels. In the lower picture the bakers are shoving the bread just kneaded into the oven to bake. The bearded man in the foreground at the left is the fireman who keeps the fires going. From this bakery the loaves went out, after each batch was duly weighed, to the various regiments according to the amount requisitioned by their several commissaries. It was always a happy moment for the soldiers when "fresh-bread day" came around. It varied the monotony of "hard-tack," and formed quite a luxury after the hard campaign through the Wilderness and across the James River. Soft bread was obtainable only in permanent camp. There was no time for it on the march.

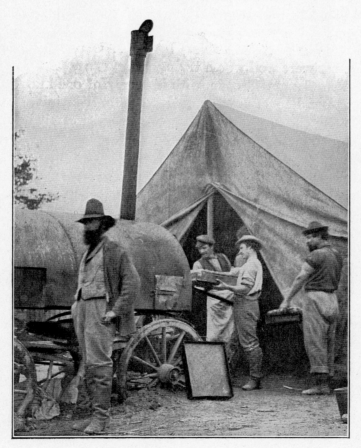

A GOVERNMENT OVEN ON WHEELS

for moving one thousand men one hundred miles by rail was far less than the cost of marching the same number of men an equivalent distance over the roads of the country.

Unfortunately, however, campaign plans, more frequently than otherwise, called for long marches between points not connected by rail. Water transportation was used by General McClellan to good advantage in beginning the Peninsula campaign; after that, the Army of the Potomac, once having made the acquaintance of Virginia mud, retained it to the end. The wagon roads of the Old Dominion were tested in all seasons and by every known form of conveyance. A familiar accompaniment of the marching troops was the inevitable wagon train, carrying subsistence, ammunition, and clothing. Twelve wagons to every thousand men had been Napoleon's rule on the march, but the highways of Europe undoubtedly permitted relatively heavier loads. For the Army of the Potomac, twenty-five wagons per thousand men was not considered an excessive allowance. No wonder these well-laden supply trains aroused the interest of daring bands of Confederate scouts! Such prizes were well worth trying for.

When General Meade, with his army of one hundred and fifty thousand men, left Brandy Station, Virginia, in May, 1864, on his march to Petersburg, each soldier carried six days' rations of hardtack, coffee, sugar, and salt. The supply trains carried ten days' rations of the same articles, and one day's ration of salt pork. For the remainder of the meat ration, a supply of beef cattle on the hoof for thirteen days' rations was driven along with the troops, but over separate roads. General Thomas Wilson, who was Meade's chief commissary, directed the movements of this great herd of beef cattle by brigades and divisions.

The Federal service required an immense number of draft animals. The Quartermaster's Department bought horses for the cavalry and artillery, and horses and mules for the trains. In 1862, the Government owned approximately

GUARDING LUMBER FOR THE GOVERNMENT

Vast quantities of lumber were used by the Union armies during the war. The Federal Government was at that time the largest builder in the world. The Engineer Corps carried interchangeable parts to replace destroyed railroad bridges, and lumber was needed for pontoons, flooring, hospital buildings, and construction of every kind necessary to the welfare of the armies. Often, when no lumber was at hand, neighboring houses had to be wrecked in order to repair a railroad bridge or furnish flooring for the pontoon-bridges. The upper photograph shows a sentry guarding the Government's lumber-yard at Washington. Much of this lumber was doubtless used in repairing the Orange & Alexandria Railroad, so frequently destroyed by both armies as they operated between Richmond and Washington. In the lower photograph a sentry is guarding a Government mill in the field.

SENTRY AT GOVERNMENT MILL

one hundred and fifty thousand horses and one hundred thousand mules. The forage for these animals was no inconsiderable item, and the shoeing, stabling, and driving of the teams gave employment to a small army of men.

The Confederate authorities were never compelled to make such extensive purchases of animals either for transportation or for strictly military uses. Under the system adopted in the Confederate army, the cavalry horses were furnished by the officers and enlisted men themselves; the Quartermaster's Department made no purchases on that account. Furthermore, since the operations were very largely conducted in the home territory, there was less demand for supply-train transportation than in the case of the Federal armies, which repeatedly made expeditions into hostile country and had to be fully provisioned for the march.

The Federal forces seem never to have been for any length of time without abundant food supplies. In the fall of 1863, while the fighting around Chattanooga was in progress, supplies were deficient, but the shortage was soon made up, and the railroads brought great quantities of meat from the West, to feed Sherman's army during its long Atlanta campaign. These commissary stores were obtained at convenient shipping-points, by contracts let after due advertisement by the commissary officers. They were apportioned by the commissary-general at Washington to the respective army commissaries and by them in turn to the corps-, division-, brigade-, and finally the regimental commissaries, who dealt out the rations to the individual soldiers, each officer being held to account for a given quota. Prices fluctuated during the war, but the market for foodstuffs in the North can hardly be said to have been in a condition of panic at any time. The Government had no difficulty in buying all the supplies it needed at prevailing prices.

In the Confederacy, the situation was different. The general system of purchasing supplies that the Richmond Government attempted to follow was essentially the same as that

LOADING SUPPLY–WAGONS FROM TRANSPORTS FOR GRANT'S ARMY—CITY POINT, 1864

PORK, HARD–TACK, SUGAR, AND COFFEE FOR THE REGIMENTAL COMMISSARY AT CEDAR LEVEL

The immense supply and transportation facilities of the North in 1864, contrasted with the situation of the Southern soldiery, recalls Bonaparte's terse speech to his army in Italy: "Soldiers! You need *everything*—the enemy *has* everything." The Confederates often acted upon the same principle. At City Point, Virginia, Grant's wagon-trains received the army supplies landed from the ships.

established at Washington, but, from the very outset, the seceding State Governments were active in provisioning the Confederate armies, and in some instances there was an apparent jealousy of authority, as when Confederate officers began the impressment of needed articles. The inflated currency and soaring prices made such action imperative, in the judgment of the Davis cabinet.

The blockade did not wholly cut off the importation of supplies from abroad. Indeed, considerable quantities were bought in England by the Confederate Subsistence Department and paid for in cotton. Early in the war the South found that its meat supply was short, and the Richmond Government went into the pork-packing business on a rather extensive scale in Tennessee. The Secretary of War made no secret of the fact that, in spite of these expedients, it was still impossible to provision the Confederate army as the Government desired, although it was said that the troops in the field were supplied with coffee long after that luxury had disappeared from the breakfast tables of the " home folks."

In the matter of clothing, the armies of both the Federal and Confederate Governments were relieved of no slight embarrassment at the beginning of the war by the prompt action of States and communities. The Quartermaster's Department at Washington was quite unequal to the task of uniforming the " three-months' men " who responded to Lincoln's first call for volunteers. This work was done by the State Governments. Wisconsin sent its first regiments to the front clad in cadet gray, but the uniforms, apart from the confusion in color, were said to have been of excellent quality, and the men discarded them with regret, after a few weeks' wear, for the flimsy blue that the enterprising contractors foisted on the Washington Government in its mad haste to secure equipment. Those were the days when fortunes were made from shoddy— an era of wholesale cheating that ended only with the accession of Stanton, Lincoln's great war secretary, who numbered

PROVISIONING BURNSIDE'S ARMY—BELLE PLAIN LANDING ON THE POTOMAC

CLOSER VIEWS OF BELLE PLAIN LANDING, LATE IN NOVEMBER, 1862

NEARER STILL—ARRIVAL OF THE WAGON-TRAINS AT BELLE PLAIN LANDING

among the special objects of his hatred the dishonest army contractor.

After the work of the Quartermaster's Department had been systematized and some effort had been made to analyze costs, it appeared that the expense incurred for each soldier's equipment, exclusive of arms, amounted to fifty dollars.

For the purchase and manufacture of clothing for the Federal army, it was necessary to maintain great depots in New York, Philadelphia, Boston, Cincinnati, Louisville, Indianapolis, St. Louis, Detroit, and Springfield, Illinois. Confederate depots for similar purposes were established at Richmond, New Orleans, Memphis, Charleston, Savannah, San Antonio, and Fort Smith. The Confederacy was obliged to import most of its shoes and many articles of clothing. Wool was brought from Texas and Mexico to mills in the service of the Confederate Quartermaster's Department. Harness, tents, and camp and garrison equipage were manufactured for the department in Virginia, Georgia, Louisiana, North Carolina, and Mississippi. The department's estimate to cover contracts made in England for supplies to run the blockade during a single six-months' period amounted to £570,000.

It is the conclusion of James Ford Rhodes, the historian of the Civil War period, that " never had an army been so well equipped with food and clothing as was that of the North; never before were the comfort and welfare of the men so well looked after." The appropriations for the Quartermaster's Department alone, during the war, aggregated more than a billion dollars. Extensive frauds were perpetrated on the Government, not only in the clothing contracts of the first year, to which reference has been made, but in the transport service and in various transactions which were not properly checked under a system of audit and disbursement that broke down altogether in the emergency of real war. In the opinion of Mr. Rhodes, the administrators of the War Department were not only efficient, but aggressively honest public servants.

MARSHALLING THE FEDERAL VOLUNTEERS

OFFICER AND SERGEANT IN '61
MEN OF THE SIXTH VERMONT NEAR WASHINGTON

A HOLLOW–SQUARE MANEUVER FOR THE NEW SOLDIERS

This regiment was organized at Bangor, Me., for three months' service, and left the State for Willett's Point, N. Y., May 14, 1861. Such was the enthusiasm of the moment that it was mustered into the United States service, part for two and part for three years, May 28, 1861. It moved to Washington on May 30th. The first camp of the regiment was on Meridian Hill, near Washington, till July 1st. The live-long days were spent in constant "drill, drill, drill" during this period. McClellan was fashioning the new levies into an army. The total population of the Northern States in 1860 was 21,184,305. New England's population was 3,135,283, or about one-seventh of the whole. New England's troops numbered 363,162, over one-tenth of its population, practically one-seventh the total muster of forces raised in the North during the war, namely, 2,778,304. The New England population was distributed as follows: Maine, 628,279; Massachusetts, 1,231,066; Vermont, 315,098; New Hampshire, 326,073; Connecticut, 460,147, and

SECOND MAINE INFANTRY AT CAMP JAMESON, 1861

Rhode Island, 174,620.   The number of troops that these States respectively furnished and the losses they incurred were: Maine, 70,107—loss, 9,398; Massachusetts, 146,730—loss, 13,942; Vermont, 33,288—loss, 5,224; New Hampshire, 33,937—loss, 4,882; Connecticut, 55,864—loss, 5,354; and Rhode Island, 23,236—loss, 1,321.   The total loss was thus 40,121.   Maine's contribution of more than 11 per cent. of its population took the form of two regiments of cavalry, one regiment of heavy artillery, seven batteries of light artillery, one battalion and a company of sharpshooters, with thirty-three regiments, one battalion, and seven companies of infantry.   The Second Maine fought with the Army of the Potomac until the battle of Chancellorsville, May 1 to 5, 1863.   The regiment was ordered home on the 20th of that month, and the three-years men were transferred to the Twentieth Maine Infantry.   The regiment was mustered out June 9, 1863, having lost four officers and 135 enlisted men, killed or mortally wounded, and by disease.

THE FIRST RHODE ISLAND INFANTRY LEAVING PROVIDENCE, APRIL 20, 1861

The sidewalks were filled with cheering throngs, and unbounded enthusiasm greeted the volunteers, as the first division of the First Regiment of Detached Rhode Island Militia left Providence for Washington April 20, 1861. At 10:30 in the morning Colonel Ambrose E. Burnside, in command, had ordered the men of the first division to assemble upon Exchange Place. The band was followed by the National Cadets and the first division was led by Colonel Burnside himself. It contained practically half of each of the ten companies, six of which were recruited in Providence and one each in Pawtucket, Woonsocket, Newport, and Westerly. The second division left four days later. The men in this photograph marched through Exchange Street to Market Square, up North Main Street and through Meeting to Benefit, and down Benefit to Fox Point.

BURNSIDE AND HIS BOYS OF THE FIRST RHODE ISLAND AFTER BULL RUN

The officers of the First Rhode Island Volunteers looked quite martial in their pleated blue blouses and gauntlets at the outset of the war. Colonel Ambrose E. Burnside sits in the center, with folded arms in front of the tree. Above his head to the right is the rude sign: "Welcome home." The little State of Rhode Island contributed three regiments and a battalion of cavalry, three regiments of heavy artillery, ten batteries of light artillery, twelve regiments of infantry, and an independent company of hospital guards to the Union cause. The first Rhode Island was a three-months regiment which was mustered out August 2, 1861. This photograph shows the young officers after the Union disaster at Bull Run. From April, 1861, to August, the regiment lost one officer and sixteen enlisted men killed and mortally wounded, and eight enlisted men by disease.

THIRD CONNECTICUT INFANTRY, CAMP DOUGLAS, 1861

Only one day after the First Regiment of Connecticut Infantry started from Hartford—May 18, 1861—the Second and Third left New Haven for the great camps that encircled Washington. All three of these three-months regiments took part in the battle of Bull Run, and all three were mustered out by the middle of August. This was one of the first steps by which the fighting men of the North were finding themselves. Con-

three batteries of light artillery, and thirty regiments of infantry to the front in the course of the war. Two of the latter, the Twenty-ninth and the Thirtieth, were colored regiments. The company of the Third in the photograph looks quite natty in its dark blue uniforms. These men have not yet heard the crash of a Confederate volley, but they are soon to do so on the disastrous field of Bull Run. They served almost three months, being mustered in on May 14, 1861, and mustered out August 12th,

OFFICERS OF THE NINTH MASSACHUSETTS INFANTRY AT CAMP CASS, 1861

A little over two months before this regiment left Boston for Washington, the Sixth Massachusetts had been defending itself against the mob in the streets of Baltimore, April 19, 1861. Massachusetts poured regiment after regiment to the front until seventy-one regiments had answered President Lincoln's calls. Besides the infantry, Massachusetts sent five regiments and three battalions of cavalry, four regiments, a battalion, and thirty unassigned companies of heavy artillery, eighteen batteries of light artillery, and two companies of sharpshooters. The Ninth Massachusetts left Boston for Washington on June 27, 1861. At the first and second Bull Run, on the Peninsula, at Antietam, Fredericksburg, Chancellorsville, Gettysburg, the Wilderness, Spotsylvania, and Cold Harbor this regiment fought bravely and well. When it was finally mustered out June 21, 1864, it had lost 15 officers, 194 enlisted men killed and mortally wounded, and 3 officers and 66 enlisted men by disease.

"GREEN
MOUNTAIN
BOYS"
AT DRILL,
1861

"I" AND "D"

COMPANIES

OF THE

SIXTH

VERMONT

THE SIXTH VERMONT INFANTRY BEFORE CAMP GRIFFIN, NEAR WASHINGTON, IN 1861

From October 19 and 22, 1861, when the Sixth Vermont Infantry left Montpelier for Washington, until its final corps-review June 8, 1865, nearly two months after Appomattox, this regiment served with the Army of the Potomac and the Army of the Shenandoah. These hardy mountain boys shown in the photograph are drilling in full accouterment, carrying their knapsacks on their sturdy backs. Clad in gray turned up with emerald, as befitted "the Green Mountain Boys," they added one more note of color to the kaleidoscope of uniforms that gathered in Washington that summer and fall.

Vermont sent one regiment of cavalry, a regiment and a company of heavy artillery, three batteries of light artillery, and eighteen regiments of infantry to the front. The Sixth Vermont fought at Yorktown, Antietam, Fredericksburg, Chancellorsville, Gettysburg, Wilderness, Spotsylvania, at Opequon, in the Shenandoah Valley, and at Petersburg, and formed part of the Sixth Corps sent to the relief of Washington when Early threatened it in July, 1864. When mustered out June 26, 1865, the Sixth had lost 12 officers and 191 enlisted men killed and wounded, and 3 officers and 212 men by disease.

MARSHALING THE FEDERAL ARMY

By Charles King
Brigadier-General, United States Volunteers

UNION men wore anxious faces early in the spring of 1861. For months the newspapers had been filled with accounts of the seizure of Government forts and arsenals all over the South. State after State had seceded, and the *New York Tribune*, edited by Horace Greeley, had bewildered the North and encouraged the South by declaring that if the latter desired to set up a government of its own it had every moral right to do so. The little garrison of Fort Moultrie, in Charleston Harbor, threatened by a superior force and powerless against land attack, had spiked its guns on Christmas night, in 1860, and pulled away for Sumter, perched on its islet of rocks a mile from shore, hoisted the Stars and Stripes, and there, in spite of pitiful numbers, with a Southern-born soldier at its head, practically defied all South Carolina.

The *Star of the West* had been loaded with soldiers and supplies at New York, and sent to Sumter's relief. Then South Carolina, duly warned, had manned the guns of Morris Island and driven her back to sea. Not content with that, South Carolina, the envy of an applauding sisterhood of Southern States, had planted batteries on every point within range of Sumter. All the North could see that its fate was sealed, and no one, when the 1st of April came, could say just how the North would take it.

The second week settled the question. With one accord, on April 12th, the Southern guns opened on the lone fortress and its puny force. The next day, with the flagstaff shot away and the interior of the fort all ablaze, the casemates thick with

THE FAMOUS NEW YORK SEVENTH, JUST AFTER REACHING WASHINGTON IN APRIL, 1861

The first New York State militia regiment to reach Washington after President Lincoln's call for troops, April 15, 1861, was the Seventh Infantry. The best blood and most honored names in New York City were prominent in its ranks. It eventually supplied no less than 606 officers to the Union army. Veterans now hail it as the highest type of the citizen soldiers who went to the front. The old armory at the foot of Third Avenue could not contain the crowds that gathered. At this writing (1911) it is just being demolished. The Seventh left for Washington April 19, 1861, and as it marched down Broadway passed such a multitude of cheering citizens that its splendid band was almost unheard through the volume of applause. On April 24th the regiment reached Annapolis Junction, Maryland. On that and the day following, with the Eighth Massachusetts for company, it had to patch the railway and open communications with Washington. The men were mustered into service on April 26th, and their camp on Meridian Hill, May 2d to 23d, was pointed out as a model. They took part in the occupation of Arlington Heights, Virginia, May 24th to May 26th, and assisted in building Fort Runyon. They returned to Camp Cameron on the latter date, and were mustered out at New York City, June 3, 1861, but those not immediately commissioned were mustered in again the following year, and in 1863.

blinding smoke, with no hope from friends, the gallant garrison could ask only the mercy of the foes, and it was given willingly—the soldier's privilege of saluting his colors and marching out with the honors of war.

And then the North awoke in earnest. In one day the streets of New York city, all seeming apathy the day before, blazed with a sudden burst of color. The Stars and Stripes were flung to the breeze from every staff and halyard; the hues of the Union flamed on every breast. The transformation was a marvel. There was but one topic on every tongue, but one thought in every heart: The flag had been downed in Charleston Harbor, the long-threatened secession had begun, the very Capitol at Washington was endangered, the President at last had spoken, in a demand for seventy-five thousand men.

It was the first call of many to follow—calls that eventually drew 2,300,000 men into the armies of the Union, but the first was the most thrilling of all, and nowhere was its effect so wonderful as in the city of New York.

Not until aroused by the echo of the guns at Sumter could or would the people believe the South in deadly earnest. The press and the prophets had not half prepared them. Southern sympathizers had been numerous and aggressive, and when the very heads of the Government at Washington were unresentful of repeated violation of Federal rights and authority, what could be expected of a people reared only in the paths of peace? The military spirit had long been dominant in the South and correspondingly dormant in the North. The South was full of men accustomed to the saddle and the use of arms; the North had but a handful. The South had many soldier schools; the North, outside of West Point, had but one worthy the name. Even as late as the winter of 1860 and 1861, young men in New York, taking counsel of far-seeing elders and assembling for drill, were rebuked by visiting pedagogues who bade them waste no time in " silly vanities."

" The days of barbaric battle are dead," said they. " The

[68]

OFFICERS OF THE SEVENTY-FIRST NEW YORK INFANTRY

The Seventy-first New York Infantry, or "Second Excelsior," was organized at Camp Scott, Staten Island, New York, as the second regiment of Sickles' brigade in June, 1861. The men left for Washington July 23d. The lower photograph shows a group off duty, lounging in the bright sunshine near their canvas houses—in this case "A" tents. They accompanied McClellan to the Peninsula, and served in all the great battles of the Army of the Potomac until they were mustered out at New York City, July 30, 1864. The regiment lost five officers and eighty-three enlisted men killed and mortally wounded, and two officers and seventy-three enlisted men by disease.

MEN OF THE SEVENTY-FIRST NEW YORK AT CAMP DOUGLAS IN 1861

good sense of the American people will ever stand between us and a resort to arms." The ominous rumbles from Pensacola, Augusta, Baton Rouge, and San Antonio meant nothing to these peace proclaimers; it took the thunderclap of Sumter to hush them. It took the sudden and overwhelming uprising of April 15th to bring the hitherto confident backers of the South face to face with an astounding fact.

Seventy-five thousand men needed at once!—the active militia called instantly to the front! Less than fifteen thousand regulars scattered far and wide—many of them in Texas, but mainly on the Indian frontier—could the Nation muster in gathering toils. Many a Southern-born officer had resigned and joined the forces of his native State, but the rank and file, horse, foot, and gunners stood sturdily to their colors. Still, these tried and disciplined men were few and far between.

Utterly unprepared for war of any kind, the Union leaders found themselves forced to improvise an army to defend their seat of Government—itself on Southern soil, and compassed by hostile cities. The new flag of the seceding States was flaunted at Alexandria, in full view of the unfinished dome of the Capitol. The colors of the South were openly and defiantly worn in the streets of Baltimore, barring the way of the would-be rescuers.

The veteran Virginian, General Winfield Scott, at the head of the United States army, had gathered a few light guns in Washington. His soldierly assistant, Colonel Charles P. Stone, had organized, from department clerks and others, the first armed body of volunteers for the defense of the threatened center, and within a few months the first-named was superseded as too old, the second imprisoned as too Southern— an utterly baseless charge. The one hope to save the capital lay in the swift assembling of the Eastern militia, and by the night of April 15th the long roll was thundering from the walls of every city armory. From Boston Common to the Mississippi, loyal States were wiring assurance of support.

THE WEST IN 1861—BOYS OF THE FOURTH MICHIGAN INFANTRY

While the East was pouring its thousands to Washington, the West, an unknown quantity to the Confederacy, was rapidly organizing and sending forward its regiments. In 1860, the population of Michigan was 748,112. In the course of the war Michigan furnished 87,364 soldiers, of which 14,753 gave their lives. At the outbreak of the war the State had a militia strength of only twenty-eight companies, aggregating 1,241 officers and men. The State appropriation for military service was only $3,000 a year. At the President's call for troops on April 15th, Michigan's quota was only one infantry regiment. On May 7th the Legislature met and passed an Act giving the Governor power to raise ten regiments and make a loan of $1,000,000. On May 13th, the first regiment left for the seat of war, fully armed and equipped. Public subscriptions were started at all centers. Detroit raised $50,000 in one day as a loan to the State.

And that night the muster began, Massachusetts promptly rallying her old line-militia in their quaint, high-topped shakos and long gray overcoats—the Sixth and Eighth regiments mustering at once. New York city was alive with eager but untried soldiery. First and foremost stood her famous Seventh, the best blood and most honored names prominent in its ranks. The old armory at the foot of Third Avenue could not contain the crowds that gathered. Close at hand mustered the Seventy-first—the "American Guard" of the ante-bellum days. But a few streets away, with Centre Market as a nucleus, other throngs were cheering about the hall where Michael Corcoran, suspended but the year before because his Irishmen would not parade in honor of the Prince of Wales, was now besieged by fellow countrymen, eager to go with him and his gallant Sixty-ninth. Four blocks further, soon to be led by Cameron, brother to the Pennsylvania Secretary of War, the Highlanders were forming to the skirl of the piper and under the banner of the Seventy-ninth. West of Broadway, Le Gal and DeTrobriand were welcoming the enthusiastic Frenchmen who made up the old "red-legged Fifty-fifth," while, less noisily, yet in strong numbers, the Eighth, the Twelfth, and in Brooklyn the Fourteenth, were flocking to their armories and listening with bated breath to the latest news and orders from Washington.

Orders came soon enough. First to march from the metropolis for the front was New York's soldierly Seventh, striding down Broadway through countless multitudes of cheering citizens, their splendid band almost unheard through the volume of applause. Never before had New York seen its great thoroughfare so thronged; never had it shown such emotion as on that soft April afternoon of the 19th. Prompt as had been the response to marching orders, the gray column of the Seventh was not the first to move. The Massachusetts Sixth had taken the lead one day earlier, and was even now battling its way through the streets of Baltimore. Barely

A YOUNG VOLUNTEER FROM THE WEST

This youthful warrior in his "hickory" shirt looks less enthusiastic than his two comrades of the Fourth Michigan Infantry shown on the previous page. Yet the Fourth Michigan was with the Army of the Potomac from Bull Run to Appomattox. The regiment was organized at Adrian, Mich., and mustered in June 20, 1861. It left the State for Washington on June 26th, and its first service was the advance on Manassas, July 16th to 21, 1861. It participated thereafter in every great battle of the Army of the Potomac until it was relieved from duty in the trenches before Petersburg, June 19, 1864. The veterans and recruits were then transferred to the First Michigan Infantry. The regimental loss was heavy. Twelve officers and 177 enlisted men were killed or mortally wounded, and the loss by disease was one officer and 107 enlisted men.

had the Cortlandt Street Ferry borne the last detachment of the Seventh across the Hudson when the newsboys were shrieking the tidings of the attack on the men of New England by the mob of " blood-tubs " and " plug-uglies " in the Maryland city.

It takes five hours to go from New York to Washington to-day; it took six days that wild week in 1861. The Seventh, with the Massachusetts Eighth for company, had to patch the railway and trudge wearily, yet manfully, from Annapolis to the junction of the old Baltimore and Washington Railroad, before it could again proceed by rail to its great reception on Pennsylvania Avenue in Washington. Then New York's second offering started—another wonderful day in Gotham. In less than a week from the original call, the active militia was under arms in full ranks, and most of it en route for the front.

Farther west the Lake cities—Buffalo, Cleveland, Detroit, Milwaukee, Chicago—each had mustered a regiment with its own favorite companies—Continentals, Grays or Light Guards as a nucleus. Michigan, Wisconsin, Iowa, and Minnesota each had been called upon for a regiment, and the response was almost instantaneous. Ohio, Indiana, and Illinois, more populated, had tendered more than the thousands demanded.

By the 1st of June, there was camped or billeted about Washington the cream of the State soldiery of every commonwealth east of the Ohio and north of the Potomac—except Maryland. Maryland held aloof. Pennsylvania, asked for twelve thousand men, had rushed twenty thousand to the mustering officers. Massachusetts, called on for fifteen hundred, sent more than twice that number within two days. Ohio, taxed for just ten thousand, responded with twelve thousand, and Missouri, where Southern sentiment was rife and St. Louis almost a Southern stronghold, tumultuously raised ten thousand men, unarmed, undrilled, yet sorely needed. But for Nathaniel Lyon of the regular army, and the prompt muster

SOLDIERS FROM THE WEST IN 1861—FOURTH MICHIGAN INFANTRY

No less enthusiastic than the sister State across Lake Michigan was the then far-Western State of Wisconsin. Its population in 1860 was 305,391, and the State furnished during the war 91,327 men, or nearly 30 per cent. of the population. The State's loss in men was 12,301. Within a week after the President's call for 75,000 men, April 15, 1861, Governor Randall, of Wisconsin, had thirty-six companies offered him, although only one regiment was Wisconsin's quota under the Federal Government's apportionment. Within six days the first regiment was enrolled. Wisconsin suffered a financial panic within a fortnight after the fall of Fort Sumter. Thirty-eight banks out of one hundred and nine suspended payment, but the added burden failed to check the enthusiasm of the people. The State contained large and varied groups of settlers of foreign birth. Among its troops at the front, the Ninth, Twenty-sixth, and Forty-sixth Regiments were almost wholly German; the Twelfth Regiment was composed of French Canadians; the Fifteenth of Scandinavians; the Seventeenth of Irish, and the Third, Seventh, and Thirty-seventh contained a large enrollment of Indians. Wisconsin's contribution of troops took the form of four regiments of cavalry, one regiment of heavy artillery, thirteen batteries of light artillery, one company of sharpshooters, and fifty-four regiments of infantry. Such unanimity for the Union cause surprised the Confederacy.

of her Union men, Missouri would early have been lost to the Nation. And as for Kentucky, though in grand numbers and gallant services her sons repudiated his action, Governor Magoffin refused a man for the defense of the general Government, or what he called the "coercion" of the Southern States.

But it was a motley concourse, that which gathered at Washington where all eyes were centered. The call for seventy-five thousand militia for three months was quickly followed by the call for five hundred thousand volunteers for three years, and such was the spirit and enthusiasm of the North that, as fast as they could be uniformed, faster than they could be armed, the great regiments of State volunteers came dustily forth from the troop trains and went trudging along the length of Pennsylvania Avenue, out to the waiting camps in the suburbs. Within the month of its arrival, the Seventh New York, led by engineers and backed by comrade militiamen, had crossed the Potomac, invaded the sacred soil of Virginia, and tossed the red earth into rude fortifications. Then it had been sent home for muster-out as musketmen, but, let this ever be remembered, to furnish almost instantly seven hundred officers for the newly organizing regiments, regular and volunteer.

Two little classes of West Point cadets, graduated in May and June respectively, brave boys just out of their bell-buttoned coatees, were set in saddle and hard at work drilling whole battalions of raw lads from the shops and farms, whose elected officers were to the full as untaught as their men. Local fame as a drillmaster of cadets or Zouaves gave many a young fellow command of a company; some few, indeed, like Ellsworth, even of a regiment. Foreign soldiers of fortune, seeing their chance, had hurried to our shores and tendered their swords, many of them who could barely speak English receiving high commissions, and swaggering splendidly about the camps and streets. Many of the regiments came headed by local politicians, some who, but the year gone by, had been fervent supporters of Southern rights and slavery. A favored

IN THE QUOTA FROM MICHIGAN

WOODSMEN OF THE NORTH WITH THEIR TASSELED CAPS

An officer, privates, and bandsmen of the Fourth Michigan Infantry, who came from the West in their tasseled caps to fight for the Union cause. By the close of the war Michigan had sent eleven regiments and two companies of cavalry, a regiment of heavy artillery, fourteen batteries of light artillery, a regiment and a company of engineers, a regiment and eight companies of sharpshooters, and thirty-five regiments and two companies of infantry to the front. In

face of the fact that the original demand upon the State of Michigan had been for one company of infantry, this shows something of the spirit of the West. This was one of the earliest regiments sent to the front by the State of Michigan. Some of its companies were dressed in a sort of Zouave uniform, as shown above, that is, Canadian caps without visors, and short leggings; while other companies were dressed in the ordinary uniform of the volunteer regiments.

few came under command of soldierly, skilled young officers from the regular service, and most of them led by grave, thoughtful men in the prime of life who realized their responsibility and studied faithfully to meet the task.

Then wonderful was the variety of uniform! It was marked even before McDowell led forth the raw levies to try their mettle at Bull Run. Among the New Yorkers were Highlanders in plaid "trews" (their kilts and bonnets very properly left at home), the blue jackets of the Seventy-first, the gray jackets of the Eighth, and Varian's gunners—some of whom bethought them at Centreville that their time was up and it would be pleasanter " going home than hell-ward," as a grim, red-whiskered colonel, Sherman by name, said they surely would if they didn't quit straggling. There were half-fledged Zouaves, like the Fourteenth New York (Brooklyn), and full-rigged Zouaves, albeit their jackets and " knickers " were gray and only their shirts were red—the First " Fire " of New York, who had lost their martial little colonel—Ellsworth—before Jackson's shotgun in Alexandria. There were Rhode Islanders in pleated blue blouses—Burnside's boys; there were far Westerners from Wisconsin, in fast-fading gray. Michigan and Minnesota each was represented by a strong regiment. Blenker's Germans were there, a reserve division in gray from head to foot. There were a few troops of regular cavalry, their jackets gaudy with yellow braid and brazen shoulder scales. There were the grim regular batteries of Carlisle, Ricketts, and Griffin, their blouses somber, but the cross cannon on their caps gleaming with polish, such being the way of the regular. It was even more marvelous, later, when McClellan had come to organize the vast array into brigades and divisions, and to bring order out of chaos, for chaotic it was after Bull Run.

The States were uniforming their soldiery as best they could in that summer of 1861. New York, Massachusetts, and Pennsylvania usually in blue, the Vermonters in gray, turned-up with emerald, as befitted the Green Mountain boys. The

FIRST MINNESOTA INFANTRY AT CAMP STONE, NEAR POOLES–VILLE, MARYLAND, IN JANUARY, 1862

The First Minnesota Infantry was the first regiment tendered to the Government, April 14, 1861. It was mustered into the service April 29, 1861, fourteen days after the President's proclamation. The regiment embarked June 22, 1861, for Prairie du Chien, whence it proceeded by rail to Washington. Its first uniforms furnished by the State were black felt hats, black trousers, and red flannel shirts. It served throughout the war. The population of Minnesota in 1860 was 172,023, including 2,369 Indians. It furnished 24,020 soldiers, of whom 2,584 were lost. While the whole people of Minnesota were striving night and day to fill up new regiments to reënforce the national armies, they had to maintain garrisons along the Indian frontiers. One garrison was at Fort Ripley, below Crow Wing, and another at Fort Ridgly, in Nicolett County. Fort Abercrombie and a post on the Red River fifteen miles north of Breckinridge were strongly fortified. In the Sioux war of 1861, from one thousand to fifteen hundred persons were killed, and property to the value of over half a million dollars destroyed. Most of the regiments raised for the war saw some service at home, fighting the Indians within the borders of the State. Thus the First Minnesota sent two companies to Fort Ridgly, one to Fort Ripley, and two to Fort Abercrombie to quell Indian uprisings before they dared to gather at Fort Snelling to leave the State for the struggle with the South. Minnesota sent two regiments and two battalions of cavalry, one regiment of heavy artillery, three batteries of light artillery, two companies of sharpshooters, and eleven infantry regiments to the front during the war.

one Western brigade in the newly formed Army of the Potomac came clad in gray throughout, not to be changed for the
blue until late in September.

But for variety, New York city led the country. A second regiment of Fire Zouaves had been quickly formed, as
dashing in appearance as the first. Abram Duryée of the old
militia (with a black-eyed, solemn-faced little regular as second in command, soon to become famous as a corps leader)
marched forth at the head of a magnificent body of men, the
color-guard, nearly all seven-footers, all in the scarlet fez and
breeches of the favorite troops of France. Zouave rig was by
long odds the most pleasing to the popular eye in the streets
of the big city—and, less happily, to Southern marksmen later
—for all in a day the improvised wooden barracks were thronging with eager lads seeking enlistment in the Zouave regiments. Baxter's in Philadelphia, Farnsworth's (Second
Fire), Duryée's (Fifth New York), Bendix's, Hawkins', and
" Billy Wilson's " in New York.

To cater still further to the love for the spectacular and
the picturesque, still more distinctive regiments were authorized—the Garibaldi Guard—mainly Italians, under Colonel
D'Utassy, in a dress that aped the Bersaglieri. The D'Epi-
neul Zouaves, French and would-be Frenchmen, in the costliest costume yet devised, and destined to be abandoned before
they were six months older. Still another French battalion,
also in Algerian campaign rig—" *Les Enfants Perdus.*" Lost
Children, indeed, once they left New York and fell in with the
campaigners of Uncle Sam. Then came the Chasseurs, in very
natty and attractive dress, worn like the others until worn out
in one real campaign, when its wearers, like the others, lost their
identity in the universal, most unbecoming, yet eminently serviceable blue-flannel blouse and light-blue kersey trousers, with
the utterly ugly forage cap and stout brogans of the Union
army.

Fanciful names they took, too, at the start, and bore

THE GUARD EXAMINING PASSES AT GEORGETOWN FERRY

So expert became the patrols of the provost-guard, and so thorough the precautions at headquarters during the first half-year of drill and picket duty along the Potomac, that straggling from camp to camp, especially from camp to town, became a thing of the past. Guards were stationed at the bridges and ferry-boats to examine all passes. These were granted by the regimental, brigade, or division commanders—or by all three—and prescribed the time of departure and also the time of return. The holder was liable also to be stopped by a patrol of the provost-guard in Washington and required to show it again. Attempts were frequently made by officers and men who had overstayed their leave to tamper with the dates on their passes, but these seldom succeeded. Several officers were dismissed the service, and many a soldier suffered punishment of hard labor for this offense. Among old army men of 1861–62 located near Washington, the signature of Drake de Kay, Adjutant-General of the War Department, became well-known. His signature was considerably larger even than the renowned signature of John Hancock, who made his name under the Declaration of Independence an inscription so enormous that "King George would not have to take off his glasses to read it," and one not easily mistaken.

SERGEANT AND SENTRY ON GUARD AT LONG BRIDGE

proudly at home but meekly enough at the front, where speedily the "Ellsworth Avengers" became the Forty-fourth; the "Brooklyn Phalanx," the Sixty-seventh; the "Engineers," the Thirty-eighth; the "Lancers," the Sixth Pennsylvania. Dick Rush's gallant troopers were soon known as the "Seventh Regulars," and well did they earn the title. So, too, in the West, where the "Guthrie Grays," once Cincinnati's favorite corps, were swallowed up in the Sixth Ohio, and in St. Louis, where the "Fremont Rifles," "Zagonyi Guards," and "Foreign Legions" drew many an alien to the folds of the flag, and later to the dusty blue of the Union soldier.

As for arms, the regiments came to the front with every conceivable kind, and some with none at all. The regular infantry, what there was of it, had but recently given up the old smooth-bore musket for the Springfield rifle, caliber 58, with its paper cartridge and conical, counter-sunk bullet; but Harper's Ferry Arsenal had been burned, Springfield could not begin to turn out the numbers needed; Rock Island Arsenal was not yet built, and so in many a regiment, flank companies, only, received the rifle, the other eight using for months the old smooth-bore with its "buck-and-ball" cartridge, good for something within two hundred yards and for nothing beyond.

Even of these there were enough for only the first few regiments. Vast purchases, therefore, were made abroad, England selling us her Enfields, with which the fine Vermont brigade was first armed, and France and Belgium parting with thousands of the huge, brass-bound, ponderous *carabines à tige*"—the Belgian guns with a spike at the bottom to expand the soft leaden bullet when "rammed home." With this archaic blunderbus whole regiments were burdened, some foreign-born volunteers receiving it eagerly as "from the old country," and therefore superior to anything of Yankee invention. But their confidence was short lived. One day's march, one

TASTING THE SOUP
A FORMALITY SOON ABANDONED

One of the formalities soon abandoned after the soldiers took the field was that of tasting the soup. Here it appears as observed at the camp of the 31st Pennsylvania near Washington, in 1861. This duty fell to one of the officers of each company, and its object was to discover whether the soup was sufficiently strong to pass muster with the men, but as the war went on the men themselves became the only "tasters." The officers had too many other pressing duties to perform, and the handling of the soup, when there was any, became the simple matter of ladling it out to men who were only too glad to fill up their cans and devour the contents. The hunting-horn on the hat of the man leaning on his gun just behind the officer betokens the infantry. It was a symbol adopted from European armies, where the hunter became by a natural process of evolution the *chasseur* or light infantryman. In the Union armies the symbol was stretched to cover all the infantry. The presence of the feather in his hat also indicates that this photograph was taken early in the war. After the first campaign such superfluous decorative insignia were generally discarded.

short hour's shooting, and all predilection for such a weapon was gone forever.

And then the shoes with which the Federals reached the front! Not one pair out of four would have borne the test of a ten-mile tramp, not one out of ten would have stood the strain of a ten-days' march, and those that first took their places, the make of contractors, were even worse. Not until the "Iron Secretary," Stanton, got fairly into swing did contractors begin to learn that there was a man to dread in the Department of War, but Stanton had not even been suggested in the fall of 1861. Simon Cameron, the venerable Pennsylvania politician, was still in office. McClellan, the young, commanding general was riding diligently from one review to another, a martial sight, accompanied by his staff, orderlies, and escort.

The weather was perfect along the Potomac that gorgeous early autumn of 1861. The beautiful wooded heights were crowned with camps; the plains and fields were white with snowy tentage; the dust hung lazily over countless drill-grounds and winding roadways; the bands were out in force on every afternoon, filling the soft, sunshiny air with martial melody; the camps were thronged with smile-wreathed visitors, men and women from distant homes; the streets of Washington were crowded, and its famous old caravanseries prospered, as never before, for never had the Nation mustered in such overwhelming strength as here about the sleepy old Southern "city of magnificent distances"—a tawdry, shabby town in all conscience, yet a priceless something to be held against the world in arms, for the sacred flag that floated over the columned White House, for the revered and honored name it bore.

In seven strong divisions, with three or four brigades in each, "Little Mac," as the volunteers rejoiced to call him, had organized his great army as the autumn waned, and the livelong days were spent in the constant drill, drill that was absolutely needed to impart cohesion and discipline to this vast

OFFICERS OF THE FOURTH NEW JERSEY REGIMENT, 1861

This three-months regiment was formed at Trenton, N. J., in April, 1861, and arrived at Washington on May 6th. It was on duty at Meridian Hill until May 24th, when it took part in the occupation of Arlington Heights. It participated in the battle of Bull Run, July 21st, and ten days later was mustered out at the expiration of its term of service. New Jersey contributed three regiments of cavalry, five batteries of light artillery, and forty-one regiments of infantry to the Union armies during the war.

THE FOURTH NEW JERSEY ON THE BANKS OF THE POTOMAC, 1861

array, mostly American bred, and hitherto unschooled in discipline of any kind. When McDowell marched his militiamen forward to attack Beauregard at Bull Run, they swarmed all over the adjacent country, picking berries, and plundering orchards. Orders were things to obey only when they got ready and felt like it, otherwise " Cap "—as the company commander was hailed, or the " orderly," as throughout the war very generally and improperly the first sergeant was called—might shout for them in vain. " Cap," the lieutenant, the sergeant—all, for that matter—were in their opinion creatures of their own selection and, if dissatisfied with their choice, if officer or non-commissioned officer ventured to assert himself, to " put on airs," as our early-day militiamen usually expressed it, the power that made could just as soon, so they supposed, unmake.

It took many weeks to teach them that, once mustered into the service of " Uncle Sam," this was by no means the case. They had come reeling back from Bull Run, a tumultuous mob of fugitives, some of whom halted not even on reaching Washington. It took time and sharp measures to bring them back to their colors and an approximate sense of their duties. One fine regiment, indeed, whose soldierly colonel was left dead, found itself disarmed, deprived of its colors, discredited, and a dozen of its self-selected leaders summarily court-martialed and sentenced for mutiny. It took time and severe measures to bring officers and men back from Washington to camp, thereafter to reappear in town only in their complete uniform, and with the written pass of a brigade commander.

It took more time and many and many a lesson, hardest of all, to teach them that the men whom they had known for years at home as " Squire " or " Jedge," " Bob " or " Billy," could now only be respectfully addressed, if not referred to, as captain, lieutenant, or sergeant. It took still longer for the American man-at-arms to realize that there was good reason why the self-same " Squire " or " Jedge " or even a " Bob "

OFFICERS OF THE EIGHTH NEW YORK STATE MILITIA INFANTRY, ARLINGTON HEIGHTS, VIRGINIA, 1861

There were three organizations from New York State known as the Eighth Infantry—the Eighth Regiment State Militia Infantry, or "Washington Grays"; the Eighth Regiment Infantry, or "First German Rifles"; and the Eighth Regiment National Guard Infantry. The second of these was organized at New York and mustered in April 23, 1861. It left for Washington on May 26th, and served for two years. It served in the defenses of Washington till July 16, 1861; advanced to Manassas, Va., on that date, and took part in the battle of Bull Run July 21st. It did duty in the defenses of Washington, with various scouts and reconnaissances, till April, 1862, and then went to the Shenandoah Valley, where it fought in the battle of Cross Keys. Back to the Rappahannock, and service at Groveton and second Bull Run, and it was mustered out on April 23, 1863. The day before being mustered out, the three-years men were consolidated into a company and transferred to the Sixty-eighth Regiment of New York Infantry, May 5, 1863. The regiment lost ninety men, killed and wounded, and one officer and forty-two enlisted men by disease. The third organization was a three months regiment, organized May 29, 1862, which did duty in the defenses of Washington till September 9th of that year, and was again mustered into service for thirty days in June, 1863, and sent to Harrisburg, Pa. It was mustered out at New York City, July 23, 1863.

or "Billy" of the year agone, could not now be accosted or even passed without a soldierly straightening-up, and a prompt lifting of the open hand to the visor of the cap.

All through the months of August and September, the daily grind of drill by squad, by company, by battalion was pursued in the "hundred circling camps" about Washington. Over across the Long Bridge, about the fine old homestead of the Lees, and down toward Alexandria the engineers had traced, and the volunteers had thrown up, strong lines of fortification. Then, as other brigades grew in discipline and precision, the lines extended. The Vermonters, backed by the Western brigade, crossed the Chain Bridge one moonless night, seized the opposite heights, and within another day staked out Forts Ethan Allen and Marcy, and ten strong regiments fell to hacking down trees and throwing up parapets. Still further up the tow-path of the sleepy old Chesapeake and Ohio Canal, the men of Massachusetts, New York, and Minnesota made their lodgment opposite Edwards' Ferry, and presently from Maryland Heights down to where Anacostia Branch joins the Potomac, the northern shore bristled everywhere with the bayonets of the Union, and with every sun the relentless drill, drill, drill went on.

At break of day, the soldier lads were roused from slumber by the shrill rattle of the reveille. Following the methods of the Mexican War, every regiment had its corps of drummers and fifers, and stirring music did the youngsters make. The mists rolled lazily from the placid reaches of the Potomac until later banished by the sun, and doctors agreed that miasma lurked in every breath, and that coffee, piping hot, was the surest antidote. And so each company formed for reveille roll-call, tin cup in hand, or slung to the haversack in those regiments whose stern, far-sighted leaders required their men to appear full panoplied, thereby teaching them the soldier lesson of keeping arms, equipment, and clothing close at hand, where they could find them instantly, even in the dark. It

TWELFTH NEW YORK INFANTRY AT CAMP ANDERSON, 1861

The painfully new uniforms, and the attitudes that show how heavy the gold lace lay on unaccustomed arms, betoken the first year of the war. This three-months regiment sailed from New York for Fortress Monroe, Virginia, April 21, 1861; it arrived April 23d, and continued to Annapolis and Washington. It was mustered in on May 2, 1861, and assigned to Mansfield's command. It took part in the advance into Virginia May 23d, and the occupation of Arlington Heights the following day. It was there that, under the supervision of the Engineer Corps, its members learned that a soldier must dig as well as fight, and their aching backs and blistered hands soon made them forget their spruce, if awkward, appearance indicated in this photograph. Ten strong regiments were set to hacking down trees and throwing up parapets for Forts Ethan Allen and Marcy, staked out by the boys from Vermont. These New York volunteers were ordered to join Patterson's army on July 6th, and were part of the force that failed to detain Johnston in the Shenandoah Valley. With his fresh troops Johnston was able to turn the tide in favor of the Confederates on the field of Bull Run, July 21st. They bore themselves well in a skirmish near Martinsburg, Va., on July 12th. On the 5th of August they were mustered out at New York City. Many, however, reënlisted.

was not the best of coffee the commissaries served in 1861, but never did coffee taste better than in the keen air of those early misty mornings, and from those battered mugs of tin.

Customs varied according to the caprice of brigade or regimental commander, but in many a battalion in that early-day Army of the Potomac, a brief, brisk drill in the manual followed reveille; then " police " and sprucing-up tents and camp, then breakfast call and the much relished, yet often anathematized, bacon, with abundant loaves from Major Beckwith's huge Capitol bakery, and more steaming tins of coffee. Then came guard-mounting, with the band out, and the details in their best blue and brightest brasses, with swarms of men from every company, already keen critics of the soldiership of the adjutant, the sergeants, and rival candidates for orderly, for the colonel and the officer-of-the-day.

Later still, the whole regiment formed on the color line, and with field-officers in saddle—many of them mightily unaccustomed thereto—and ten stalwart companies in line, started forth on a two or three hours' hard battalion drill, field-officers furtively peeping at the drill books, perhaps, yet daily growing more confident and assured, the men speedily becoming more springy and muscular, and companies more and more machine-like.

Back to camp in time for a brush-off, and then " fall to " with vigorous appetite for dinner of beef and potatoes, pork and beans, and huge slabs of white bread, all on one tin plate, or a shingle. Then time came for a " snooze," or a social game, or a stroll along the Potomac shore and a call, perhaps, on a neighboring regiment; then once again a spring to ranks for a sharp, spirited drill by company; and then the band would come marching forth, and the adjutant with his sergeant-major, and " markers," with their little guidons, would appear; the colonel and his field seconds would sally forth from their tents, arrayed in their best uniforms, girt with sash and sword, white-gloved and precise, and again the long line would

EIGHTH NEW YORK, 1861

This regiment was organized for three months' service in April, 1861, and left for Washington on April 20th. It was known as the "Washington Grays." It did duty in the defenses of Washington until July, and took part in the battle of Bull Run on July 21st. It was attached to Porter's first brigade, Hunter's second division, McDowell's Army of Northeast Virginia. On August 2, 1861, it was mustered out at New York City. All of the fanciful regimental names, as well as their variegated uniforms, disappeared soon

after the opening of the war, and the "Grays," "Avengers," "Lancers," and "Rifles" became mere numerical units, while the regiments lost their identity in the universal blue flannel blouse and light-blue kersey trousers, with the utterly ugly forage cap and stout brogans of the Union armies—a uniform that was most unbecoming, yet eminently serviceable for rough work and actual warfare. The Eighth New York, for instance, at the battle of Bull Run, was mistaken several times for a Confederate regiment, although the error was always discovered in the nick of time.

MEN OF THE EIGHTH REGIMENT, NEW YORK STATE MILITIA INFANTRY, 1861 form for the closing, stately ceremony of the day—the martial dress-parade.

It was at this hour that the great army, soon to be known as the Army of the Potomac, seemed at its best. Many of the regiments had been able to draw the picturesque black felt hat and feather, the ugly, straight-cut, single-breasted coat of the regular service, and, with trousers of sky blue, and glistening black waist, and shoulder-belt, and spotless white gloves, to pride themselves that they looked like regulars. Many of them did.

Excellent were the bands of some of the Eastern regiments, and throngs of visitors came out from Washington to hear the stirring, spirited music and to view the martial pageant. Often McClellan, always with his staff, would watch the work from saddle, his cap-visor pulled well down over his keen eyes. Occasionally some wandering soldier, on pass from neighboring camp, would shock the military sensibilities of veteran officers by squirming through the guard lines and offering the little general-in-chief a chance to " shake hands with an old Zouave."

Once it happened in front of a whole brigade, and I heard him say "Certainly" before a scandalized aide-de-camp, or corporal of the guard, could hustle the intruder, grinning and triumphant, away from the imposing front of the cavalcade.

Time and again, in open barouche, with not a sign of escort, guard, or secret-service officer, there would come the two foremost statesmen of the day; one of them just rising above his companion and great rival of the East—as he had already overcome his great antagonist, the " Little Giant of the West "—and rising so steadily, rising so far above any and all contemporaries that, within another year, there lived no rival to his place in the hearts of the Nation, and within the compass of the two generations that followed, none has yet approached it. Tall, lank, angular, even awkward, but simple and unpretentious, cordial and kindly and sympathetic alike

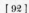

SCIENCE IN
THE TRAINING
OF AN ARMY

The stout sergeant in front of the adjutant's tent probably lost some weight during the process used by General George B. McClellan to make an army out of the raw material which flocked to Washington in the summer and fall of 1861. Through constant drill the volunteers speedily became more springy and muscular, and the companies daily more and more machine-like. The routine was much the same throughout the various camps. At break of day the soldier lads were roused by the hurried notes of the reveille. Hot coffee was served to guard against the miasmatic mists, and the regiments were required by their stern, far-sighted leaders to appear full-panoplied, thereby learning the soldier lesson of keeping arms,

A VOLUNTEER ABOUT TO LOSE SOME WEIGHT

THE EIGHTH NEW YORK GETTING INTO SHAPE

equipment, and clothing close at hand, where they could be found instantly, even in the dark. This was a lesson which proved invaluable many a time later in the war. In many a regiment a brief, brisk drill in the manual followed reveille; then "police" and sprucing up tents and camp, then breakfast call. Next came guard mounting, and later still the whole regiment formed on the color line, and started forth on a two or three hours' hard battalion drill. By the time General McClellan was ready to move his army to the Peninsula they had learned much of the lesson that they were to put to practical use. They could march under the burning sun or through the drenching rain with equal indifference, and their outdoor life had inured them to exposure that would have meant sunstroke on one hand, or pneumonia and death on the other, a few months earlier in the war.

to colonel, corporal, or drum-boy, Abraham Lincoln sprawled at his ease, with William H. Seward sitting primly by his side —the President and the Premier—the Commander-in-Chief and the Secretary of State—the latter, his confident opponent for the nomination but the year agone, his indulgent adviser a few months back, but now, with wisdom gained through weeks of mental contact, his admiring and loyal second.

It was characteristic of our people that about the knoll where sat McClellan, in statuesque and soldierly pose, his aides, orderlies, and escort at his back, there should gather an admiring throng, while about the carriage of the dark-featured, black-whiskered, black-coated, tall-hatted civilian there should be but a little group. It was characteristic of McClellan that he should accept this homage quite as his due. It was characteristic of Lincoln that he did not seem to mind it. " I would hold McClellan's horse for him," he was sadly saying, just one year later, " if he would only *do* something."

Only a few days after this scene at Kalorama, all the camps along the Potomac about the Chain Bridge were roused to a sudden thrill of excitement at the roar of cannon in brisk action on the Lewinsville road. General " Baldy " Smith had sent out a reconnaissance. It had stumbled into a hornet's nest of Confederates; it needed help, and Griffin's regulars galloped forward and into battery. For twenty minutes there was a thunderous uproar. A whole division stood to arms. The firing ended as suddenly as it began, but not so the excitement. To all but two regiments within hearing that was the first battle-note their ears had ever known—how fearfully familiar it was soon to be!—and then, toward sunset, who should come riding out from Washington, with a bigger staff and escort than ever, but our hero, " Little Mac," and with enthusiasm unbounded, five thousand strong, the " boys " flung themselves about him, cheering like mad, and, after the American manner, demanding " speech." That was the day he said, " We've had our last defeat; we have made our last retreat," and then

PLEASANT DAYS IN '61 FOR VOLUNTEERS FROM EAST AND WEST

After the various drills through the day in the camps about Washington in the fall of 1861, the men had time for a "snooze" or a social game. They would stroll along the shore of the Potomac, their minds full of the great battles to come—how great and terrible they little knew—or call perhaps on friends in a neighboring regiment to discuss what McClellan was going to do to the Confederates with his well-disciplined army in the spring. They did not suspect that "Little Mac" was to be deposed for Burnside, and that the command of the Army of the Potomac was to pass on to Hooker and then to Meade. In the meantime, the star of Grant was to rise steadily in the West, and he was finally to guide the Army of the Potomac to victory. All these things were hidden to these men of the Eighth New York State Militia Infantry in their picturesque gray uniforms. They have

already some of the rough and ready veteran appearance, as have their Western comrades (Fourth Michigan) in the smaller picture. At the outset of the war there was no regular or prescribed uniform, and in many regiments each company varied from the others. One company might even be clad in red, another in gray, another in blue, and still another in white. Since the South had regiments in gray uniform and many of the men of the North were clad in gray, at the first battle of Bull Run some fatal mistakes occurred, and soldiers fired upon their own friends. Thereafter all the soldiers of the Union army were dressed practically alike in blue, with slight variations in the color of insignia to designate cavalry, artillery, and infantry. Head covering varied, many regiments wearing black hats. During the last years of the war individual soldiers wore hats—usually black—on the march.

followed the confident prediction that the war would be " short, sharp, and decisive." In unbounded faith and fervor, old and young, they yelled their acclamations. Was there ever a commander by whom " the boys " stood more loyally or lovingly?

A few days later still, on the Virginia slopes south of the Chain Bridge, where was stationed a whole brigade of " the boys "—Green Mountain boys principally, though stalwart lads from Maine, Wisconsin, New York, and Pennsylvania, were there also, preparations were in progress for a tragic scene. There had been some few instances of sentries falling asleep. Healthy farm-boys, bred to days of labor in the sunshine, and correspondingly long hours of sleep at night, could not always overcome the drowsiness that stole upon them when left alone on picket. An army might be imperiled—a lesson must be taught. A patrol had come upon a young Vermonter asleep on post. A court martial had tried and sentenced, and to that sentence General Smith had set the seal of his approval. For the soldier-crime of sleeping on guard, Private Scott was to be shot to death in sight of the Vermont brigade.

A grave would be dug; a coffin set beside it; the pale-faced lad would be led forth; the chaplain, with bowed head and quivering lips, would speak his final word of consolation; the firing-party—a dozen of his own brigade—would be marched to the spot, subordinate, sworn to obey, yet dumbly cursing their lot; the provost-marshal would give the last order, while all around, in long, rigid, yet trembling lines, a square of soldiery would witness a comrade's death. But on the eve of the appointed day, the great-hearted Lincoln, appealed to by several of the lad's company, went himself to the Chain Bridge, had a long conversation with the young private and sent him back to his regiment, a free man. The President of the United States could not suffer it that one of his boys should be shot to death for being overcome by sleep. He gave his young soldier life only that the lad might die gloriously a few months later, heading the dash of his comrades upon the Southern line at

OFFICERS OF "THE RED–LEGGED FIFTY–FIFTH" NEW YORK AT FORT GAINES, 1861

Right royally did Washington welcome the Fifty-fifth New York Infantry, surnamed "Garde de Lafayette" in memory of that distinguished Frenchman's services to our country in Revolutionary days, in September, 1861. The "red-legged Fifth-fifth" was organized in New York City by Colonel Philip Regis de Trobriand (who ended the war as a brevet major-general of volunteers, a rank bestowed upon him for highly meritorious services during the Appomattox campaign) and left for Washington August 31st. The French uniforms attracted much attention and elicited frequent bursts of applause as the crowds on Pennsylvania Avenue realized once again how many citizens from different lands had rushed to the defense of their common country. The Fifty-fifth accompanied McClellan to the Peninsula, and took part in the desperate assault on Marye's Heights at Fredericksburg, after which it was consolidated, in four companies, with the Thirty-eighth New York December 21, 1862. The regiment lost during service thirty-three enlisted men killed and mortally wounded, and twenty-nine enlisted men by disease. Its gallant colonel survived until July 15, 1897.

Lee's Mill—sending, with his last breath, a message to the President that he had tried to live up to the advice he had given.

It was indeed a formative period, that first half-year of drill, picket duty, and preparation along the Potomac, and so expert became the patrols of the provost guard, so thorough the precautions at headquarters, that straggling from camp to camp, especially from camp to town, became a thing of the past. Except a favored few, like the mounted orderlies, or messengers, men of one brigade knew next to nothing of those beyond their lines. Barely three miles back from the Potomac, up the valley of Rock Creek, was camped an entire division, the Pennsylvania Reserves, in which the future leader of the Army of the Potomac was modestly commanding a brigade.

Just across the Chain Bridge, he who was destined to become his great second, proclaimed " superb " at Gettysburg, was busily drilling another, yet the men under George G. Meade and those under Winfield S. Hancock saw nothing of each other in the fall of 1861.

Over against Washington, the Jerseymen under dashing Philip Kearny brushed with their outermost sentries the picket lines of " Ike Stevens' Highlanders," camped at Chain Bridge, yet so little were the men about Arlington known to these in front of the bridge, that a night patrol from the one stirred up a lively skirmish with the other. In less than a year those two heroic soldiers, Kearny and Stevens, were to die in the same fight only a few miles farther out, at Chantilly. Only for a day or two did the " Badgers," the " Vermonters," and the " Knickerbockers " of King's, Smith's, and Stevens' brigades compare notes with the so-called " California Regiment," raised in the East, yet led by the great soldier-senator from the Pacific slope, before they, the " Californians," and their vehement colonel marched away along the tow-path to join Stone's great division farther up stream.

Three regiments, already famous for their drill and discipline had preceded them, the First Minnesota, the Fifteenth

[98]

A DRESS PARADE OF THE SEVENTEENTH NEW YORK IN 1861

New York's Seventeenth Infantry Volunteers entered the war as the "Westchester Chasseurs." It was organized at New York City and mustered in for two years, Colonel H. Seymour Lansing in command. The regiment left for Washington June 21, 1861, and was stationed near Miner's Hill, just across the District of Columbia line, a mile and a half from Falls Church. It fought on the Peninsula, at the second Bull Run, at Antietam, Fredericksburg, and Chancellorsville, and took part in the famous "mud march" January 20 to 24, 1863. On May 13, 1863, the three-years men were detached and assigned to a battalion of New York volunteers, and on June 23, 1863, were transferred to the 146th New York Infantry. The regiment was mustered out June 2, 1863, having lost during service five officers and thirty-two enlisted men killed and mortally wounded, and three officers and thirty-seven enlisted men by disease.

THE SEVENTEENTH NEW YORK AT MINER'S HILL, NEAR WASHINGTON

It was not often during army life that the advantage of churches or places of religious worship were available to the troops in the field. When chaplains were connected with regiments in active service, any improvised tent or barrel for an altar or pulpit was utilized for the minister's benefit. The question of denomination rarely entered the minds of the men. Where a church edifice was near the camps, or when located near some village or city, services were held within the edifice, but this was very infrequent. The camp at Arlington Heights was located directly opposite Washington and Georgetown, D. C., overlooking the banks of the Potomac River on the Virginia side. The Ninth Massachusetts was a regiment composed of Irish volunteers from the vicinity of Boston. The Catholic chaplains were very assiduous in their attention to the ritual of the Church, even on the tented field. Many of these chaplains have

FATHER SCULLY PREACHING TO THE NINTH
MASSACHUSETTS REGIMENT

since risen to high positions in the Church. Archbishop Ireland was one of these splendid and devoted men. An example of the fearless devotion of the Catholic chaplains was the action of Father Corby, of the Irish Brigade, at the battle of Gettysburg. As the brigade was about to go into the fiercest fighting at the center of the Federal line and shot and shell were already reaching its ranks, at the solicitation of Father Corby it was halted, and knelt; standing upon a projecting rock, the brave father rendered absolution to the soldiers according to the rites of the Catholic Church. A few minutes later the brigade had plunged to the very thick of the fierce fighting at the "Loop."

SERVICE FOR THE RECRUITS AT CAMP CASS, ARLINGTON HEIGHTS, VIRGINIA, 1861

Attentive and solemn are the faces of these men new to warfare, facing dangers as yet unknown, while they listen to Father Scully's earnest words. Not a few of the regiments in the Union armies were led by ministers who assisted in organizing them, and then accepted the command. When the Fiftieth New York Engineers were stationed in front of Petersburg, Virginia, they made a rustic place of worship, spire and all, after the model of their winter-quarters. A photograph of this soldier-built edifice is shown on page 257. The muskets and glistening bayonets of the soldiers, leaning against the fence in the foreground of the Petersburg picture, contrast vividly with the peaceful aspect of the little church—an oasis in a desert.

BLAIR, OF MISSOURI

Although remaining politically neutral throughout the war, Missouri contributed four hundred and forty-seven separate military organizations to the Federal armies, and over one hundred to the Confederacy. The Union sentiment in the State is said to have been due to Frank P. Blair, who, early in 1861, began organizing home guards. Blair subsequently joined Grant's command and served with that leader until Sherman took the helm in the West. With Sherman Major-General Blair fought in Georgia and through the Carolinas.

BAKER, OF CALIFORNIA

California contributed twelve military organizations to the Federal forces, but none of them took part in the campaigns east of the Mississippi. Its Senator, Edward D. Baker, was in his place in Washington when the war broke out, and, being a close friend of Lincoln, promptly organized a regiment of Pennsylvanians which was best known by its synonym "First California." Colonel Baker was killed at the head of it at the battle of Ball's Bluff, Virginia, October 21, 1861. Baker had been appointed brigadier-general but declined.

KELLEY, OF WEST VIRGINIA

West Virginia counties had already supplied soldiers for the Confederates when the new State was organized in 1861. As early as May, 1861, Colonel B. F. Kelley was in the field with the First West Virginia Infantry marshalled under the Stars and Stripes. He served to the end of the war and was brevetted major-general. West Virginia furnished thirty-seven organizations of all arms to the Federal armies, chiefly for local defense and for service in contiguous territory. General Kelley was prominent in the Shenandoah campaigns.

SMYTH, OF DELAWARE

Little Delaware furnished to the Federal armies fifteen separate military organizations. First in the field was Colonel Thomas A. Smyth, with the First Delaware Infantry. Early promoted to the command of a brigade, he led it at Gettysburg, where it received the full force of Pickett's charge on Cemetery Ridge, July 3, 1863. He was brevetted major-general and fell at Farmville, on Appomattox River, Va., April 7, 1865, two days before the surrender at Appomattox. General Smyth was a noted leader in the Second Corps.

MITCHELL, OF KANSAS

The virgin State of Kansas sent fifty regiments, battalions, and batteries into the Federal camps. Its Second Infantry was organized and led to the field by Colonel R. B. Mitchell, a veteran of the Mexican War. At the first battle in the West, Wilson's Creek, Mo. (August 10, 1861), he was wounded. At the battle of Perryville, Brigadier-General Mitchell commanded a division in McCook's Corps and fought desperately to hold the Federal left flank against a sudden and desperate assault by General Bragg's Confederates.

CROSS, OF NEW HAMPSHIRE

New Hampshire supplied twenty-nine military organizations to the Federal armies. To the Granite State belongs the grim distinction of furnishing the regiment which had the heaviest mortality roll of any infantry organization in the army. This was the Fifth New Hampshire, commanded by Colonel E. E. Cross. The Fifth served in the Army of the Potomac. At Gettysburg, Colonel Cross commanded a brigade, which included the Fifth New Hampshire, and was killed at the head of it near Devil's Den, on July 2, 1863.

| PEARCE, OF ARKANSAS | STEUART, OF MARYLAND | CRITTENDEN, THE CONFEDERATE |

Arkansas entered into the war with enthusiasm, and had a large contingent of Confederate troops ready for the field in the summer of 1861. At Wilson's Creek, Missouri, August 10, 1861, there were four regiments and two batteries of Arkansans under command of Brigadier-General N. B. Pearce. Arkansas furnished seventy separate military organizations to the Confederate armies and seventeen to the Federals. The State was gallantly represented in the Army of Northern Virginia, notably at Antietam and Gettysburg.

Maryland quickly responded to the Southern call to arms, and among its first contribution of soldiers was George H. Steuart, who led a battalion across the Potomac early in 1861. These Marylanders fought at First Bull Run, or Manassas, and Lee's army at Petersburg included Maryland troops under Brigadier-General Steuart. During the war this little border State, politically neutral, sent six separate organizations to the Confederates in Virginia, and mustered thirty-five for the Federal camps and for local defense.

Kentucky is notable as a State which sent brothers to both the Federal and Confederate armies. Major-General George B. Crittenden, C. S. A., was the brother of Major-General Thomas L. Crittenden, U. S. A. Although remaining politically neutral throughout the war, the Blue Grass State sent forty-nine regiments, battalions, and batteries across the border to uphold the Stars and Bars, and mustered eighty of all arms to battle around the Stars and Stripes and protect the State from Confederate incursions.

| RANSOM, OF NORTH CAROLINA | FINEGAN, OF FLORIDA | CLEBURNE, OF TENNESSEE |

The last of the Southern States to cast its fortunes in with the Confederacy, North Carolina vied with the pioneers in the spirit with which it entered the war. With the First North Carolina, Lieut.-Col. Matt W. Ransom was on the firing-line early in 1861. Under his leadership as brigadier-general, North Carolinians carried the Stars and Bars on all the great battlefields of the Army of Northern Virginia. The State furnished ninety organizations for the Confederate armies, and sent eight to the Federal camps.

Florida was one of the first to follow South Carolina's example in dissolving the Federal compact. It furnished twenty-one military organizations to the Confederate forces, and throughout the war maintained a vigorous home defense. Its foremost soldier to take the field when the State was menaced by a strong Federal expedition in February, 1864, was Brigadier-General Joseph Finegan. Hastily gathering scattered detachments, he defeated and checked the expedition at the battle of Olustee, or Ocean Pond, on February 20.

Cleburne was of foreign birth, but before the war was one year old he became the leader of Tennesseeans, fighting heroically on Tennessee soil. At Shiloh, Cleburne's brigade, and at Murfreesboro, Chattanooga, and Franklin, Major-General P. R. Cleburne's division found the post of honor. At Franklin this gallant Irishman "The 'Stonewall' Jackson of the West," led Tennesseeans for the last time and fell close to the breastworks. Tennessee sent the Confederate armies 129 organizations, and the Federal fifty-six, and Twentieth Massachusetts, followed by longing hearts and admiring eyes, for rumors from Edwards' Ferry told of frequent forays of Virginia horse, and the stories were believed and these noted regiments envied by those held back here for other duty. The Fortieth New York, too, had gone—Tammany Hall's contribution to the Union cause—Tammany that a year back had been all pro-slavery. Something told the fellows that grand opportunity awaited those favored regiments, and something like a pall fell over the stunned and silent camps when late October brought the news of dire disaster at Ball's Bluff. Baker, the brave Union leader, the soldier-senator, the hero of Cerro Gordo, the intimate friend of Abraham Lincoln, shot dead, pierced by many a bullet—Raymond Lee and many of his best officers wounded or captured—the Fifteenth and Twentieth Massachusetts tricked, ambushed, and driven in bewilderment into the Potomac, brave and battling to the last, yet utterly overwhelmed.

No wonder there was talk of treachery! No wonder the young faces in our ranks were grave and sad! Big Bethel, Bull Run, Ball's Bluff—three times had the Federals clashed with these nimble foemen from the South, and every clash had wrought humiliation. No wonder the lessons sank home, for young hearts are impressionable, and far more than half the rank and file of the Army of the Potomac was under twenty-one—far more than a third not then nineteen years of age. With all its fine equipment, its rapidly improving arms, its splendid spirit that later endured through every trial, defeat and disaster, with all its drills, discipline, and preparation, the army East and West—Potomac, Ohio, or Tennessee, had yet to learn the bitter lessons of disastrous battle, had yet to withstand the ordeal by fire. It took all the months of that formative period, and more, to fit that army for the fearful task before it, but well did it learn its lesson, and nobly did it do its final duty.

PART I
SOLDIER LIFE

GLIMPSES OF
THE CONFEDERATE
ARMY

THE FIRST HISTORICAL PUBLICATION OF SCENES PHOTOGRAPHED WITHIN THE CONFEDERATE LINES, DURING THE CIVIL WAR, MAY BE FOUND IN THE ILLUSTRATIONS TO THE CHAPTERS BY ADMIRAL FRENCH E. CHADWICK AND GENERAL MARCUS J. WRIGHT, ON PAGES 86–110 OF VOLUME I. MORE OF SUCH PREVIOUSLY UNPUBLISHED PHOTOGRAPHS APPEAR IN VOLUME III, PAGES 169–171. WITH THE THREE CHAPTERS THAT FOLLOW ARE PRESENTED AN EVEN LARGER NUMBER OF WAR-TIME CONFEDERATE PHOTOGRAPHS. ALL THE SERIES ABOVE REFERRED TO WERE NEVER BEFORE REPRODUCED, OR EVEN COLLECTED; IN FACT, THE VERY EXISTENCE OF SUCH FAITHFUL CON-TEMPORARY RECORDS REMAINED UNKNOWN TO MOST VETERANS AND HIS-TORIANS UNTIL THE PUBLICATION OF THIS "PHOTOGRAPHIC HISTORY." THE OPPORTUNITY THUS FURNISHED TO STUDY THE VOLUNTEERS OF THE CON-FEDERACY AS THEY CAMPED AND DRILLED AND PREPARED FOR WAR IS UNIQUE.

A VIVID "GLIMPSE OF THE CONFEDERATE ARMY"—1861

This spirited photograph by Edwards of New Orleans suggests more than volumes of history could tell of the enthusiasm, the hope, with which the young Confederate volunteers, with their queerly variegated equipment, sprang to the defense of their land in '61.   Around this locality in Florida some of the very earliest operations centered.   Fort McRee and the adjacent batteries had passed into Confederate hands on January 12, 1861, when Lieutenant Adam J. Slemmer withdrew with his eighty-two men to Fort Pickens in Pensacola Harbor.   The lack of conventional military uniformity shown above must not be thought exceptional.   Con-

INSIDE THE BATTERY NORTH OF FORT McREE AT PENSACOLA

federate camps and men in general pretended to nothing like the "smartness" of the well-equipped boys in blue. Weapons, however, were cared for. All through the Southern camps, soldiers could be found busily polishing their muskets, swords, and bayonets with wood ashes well moistened. "Bright muskets" and "tattered uniforms" went together in the Army of Northern Virginia. Swords, too, were bright in Florida, judging from the two young volunteers flourishing theirs in the photograph. This is one of the batteries which later bombarded Fort Pickens and the Union fleet. It was held by the Confederates until May 2, 1862.

GLIMPSES OF THE CONFEDERATE ARMY

By Randolph H. McKim, D.D.

Late First Lieutenant, and A. D. C. 3d Brigade, Army of Northern Virginia

[This chapter was prepared by Dr. McKim at the request of the Editors of the "Photographic History of the Civil War" to describe the Confederate army from the standpoint of the individual and to bring out conditions under which the war was waged by that army, as well as to show the differences between those conditions and the life and activity of the Union army. The following pages are written under the limitations imposed by these conditions.]

WRITERS on the Civil War frequently speak of the Southern army as "the Secession army." Yet the most illustrious leaders of that army, Robert E. Lee and "Stonewall" Jackson, to name no more, were in fact opposed to secession; though when Virginia at length withdrew from the Union, they felt bound to follow her. I think it likely indeed that a very large proportion of the conspicuous and successful officers, and a like proportion also of the men who fought in the ranks of the Confederate armies were likewise originally Union men—opposed, at any rate, to the exercise of the right of secession, even if they believed that the right existed.

It will be remembered that months elapsed between the secession of the Gulf States and that of the great border States, Virginia, North Carolina, and Tennessee, which furnished so large a proportion of the soldiers who fought for the Southern Confederacy. But, on the 15th of April, 1861, an event occurred which instantly transformed those great States into Secession States—the proclamation of Abraham Lincoln calling

THE DRUM–MAJOR OF THE FIRST VIRGINIA, APRIL, 1861

C. R. M. Pohlé of Richmond, Virginia, drum-major of the crack Richmond regiment, the First Virginia, presented a magnificent sight indeed, when this photograph was taken in April, 1861. The Army of Northern Virginia did not find bands and bearskin hats preferable to food, and both the former soon disappeared, while the supply of the latter became only intermittent. Bands, however, still played their part now and then in the Virginia men's fighting. David Homer Bates records that when Early descended on Washington a scout reported to General Hardin at Fort Stevens: "The enemy are preparing to make a grand assault on this fort to-night. They are tearing down fences and are moving to the right, their bands playing. Can't you hurry up the Sixth Corps?" Many of the regiments raised among men of wealth and culture in the larger cities of the Confederacy were splendidly equipped at the outset of the war. Captain Alexander Duncan of the Georgia Hussars, of Savannah, is authority for the statement that the regiment spent $25,000 on its initial outfit. He also adds that at the close of the war the uniforms of this company would have brought about twenty-five cents.

upon them to furnish their quota of troops to coerce the seceded States back into the Union. Even the strongest Federalists, like Hamilton, had, in the discussions in the Constitutional Convention, utterly repudiated and condemned the coercion of a State. It was not strange, then, that the summons to take up arms and march against their Southern brethren, aroused deep indignation in these States, and instantly transformed them into secession states. But for that proclamation, the Southern army would not have been much more than half its size, and would have missed its greatest leaders.

A glance at its personnel will perhaps be instructive. In its ranks are serving side by side the sons of the plain farmers, and the sons of the great landowners—the Southern aristocrats. Not a few of the men who are carrying muskets or serving as troopers are classical scholars, the flower of the Southern universities. In an interval of the suspension of hostilities at the battle of Cold Harbor, a private soldier lies on the ground poring over an Arabic grammar—it is Crawford H. Toy, who is destined to become the famous professor of Oriental languages at Harvard University. In one of the battles in the Valley of Virginia a volunteer aid of General John B. Gordon is severely wounded—it is Basil L. Gildersleeve, who has left his professor's chair at the University of Virginia to serve in the field. He still lives (1911), wearing the laurel of distinction as the greatest Grecian in the English-speaking world. At the siege of Fort Donelson, in 1862, one of the heroic captains who yields up his life in the trenches is the Reverend Dabney C. Harrison, who raised a company in his own Virginia parish, and entered the army at its head. In the Southwest a lieutenant-general falls in battle—it is General Leonidas Polk, who laid aside his bishop's robes to become a soldier, having been educated to arms at West Point.

It is a striking fact that when Virginia threw in her lot with her Southern sisters in April, 1861, practically the whole body of students at her State University, 515 out of 530 who

CONFEDERATE VOLUNTEERS OF '61—OFFICERS OF THE "NOTTAWAY GRAYS"

CAPTAIN R. CONNALLY

CAPTAIN ARCH. CAMPBELL

After John Brown's attempt at Harper's Ferry, the people of the border states began to form military companies in almost every county and to uniform, arm, and drill them. In the beginning, each of these companies bore some designation instead of a company letter. There were various "Guards," "Grays," and "Rifles"— the last a ludicrous misnomer, the "rifles" being mostly represented by flint-lock muskets, dating from the War of 1812, resurrected from State arsenals and carrying the old "buck and ball" ammunition, "caliber '69." On this and the following illustration page are shown some members of Company G, Eighteenth Virginia Regiment, first called Nottaway Rifle Guards and afterward Nottaway Grays. The company was organized on the 12th of January, 1861. Its original roll was signed by fifty men. April 13, 1861, its services were tendered to Governor Letcher "to repel every hostile demonstration, either upon Virginia or the Confederate States." This sentiment of home defense animated the Confederate armies to heroic deeds. The company from Nottaway, for example, was active in every important combat with the Army of Northern Virginia; yet it was composed of citizens who had, with possibly one exception, no military education, and who, but for the exigencies of the time, would never have joined a military company.

were registered from the Southern States, enlisted in the Confederate army. This army thus represented the whole Southern people. It was a self-levy *en masse* of the male population in all save certain mountain regions in Virginia, North Carolina, Tennessee, Alabama, and Georgia.

One gets a perhaps new and surprising conception of the character of the rank and file of the Southern army in such incidents as the following: Here are mock trials going on in the moot-court of a certain artillery company, and the discussions are pronounced by a competent authority "brilliant and powerful." Here is a group of privates in a Maryland infantry regiment in winter-quarter huts near Fairfax, Virginia; and among the subjects discussed are the following: Vattel and Philmore on international law; Humboldt's works and travels; the African explorations of Barth; the influence of climate on the human features; the culture of cotton; the laws relating to property. Here are some Virginia privates in a howitzer company solemnly officiating at the burial of a tame crow; and the exercises include an English speech, a Latin oration, and a Greek ode!

These Confederate armies must present to the historian who accepts the common view that the South was fighting for the perpetuation of the institution of slavery a difficult—in fact, an insoluble—problem. How could such a motive explain the solidarity of the diverse elements that made up those armies? The Southern planter might fight for his slaves; but why the poor white man, who had none? How could slavery generate such devotion, such patient endurance, such splendid heroism, such unconquerable tenacity through four long years of painfully unequal struggle? The world acknowledges the superb valor of the men who fought under the Southern Cross—and the no less superb devotion of the whole people to the cause of the Confederacy.

Colonel Theodore Roosevelt has written, "The world has never seen better soldiers than those who followed Lee."

LIEUTENANT
R. FERGUSON

LIEUTENANT
E. H. MUSE

LIEUTENANT
AL. CAMPBELL

COMPANY G
OF THE
EIGHTEENTH VIRGINIA
"OLD IRONSIDES"

A look at these frank, straightforward features conveys at a glance the caliber of the personnel in the Army of Northern Virginia. Good American faces they are, with good old-fashioned Anglo-Saxon names—Campbell, Ferguson, Hardy, Irby, Sydnor. They took part in the first battle of Bull Run, and "tasted powder." In the fall of '61 First-Lieutenant Richard Irby resigned to take his seat in the General Assembly of Virginia, but on April 20, 1862, he was back as captain of the company. He was wounded twice at Second Manassas and died at last of prison fever. Company G took part in Pickett's charge at Gettysburg. Of the men who went into the battle, only six came out unhurt. Eleven were killed or mortally wounded, and nineteen were wounded. The company fought to the bitter end; Captain Campbell (page 111) was killed at Sailor's Creek, only three days before Appomattox.

LIEUTENANT
SAMUEL HARDY

CAPTAIN
P. F. ROWLETT

CAPTAIN
RICHARD IRBY

LIEUTENANT
A. D. CRENSHAW

LIEUTENANT
J. E. IRVIN

COLOR–SERGEANT
E. G. SYDNOR

General Hooker has testified that "for steadiness and efficiency" Lee's army was unsurpassed in ancient or modern times. "We have not been able to rival it." And General Charles A. Whittier of Massachusetts has said, "The Army of Northern Virginia will deservedly rank as the best army which has existed on this continent, suffering privations unknown to its opponent."

Nor is it credible that such valor and such devotion were inspired by the desire to hold their fellow men in slavery? Is there any example of such a phenomenon in all the long records of history?

Consider, too, another fact for which the historians must assign a sufficient motive. On the bronze tablets in the rotunda of the University of Virginia, memorializing the students who fell in the great war, there are upwards of five hundred names, and, of these, two hundred and thirty-three were still privates when they fell; so that, considering the number of promotions from the ranks, it is certain that far more than half of those alumni who gave up their lives for the Southern cause, volunteered as private soldiers. They did not wait for place or office, but unhesitatingly entered the ranks, with all the hardships that the service involved.

Probably no army ever contained more young men of high culture among its private soldiers—graduates in arts, in letters, in languages, in the physical sciences, in the higher mathematics, and in the learned professions—as the army that fought under the Southern Cross. And how cheerful—how uncomplaining—how gallant they were! They marched and fought and starved, truly without reward. Eleven dollars a month in Confederate paper was their stipend. Flour and bacon and peanut-coffee made up their bill of fare. The hard earth, or else three fence-rails, tilted up on end, was their bed, their knapsacks their pillows, and a flimsy blanket their covering. The starry firmament was often their only tent. Their clothing—well, I cannot describe it. I can only say it was "a thing of shreds and patches," interspersed with rents.

A FINE–LOOKING GROUP OF CONFEDERATE OFFICERS

The officers in camp at the east end of Sullivan's Island, near Charleston, illustrate forcibly Dr. McKim's description of the personnel of the Confederate army. The preservation of the photograph is due to the care of the Washington Light Infantry of Charleston, S. C., in which these men were officers. To the left stands M. Master, and in front of him are Lieutenant Wilkie, R. Choper, and Lieutenant Lloyd. Facing them is Captain Simmonton, and the soldier shading his eyes with his hand is Gibbs Blackwood. It is easy to see from their fine presence and bearing that these were among the many thousands of Southerners able to distinguish themselves in civil life who nevertheless sprang to bear arms in defense of their native soil. "In an interval of the suspension of hostilities at the battle of Cold Harbor," writes Randolph H. McKim in the text of this volume, "a private soldier lies on the ground poring over an Arabic grammar— it is Crawford H. Toy, who is destined to become the famous professor of Oriental languages at Harvard University. In one of the battles in the Valley of Virginia, a volunteer aid of General John B. Gordon is severely wounded—it is Basil L. Gildersleeve, who has left his professor's chair at the University of Virginia to serve in the field. He still lives (1911), wearing the laurel of distinction as the greatest Grecian in the English-speaking world. At the siege of Fort Donelson, in 1862, one of the heroic captains who yields up his life in the trenches is the Reverend Dabney C. Harrison, who raised a company in his own Virginia parish and entered the army at its head. In the Southwest a lieutenant-general falls in battle—it is General Leonidas Polk, who laid aside his bishop's robes to become a soldier in the field."

But this was not all. They had not even the reward which is naturally dear to a soldier's heart—I mean the due recognition of gallantry in action. By a strange oversight there was no provision in the Confederate army for recognizing either by decoration or by promotion on the field, distinguished acts of gallantry. No "Victoria Cross," or its equivalent, rewarded even the most desperate acts of valor.

Now with these facts before him, the historian will find it impossible to believe that these men drew their swords and did these heroic deeds and bore these incredible hardships for four long years for the sake of the institution of slavery. Everyone who was conversant, as I was during the whole war, with the opinions of the soldiers of the Southern army, knows that they did not wage that tremendous conflict for slavery. That was a subject very little in their thoughts or on their lips. Not one in twenty of those grim veterans, who were so terrible on the battlefield, had any financial interest in slavery. No, they were fighting for liberty, for the right of self-government. They believed the Federal authorities were assailing that right. It was the sacred heritage of Anglo-Saxon freedom, of local self-government, won at Runnymede, which they believed in peril when they flew to arms as one man, from the Potomac to the Rio Grande. They may have been right, or they may have been wrong, but that was the issue they made. On that they stood. For that they died.

Not until this fact is realized by the student of the great war will he have the solution of the problem which is presented by the qualities of the Confederate soldier. The men who made up that army were not soldiers of fortune, but soldiers of duty, who dared all that men can dare, and endured all that man can endure, in obedience to what they believed the sacred call of Country. They loved their States; they loved their homes and their firesides; they were no politicians; many of them knew little of the warring theories of Constitutional interpretation. But one thing they knew—armed legions were

[116]

TALENTED YOUNG VOLUNTEERS UNDER THE SOUTHERN CROSS
IN THE FIRST YEAR OF THE WAR

There is an artist among the young Confederate volunteers, judging from the device on the tent, and the musicians are betrayed by the violin and bugle. This photograph of '61 is indicative of the unanimity with which the young men of the South took up the profession of arms. An expensive education, music, art, study abroad, a knowledge of modern and ancient languages—none of these was felt an excuse against enlisting in the ranks, if no better opportunity offered. As the author of the accompanying article recalls: "When Virginia threw in her lot with her Southern sisters in April, 1861, practically the whole body of students at her State University, 515 out of 530 men who were registered from the Southern States, enlisted in the Confederate army. This army thus represented the whole Southern people. It was a self-levy *en masse* of the male population." The four men in the foreground of the photograph are H. H. Williams, Jr., S. B. Woodberry, H. I. Greer, and Sergeant R. W. Greer of the Washington Light Infantry of Charleston, S. C.

marching upon their homes, and it was their duty to hurl them back at any cost!

Such were the private soldiers of the Confederacy as I knew them. Not for fame or for glory, not lured by ambition or goaded by necessity, but, in simple obedience to duty as they understood it, these men suffered all, sacrificed all, dared all—and died! I would like to add a statement which doubtless will appear paradoxical, but which my knowledge of those men, through many campaigns, and on many fields, and in many camps, gives me, I think, the right to make with confidence, viz.: *the dissolution of the Union was not what the Southern soldier had chiefly at heart. The establishment of the Southern Confederacy was not, in his mind, the supreme issue of the conflict. Both the one and the other were secondary to the preservation of the sacred right of self-government. They were means to the end, not the end itself.*

I place these statements here in this explicit manner because I believe they must be well considered by the student of the war, in advance of all questions of strategy, or tactics, or political policy, or racial characteristics, as explanatory of what the Confederate armies achieved in the campaigns and battles of the titanic struggle.

The spirit—the motives—the aims—of the Southern soldier constituted the moral lever that, more than anything else, controlled his actions and accounted for his achievements.

A conspicuous feature of this Southern army is its Americanism. Go from camp to camp, among the infantry, the cavalry, the artillery, and you are impressed with the fact that these men are, with very few exceptions, Americans. Here and there you will encounter one or two Irishmen. Major Stiles tells a story of a most amusing encounter between two gigantic Irishmen at the battle of Gettysburg—the one a Federal Irishman, a prisoner, and the other a Rebel Irishman, private in the Ninth Louisiana—a duel with fists in the midst

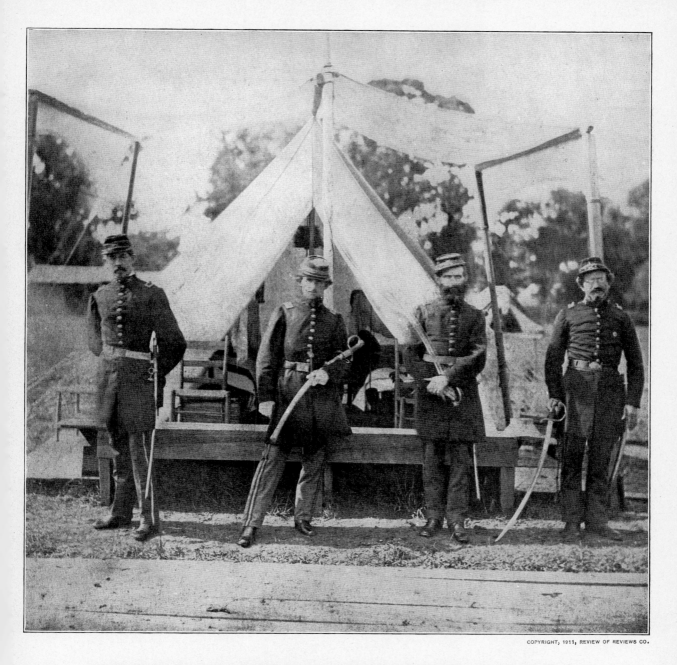

OFFICERS OF THE WASHINGTON ARTILLERY OF NEW ORLEANS

This photograph shows officers of the Fifth Company, Washington Artillery of New Orleans, in their panoply of war, shortly before the battle of Shiloh. On the following page is a photograph of members of the same organization as they looked after passing through the four terrible years. Nor were such force and ability as show in the expressions of these officers lacking in the gray-clad ranks. "And how cheerful—how uncomplaining—how gallant they were!" Dr. McKim records. "They had not even the reward which is naturally dear to a soldier's heart—I mean the due recognition of gallantry in action. By a strange oversight there was no provision in the Confederate army for recognizing, either by decoration or by promotion on the field, distinguishing acts of gallantry. No 'Victoria Cross,' or its equivalent, rewarded even the most desperate acts of valor." But brave men need no such artificial incentive to defend their homes.

of the roar of the battle! Very, very rarely you will meet a German, like that superb soldier, Major Von Borcke, who so endeared himself to "Jeb" Stuart's cavalry. But these exceptions only accentuate the broad fact that the Confederate army was composed almost exclusively of Americans. That throws some light on its achievements, does it not?

I think the visitor to the Confederate camps would also be struck by the spirit of *bonhommie* which so largely prevailed. These "Johnnie Rebs," in their gray uniforms (which, as the war went on, changed in hue to butternut brown) are a jolly lot. They have a dry, racy humor of their own which breaks out on the least provocation. I have often heard them cracking jokes on the very edge of battle. They were soldier *boys* to the bitter end!

General Rodes, in his report, describing the dark and difficult night-passage of the Potomac on the retreat from Gettysburg, says, " All the circumstances attending this crossing combined to make it an affair not only involving great hardship, but one of great danger to the men and company officers; but, be it said to the honor of these brave fellows, they encountered it not only promptly, but actually with cheers and laughter."

On the other hand, some from the remote country districts were like children away from home. They could not get used to it—and often they drooped, and sickened and died, just from *nostalgia*. In many of the regiments during the first six months or more of the war, there were negro cooks, but as time went on these disappeared, except in the officers' mess. Among the Marylanders, where my service lay, it was quite different. We had to do our own cooking. Once a week, I performed that office for a mess of fifteen hungry men. At first we lived on "slapjacks"—almost as fatal as Federal bullets!—and fried bacon; but by degrees we learned to make biscuits, and on one occasion my colleague in the culinary business and I created an apple pie, which the whole mess

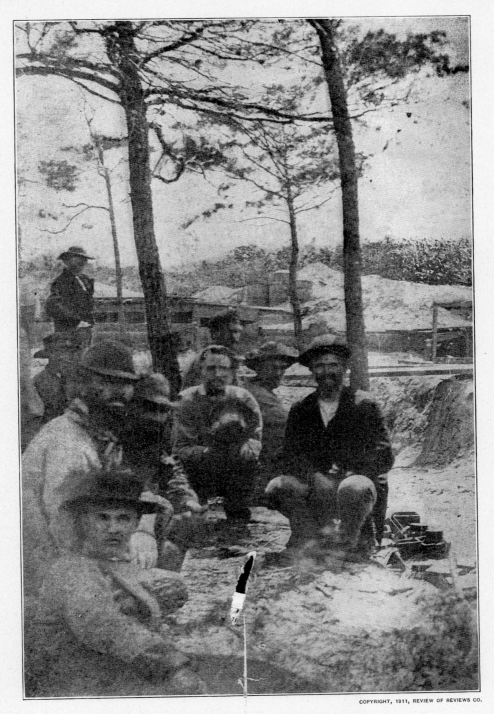

COPYRIGHT, 1911, REVIEW OF REVIEWS CO.

"THESE 'JOHNNIE REBS' ARE A JOLLY LOT"

This quotation from the accompanying text is thoroughly illustrated by the photograph reproduced above. It was taken in 1861 by J. D. Edwards, a pioneer camera-man of New Orleans, within the Barbour sand-batteries, near the lighthouse in Pensacola harbor. Nor was the Confederate good humor merely of the moment. Throughout the war, the men in gray overcame their hardships by a grim gaiety that broke out on the least provocation—at times with none at all as when, marching to their armpits in icy water, for lack of bridges they invented the term "Confederate pontoons" in derision of the Federal engineering apparatus. Or while a Federal brigade magnificently led—and clad—swept on to the charge, the ragged line in gray, braced against the assault, would crackle into amazing laughter with shouts of "Bring on those good breeches!" "Hey, Yank, might as well hand me your coat now as later!"

considered a *chef d'œuvre!* May I call your attention to those ramrods wrapped round with dough and set up on end before the fire? The cook turns them from time to time, and, when well browned, he withdraws the ramrod, and, lo! a loaf of bread, three feet long and hollow from end to end.

The general aspect of the Confederate camps compared unfavorably with those of the men in blue. They were not, as a rule, attractive in appearance. The tents and camp equipage were nothing like so " smart," so spick and span—very far from it, indeed! Our engineer corps were far inferior, lacking in proper tools and equipment. The sappers and miners of the Federal army on Cemetery Hill, at Gettysburg, did rapid and effective work during the night following the first day's battle, as they had previously done at Chancellorsville—work which our men could not begin to match. When we had to throw up breastworks in the field, as at Hagerstown, after Gettysburg, it had usually to be done with our bayonets. Spades and axes were luxuries at such times. Bands of music were rare, and generally of inferior quality; but the men made up for it as far as they could by a gay *insouciance,* and by singing in camp and on the march. I have seen the men of the First Maryland Infantry trudging wearily through mud and rain, sadly bedraggled by a long march, strike up with great gusto their favorite song, " Gay and Happy."

> So let the wide world wag as it will,
> We'll be gay and happy still.

The contrast between the sentiment of the song and the environment of the column was sufficiently striking. In one respect, I think, our camps had the advantage of the Union camps—we had no sutlers, and we had no camp-followers.

But though our camp equipage and equipment were so inferior to those of our antagonists, I do not think any experienced soldier, watching our marching columns of infantry or cavalry, or witnessing our brigade drills, could fail to be

CONFEDERATE TYPES—"GAY AND HAPPY STILL"

A conspicuous feature of the Southern army was its Americanism. In every camp, among the infantry, the cavalry and the artillery, the men were, with few exceptions, Americans. In spite of deprivations, the men were light-hearted; given a few days' rest and feeding, they abounded in fun and jocularity and were noted for indulgence in a species of rough humor which found suggestion in the most trivial incidents, and was often present in the midst of the most tragical circumstances. In so representative a body the type varied almost as did the individual; the home sentiment, however, pervaded the mass and was the inspiration of its patriotism—sectional, provincial, call it what you will. This was true even in the ranks of those knight-errants from beyond the border: Missourians, Kentuckians, Marylanders. The last were nameworthy sons of the sires who had rendered the old "Maryland Line" of the Revolution of 1776 illustrious, and, looking toward their homes with the foe arrayed between as a barrier, they always cherished the hope of some day reclaiming those homes—when the war should be over. To many of them the war was over long before Appomattox—when those who had "struck the first blow in Baltimore" also delivered "the last in Virginia." To the very end they never failed to respond to the call of duty, and were—to quote their favorite song, sung around many a camp-fire—"Gay and Happy Still."

thrilled by the spectacle they presented. Here at least, there was no inferiority to the army in blue. The soldierly qualities that tell on the march, and on the field of battle, shone out here conspicuously. A more impressive spectacle has seldom been seen in any war than was presented by "Jeb" Stuart's brigades of cavalry when they passed in review before General Lee at Brandy Station in June, 1863. The pomp and pageantry of gorgeous uniforms and dazzling equipment of horse and riders were indeed absent; but splendid horsemanship, and that superb *esprit de corps* that marks the veteran legion, and which, though not a tangible or a visible thing, yet stamps itself upon a marching column—these were unmistakably here. And I take leave to express my own individual opinion that the blue-gray coat of the Confederate officer, richly adorned with gold lace, and his light-blue trousers, and that rakish slouch-hat he wore made up a uniform of great beauty. Oh, it was a gallant array to look upon—that June day, so many years ago!

When our infantry soldiers came to a river, unless it was a deep one, we had to cross it on "Confederate pontoons," i. e., by marching right through in column of fours. This, I remember, we did twice on one day on the march from Culpeper to Winchester at the opening of the Gettysburg campaign.

Among the amusements in camp, card-playing was of course included; seven-up and vingt-et-un, I believe, were popular. And the pipe was "Johnnie Reb's" frequent solace. His tobacco, at any rate, was the real thing—genuine, no make-believe, like his coffee. Often there were large gatherings of the men, night after night, attending prayer-meetings, always with preaching added, for there was a strong religious tone in the Army of Northern Virginia. One or two remarkable revivals took place, notably in the winter of 1863–64.

It seems to me, as I look back, that one of the characteristics which stood out strongly in the Confederate army was the independence and the initiative of the individual soldier.

[124]

THE PRIVATE SOLDIER OF THE CONFEDERACY

This photograph shows the private soldier of the Confederacy "at home" early in 1862. The men are members of the Washington Artillery, the crack New Orleans organization. They were dandies as compared with most of the volunteers. On the mess-tent to the left, the sign announces that Hemming's mess consists of Sergeant Hemming and Privates Knight, Hoerner, and Potthoff. Even at this date there was no such commissary organization as in the North. The individuality of the Southern soldier was shown in the absence of anything like company kitchens, each mess preparing its rations to suit its own fancy, and according to what might be its special resources or luck in foraging on the road. And when the fierce struggle had swept down the rivers and closed the ports, the Confederates "marched and fought," to quote Dr. McKim, "and starved truly without reward. Eleven dollars a month in Confederate paper was their stipend. Flour and bacon and peanut coffee made up their bill of fare. The hard earth or else three fence-rails, tilted up on end, was their bed; their knapsacks, their pillows; and a flimsy blanket their covering. The starry firmament was often their only tent. Their clothing—well, I cannot describe it. I can only say it was 'a thing of shreds and patches' interspersed with rents."

It would have been a better army in the field if it had been welded together by a stricter discipline; but this defect was largely atoned for by the strong individuality of the units in the column. It was not easy to demoralize a body composed of men who thought for themselves and acted in a spirit of independence in battle.

It was a characteristic of the Confederate soldier—I do not say he alone possessed it—that he never considered himself discharged of his duty to the colors by any wound, however serious, so long as he could walk, on crutches or otherwise. Look at that private in the Thirty-seventh Virginia Infantry—he has been hit by a rifle-ball, which, striking him full between the eyes, has found its way somehow through and emerged at the back of his head. But there he is in the ranks again, carrying his musket—while a deep depression, big enough to hold a good sized marble, marks the spot where the bullet entered in its futile attempt to make this brave fellow give up his service with the Confederate banner! Look at Captain Randolph Barton, of another Virginia regiment. He is living to-day (1911) with just about one dozen scars on his body. He would be wounded; get well; return to duty, and in the very next battle be shot again! Look at that gallant old soldier, General Ewell. Like his brave foeman, General Sickles, he has lost his leg, but that cannot keep him home; he continues to command one of Lee's corps to the very end at Appomattox. Look at Colonel Snowden Andrews of Maryland. At Cedar Mountain, in August, 1862, a shell literally nearly cut him in two; but by a miracle he did not die; and in June, 1863, there he is again commanding his artillery battalion! He is bowed crooked by that awful wound; he cannot stand upright any more, but still he can fight like a lion.

As you walk through the camps, you will see many of the men busily polishing their muskets and their bayonets with wood ashes well moistened. "Bright muskets" and "tattered uniforms" went together in the Army of Northern Virginia.

CONFEDERATES WHO SERVED THE GUNS
MEMBERS OF THE FAMOUS
"WASHINGTON ARTILLERY" OF NEW ORLEANS

The young men of the cities and towns very generally chose the artillery branch of the service for enlistment; thus, New Orleans sent five batteries, fully equipped, into the field—the famous "Washington Artillery"— besides some other batteries; and the city of Richmond, which furnished but one regiment of infantry and a few separate companies, contributed no less than eight or ten full batteries. Few of the minor towns but claimed at least one. The grade of intelligence of the personnel was rather exceptionally high, so that the artillery came in time to attain quite a respectable degree of efficiency, especially after the objectionable system under which each battery was attached to an infantry brigade, subject to the orders of its commander, was abolished and the battery units became organized into battalions and corps commanded by officers of their own arm. The Confederate artillery arm was less fortunate than the infantry in the matter of equipment, of course. From start to finish it was under handicap by reason of its lack of trained officers, no less than from the inferiority of its material, ordnance, and ammunition alike. The batteries of the regular establishment were, of course, all in the United States service, commanded and served by trained gunners, and were easily distributed among the volunteer "brigades" by way of "stiffening" to the latter. This disparity was fully recognized by the Confederates and had its influence in the selection of more than one battle-ground in order that it might be neutralized by the local conditions, yet the service was very popular in the Southern army.

Swinton, the historian of the Army of the Potomac, exclaims, "Who can ever forget, that once looked upon it, that army of tattered uniforms and bright muskets, that body of incomparable infantry, the Army of Northern Virginia, which for four years carried the revolt on their bayonets, opposing a constant front to the mighty concentration of power brought against it; which, receiving terrible blows, did not fail to give the like, and which, vital in all its parts, died only with its annihilation."

Apropos of muskets, you will observe that a large portion of those in the hands of the Confederate soldiers are stamped "U. S. A."; and when you visit the artillery camps you will note that the three-inch rifles, the Napoleons, and the Parrott guns, were most of them " Uncle Sam's " property, captured in battle; and when you inspect the cavalry you will find, after the first year, that the Southern troops are armed with sabers captured from the Federals.* During the first year, before the blockade became stringent, Whitworth guns were brought in from abroad. But that soon stopped, and we had to look largely to " Uncle Sam " for our supply.

We used to say in the Shenandoah Valley campaign, of 1862, that General Banks was General Jackson's quartermaster-general—yes, and his chief ordnance officer, too. General Shields was another officer to whom we were much indebted for artillery and small arms, and later General Pope.† But these sources of equipment sometimes failed us, and so it came to pass that some of our regiments were but poorly armed even in our best brigades. For instance the Third Brigade in Ewell's corps, one of the best-equipped brigades in the army, entered the Gettysburg campaign with 1,941 men present for

*It is estimated by surviving ordnance officers that not less than two-thirds of the artillery in the Army of Northern Virginia was captured, especially the 3-inch rifles and the 10-pound Parrotts.

† General Gorgas, Chief of the Confederate Ordnance Bureau, stated that from July 1, 1861, to Jan. 1, 1865, there were issued from the Richmond arsenal 323,231 infantry arms, 34,067 cavalry arms, 44,877 swords and sabers, and that these were chiefly arms from battlefields, repaired.

"Seven Pines"

THE ONLY KNOWN PHOTOGRAPH OF TEXAS BOYS IN THE ARMY OF NORTHERN VIRGINIA

This group of the sturdy pioneers from Texas, heroes of many a wild charge over the battlefields of Virginia, has adopted as winter-quarters insignia the words "Wigfall Mess," evidently in honor of General Wigfall, who came to Virginia in command of the Texas contingent. The general was fond of relating an experience to illustrate the independence and individuality of his "boys." In company with Major-General Whiting he was walking near the railroad station at Manassas, and, according to wont, had been "cracking up" his "Lone Star" command, when they came upon a homespun-clad soldier comfortably seated with his back against some baled hay, his musket leaned against the same, and contentedly smoking a pipe. The two officers passed with only the recognition of a stare from the sentry, and Whiting satirically asked Wigfall if that was one of his people, adding that he did not seem to have been very well instructed as to his duty. To his surprise the Texan general then addressed the soldier: "What are you doing here, my man?" "Nothin' much," replied the man; "jes' kinder takin' care of this hyar stuff." "Do you know who I am, sir?" asked the general. "Wall, now, 'pears like I know your face, but I can't jes' call your name—who is you?" "I'm General Wigfall," with some emphasis. Without rising from his seat or removing his pipe, the sentry extended his hand: "Gin'ral, I'm pleased to meet you—my name's Jones." Less than a year later, this same man was probably among those who stormed the Federal entrenchments at Gaines' Mill, of whom "Stonewall" Jackson said, on the field after the battle: "The men who carried *this* position were soldiers indeed!"

duty, but only 1,480 muskets and 1,069 bayonets. But this was not all, or the worst. Our artillery ammunition was inferior to that of our antagonists, which was a great handicap to our success.

When General Alexander, Lee's chief of artillery at Gettysburg, was asked why he ceased firing when Pickett's infantry began its charge—why he did not continue shelling the Federal lines over the heads of the advancing Confederate column; he replied that his ammunition was so defective, he could not calculate with any certainty where the shells would explode; they might explode among Pickett's men, and so demoralize rather than support them. It will help the reader to realize the inequality in arms and equipment between the two armies to watch a skirmish between some of Sheridan's cavalry and a regiment of Fitzhugh Lee. Observe that the Federal cavalryman fires his rifle seven times without reloading, while the horseman in gray opposed to him fires but once, and then lowers his piece to reload. One is armed with the Spencer repeating rifle; the other with the old Sharp's rifle.

In another engagement (at Winchester, September 19, 1864), see that regiment of mounted men give way in disorder before the assault of Sheridan's cavalry, and dash back through the infantry. Are these men cowards? No, but they are armed with long cumbrous rifles utterly unfit for mounted men, or with double-barreled shotguns, or old squirrel-rifles. What chance has a regiment thus armed, and also miserably mounted, against those well-armed, well-equipped, well-mounted, and well-disciplined Federal cavalrymen? *

Another feature of the conditions prevailing in the Confederate army may be here noted. Look at Lee's veterans as

* The arms and equipment of the Confederate army will be found fully discussed by Professer J. W. Mallet, late Superintendent of the Ordnance Laboratories of the Confederate States, and Captain O. E. Hunt, U.S.A., in a chapter on the "Organization and Operation of the Ordnance Department of the Confederate Army" in the volume on "Forts and Artillery."

AMUSEMENTS IN A CONFEDERATE CAMP—1864

This camp of Confederate pickets on Stono Inlet near Charleston, S. C., was photographed by George S. Cook, the same artist who risked his life taking photographs of Fort Sumter. It illustrates the soldiers' methods of entertaining themselves when time lay heavy on their hands. Among the amusements in camp, card-playing was of course included. "Seven-up" and "Vingt-et-un" were popular. And the pipe was "Johnnie Reb's" frequent solace. His tobacco, at any rate, was the real thing—genuine, no make-believe, like his coffee. Often one might see large gatherings of the men night after night attending prayer-meetings, always with preaching added, for there was a strong religious tone among Southern soldiers, especially in the Army of Northern Virginia. One or two remarkable revivals took place, notably in the winter of 1863–64. That this photograph was taken early in the war is indicated by the presence of the Negroes. The one with an axe seems about to chop firewood for the use of the cooks. A little later, "Johnnie Reb" considered himself fortunate if he had anything to cook.

they march into Pennsylvania, in June, 1863. See how many of them are barefooted—literally hundreds in a single division. The great battle of Gettysburg was precipitated because General Heth had been informed that he could get shoes in that little town for his barefooted men!

These hardships became more acute as the war advanced, and the resources of the South were gradually exhausted, while at the same time the blockade became so effective that her ports were hermetically sealed against the world. With what grim determination the Confederate soldier endured cold and nakedness and hunger I need not attempt to describe, but there was a trial harder than all these to endure, which came upon him in the fourth year of the war. Letters began to arrive from home telling of food scarcity on his little farm or in the cabin where he had left his wife and children. Brave as the Southern women were, rich and poor alike, they could not conceal altogether from their husbands the sore straits in which they found themselves. Many could not keep back the cry: "What am I to do? Food is hard to get. There is no one to put in the crop. God knows how I am to feed the children!"

So a strain truly terrible was put upon the loyalty of the private soldier. He was almost torn asunder between love for his wife and children and fidelity to the flag under which he was serving. What wonder if hundreds, perhaps thousands, in those early spring months of 1865, gave way under the pressure, slipped out of the Confederate ranks, and went home to put in the crop for their little families, meaning to return to the colors as soon as that was done! Technically, they were deserters, but not in the heart or faith, poor fellows! Still, for Lee's army the result was disastrous. It was seen in the thinning ranks that opposed Grant's mighty host, week after week. This is the South's explanation of the fact, which the records show, that while at the close of the war there were over a million men under arms in the Federal armies, the aggregate of the Confederates was but 133,433.

RUINS OF THE TREDEGAR IRON WORKS IN RICHMOND, APRIL, 1865—THE MAIN FACTORY
FOR HEAVY CANNON IN THE SOUTH

The Tredegar Iron Works in Richmond was practically the only factory for cannon in the South, especially for pieces of heavy caliber. This supplied one of the chief reasons for the Confederate Government's orders to hold Richmond at all hazards. Thus the strategy of Confederate generals was hampered and conditioned, through the circumstance that Richmond contained in the Tredegar Works almost the only means of supplying the South with cannon. Augusta, Georgia, where the great powder factory of the Confederacy was located, was another most important point. Military strategists have debated why Sherman did not turn aside in his march to the sea in order to destroy this factory. Augusta was prepared to make a stout de-

AFTER THE GREAT RICHMOND FIRE

fense, and the Confederacy was already crumbling at this time. The Union armies were fast closing about Richmond, and possibly Sherman regarded such an attempt as a work of supererogation and a useless sacrifice of life. Only a few months more, and Richmond was to fall, with a conflagration that totally demolished the Tredegar Works. Colonel John W. Clarke, of 1103 Greene Street, an old inhabitant of Augusta, who made an excellent record in the Confederate army, tells of a story current in that city that the sparing of Augusta was a matter of sentiment. Sherman recalled his former connection with the local Military Academy for boys, and that here dwelt some of his former sweethearts and valued friends.

How could an army so poorly equipped, so imperfectly armed, so ill fed and ill clothed, win out in a contest with an army so vastly its superior in numbers and so superbly armed and equipped?* How could an agricultural people, unskilled in the mechanical arts, therefore unable to supply properly its armies with munitions and clothing, prevail against a great, rich, manufacturing section like the North, whose foreign and domestic trade had never been so prosperous as during the great war it was waging from 1861 to 1865?

Remember, also, that by May, 1862, the armies of the Union were in permanent occupancy of western and middle Tennessee, of nearly the whole of Louisiana, of parts of Florida, of the coast of North and South Carolina and of southeastern, northern, and western Virginia. Now, the population thus excluded from the support of the Confederacy amounted to not less than 1,200,000. It follows that, for the last three years of the war, the unequal contest was sustained by about 3,800,000 Southern whites with their slaves against the vast power of the Northern States. And yet none of these considerations furnishes the true explanation of the failure of the Confederate armies to establish the Confederacy. It was not superior equipment. It was not alone the iron will of Grant, or the strategy of Sherman. A power mightier than all these held the South by the throat and slowly strangled its army and its people. That power was Sea Power. The Federal navy, not the Federal army, conquered the South.

"In my opinion," said Field-Marshal Viscount Wolseley, in a private letter to me, dated November 12, 1904, "in my opinion, as a student of war, the Confederates must have won,

---

*I do not enter upon the contested question of the numbers serving in the respective armies. Colonel Livermore's Numbers and Losses in the Civil War is the authority relied upon usually by writers on the Northern side; but his conclusions have been strongly, and as many of us think, successfully challenged by Cazenove G. Lee, in a pamphlet entitled Acts of the Republican Party as Seen by History, and published (in Winchester, 1906) under the pseudo "C. Gardiner."

A FUTURE HISTORIAN, WHILE HISTORY WAS IN THE MAKING—1864

In the center of this group, taken before Petersburg, in August, 1864, sits Captain Charles Francis Adams, Jr., then of the First Massachusetts Cavalry, one of the historians referred to in the text accompanying. In his oration on General Lee, delivered October 30, 1901, Captain Adams vigorously maintains that the Union was saved not so much by the victories of its armies as by the material exhaustion of the Confederacy; a view ably elaborated by Hilary A. Herbert, former colonel of the Confederate States Army, in an address delivered while Secretary of the Navy, at the War College in 1896. A quotation from it appears on page 88, of Volume I, of the PHOTOGRAPHIC HISTORY. In the picture above, the officer on Captain Adams' left is Lieutenant G. H. Teague; on his right is Captain E. A. Flint. The fine equipment of these officers illustrates the advantage the Northern armies enjoyed through their splendid and never-failing system of supplies. The First Massachusetts was in active service at the front throughout the war and the conditions that Captain Adams actually witnessed afford a most direct basis for the truth of his conclusions.

had the blockade of the Southern ports been removed by us. . . . It was the blockade of your ports that killed the Southern Confederacy, not the action of the Northern armies." Compare with this mature opinion of the accomplished English soldier the words of Honorable Hugh McCulloch, one of Lincoln's Secretaries of the Treasury. "It was the blockade that isolated the Confederate States and caused their exhaustion. If the markets of Europe had been open to them for the sale of their cotton and tobacco, and the purchase of supplies for their armies, their subjugation would have been impossible. It was not by defeats in the field that the Confederates were overcome, but by the exhaustion resulting from their being shut up within their own domain, and compelled to rely upon themselves and their own production. Such was the devotion of the people to their cause, that the war would have been successfully maintained, if the blockade had not cut off all sources of supply and bankrupted their treasury." Again he says: "It must be admitted that the Union was not saved by the victories of its armies, but by the exhaustion of its enemies." Charles Francis Adams, in his oration on General Lee, vigorously maintains the same view, and Colonel Hilary A. Herbert, while Secretary of the Navy, delivered an elaborate address in 1896, in which he demonstrated the correctness of that interpretation of the true cause of the failure of the South.

In concluding, I may recall the well-known fact that the men in gray and the men in blue, facing each other before Petersburg, fraternized in those closing months of the great struggle. A Confederate officer, aghast at finding one night the trenches on his front deserted, discovered his men were all over in the Federal trenches, playing cards. The rank and file had made a truce till a certain hour!

[136]

PART I
SOLDIER LIFE

———

THE CONFEDERATE
OF '61

———

BUGLER IN A CONFEDERATE
CAMP—1861

THE CONFEDERATE OF '61

By Allen C. Redwood
Fifty-fifth Virginia Regiment, Confederate States Army

THE ill-fated attempt of John Brown at Harper's Ferry was significant in more directions than the one voiced in the popular lyric in the Southern States. The militia system had fallen into a condition little less than farcical, but the effect of Brown's undertaking was to awaken the public sense to an appreciation of the defenseless condition of the community, in the event of better planned and more comprehensive demonstrations of the kind in the future.

Rural populations do not tend readily to organization, and the Southerner was essentially rural, but under the impetus above indicated, and with no immediate thought of ulterior service, the people, of the border States especially, began to form military companies in almost every county, and to uniform, arm, and drill them.

The habit and temper of the men, no less than the putative intent of these organizations, gave a strong bias toward the cavalry arm. In the cities and larger towns the other branches were also represented, though by no means in the usual proportion in any regular establishment. In Virginia the mounted troops probably outnumbered the infantry and artillery combined. All were imperfectly armed or equipped for anything like actual campaigning, but at the beginning of hostilities a fair degree of drill and some approach to discipline had been attained, and these bodies formed a nucleus about which the hastily assembled levies, brought into the field by the call to arms, formed themselves, and doubtless received a degree of " stiffening " from such contact.

CONFEDERATES OF '61

THE CLINCH RIFLES ON MAY 10TH

NEXT DAY THEY JOINED A REGIMENT DESTINED TO FAME

On the day before they were mustered in as Company A, Fifth Regiment of Georgia Volunteer Infantry, the Clinch Rifles of Augusta were photographed at their home town. A. K. Clark, the boy in the center with the drum, fortunately preserved a copy of the picture. Just half a century later, he wrote: "I weighed only ninety-five pounds, and was so small that they would only take me as a drummer. Of the seventeen men in this picture, I am the only one living." Hardly two are dressed alike; they did not become "uniform" for many months. With the hard campaigning in the West and East, the weights of the men also became more uniform. The drummer-boy filled out and became a real soldier, and the stout man lying down in front lost much of his superfluous avoirdupois in the furious engagements where it earned its title as a "fighting regiment." The Confederate armies were not clad in the uniform gray till the second year of the war. So variegated were the costumes on both sides at the first battle of Bull Run that both Confederates and Federals frequently fired upon their own men. There are instances recorded where the colonel of a regiment notified his supports to which side he belonged before daring to advance in front of them.

In the beginning, each of these companies bore some designation instead of a company letter; there were various "Guards," "Grays," "Rifles"—the last a ludicrous misnomer —the "rifles" being mostly represented by flint-lock muskets, dating from the War of 1812, brought to light from State arsenals, only serviceable as issued, and carrying the old "buck-and-ball" ammunition, "Cal. .69."

Even this rudimentary armament was not always attainable. When the writer's company was first called into camp, requisition was made upon all the shotguns in the vicinity, these ranging all the way from a piece of ordnance quite six feet long and which chambered four buckshot, through various gages of double-barrels, down to a small single-barrel squirrel-gun. Powder, balls, and buckshot were served out to us in bulk, and each man made cartridges to fit the arm he bore, using a stick whittled to its caliber as a "former."

As the next step in the armament the obsolete flintlocks were converted into percussion as rapidly as the arsenals could turn them out. These difficulties were supplemented, however, by certain formidable weapons of war privately contributed— revolvers, and a most truculent species of double-edged cutlass, fashioned by blacksmiths from farrier's rasps, and carried in wooden scabbards bound with wire, like those affected by the Filipino volunteer. They proved very useful later on for cutting brush, but, so far as known, were quite guiltless of bloodshed, and soon went to the rear when the stress of active campaign developed the need of every possible reduction of *impedimenta*. One or two marches sufficed to convince the soldier that his authorized weapon and other equipment were quite as much as he cared to transport.

The old-pattern musket alone weighed in the neighborhood of ten pounds, which had a way of increasing in direct ratio with the miles covered, until every screw and bolt seemed to weigh a pound at least.

But I anticipate somewhat—we were really in our

COMPANY A, FIFTH GEORGIA VOLUNTEER INFANTRY

The photograph shows sixty-one of the ninety-five Southerners who next day—May 11, 1861—became Company A of the Fifth Georgia. An early photographer darkened the coats of the men in the pictures, but it was not tampered with otherwise, and the hopeful Georgians appear precisely as they looked just fifty years before the publication of this volume. Their attitudes are stiff, their bearing unmilitary in some respects; but glowing in their hearts was that rare courage which impelled them to the defense of their homes, and the withstanding through four long years of terrible blows from the better equipped and no less determined Northern armies, which finally outnumbered them hopelessly. As early as January 24, 1861, the Clinch Rifles had taken part in warfare—the capture of the arsenal at Augusta. By July 1, 1862, Augusta and Richmond County had twenty-four companies, more than two full regiments, in the field. Out of a white population of ten thousand, over two thousand soldiers were raised in six months—of whom 292 were killed or died in the service. This instance is typical of the ardor with which volunteers flocked to the front throughout the South. The war records do not contain any official roll of all the regiments and lesser organizations in the Confederate army, and there are big discrepancies in the lists compiled by private individuals. "The Confederate Soldier in the Civil War," edited by Ben La Bree, in 1897, gives the following number of organizations, including cavalry, partisan rangers, infantry, and light and heavy artillery from the various Confederate States: Alabama, 80; Arkansas, 70; Florida, 21; Georgia, 130; Louisiana, 75; Mississippi, 88; North Carolina, 90; South Carolina, 73; Tennessee, 129; Texas, 75; Virginia, 164; Border States, 50, and Confederate States regulars, 14. The Confederate ordnance was much inferior to the Union. It is worthy of note that this list includes only 6 batteries of heavy artillery as against 61 regiments, 8 battalions, and 36 companies of heavy artillery in the Federal service, the troops, however, often acting as infantry.

novitiate according to the dictum of Napoleon, who rightly believed that the proper school of war is *war*. By a species of *lucus a non lucendo* mode of designation, the uniforming of this inchoate force was not so irregular early in the war. Gray had been adopted as the color most serviceable, but the supply of cloth of that hue was soon exhausted under the influence of the blockade, and so numerous varieties came into use and were accepted as complying with the requirements of the service. Thus, in the writer's regiment, the companies were garbed from dark gray to almost white-kersey " nigger cloth." The facings varied from black, through various shades of blue and rifle-green, to artillery-red.

To revert to the matter of equipment, there was no official attempt in the beginning to do more than to arm the troops and to provide the purely warlike accouterments of cartridge-boxes, belts, and haversacks. Canteens and the like were provided quite as a matter of course, and, in default of blankets and waterproof coverings, requisition was made upon the household stock of the individual and duly honored—bed-quilts and homespun " spreads " were freely contributed, also buggy lap-robes, and pianos and tables were despoiled of their oilcloth covers to fend the rain from the men gone from the homes to do battle for the Cause, which was even dearer to the women left behind, who were steadfast to the end.

The minor courtesies and observances of military life were not readily inculcated in this mass of civilians as yet in process of conversion into soldiers, and this difficulty was present in a peculiar degree, perhaps, in the Confederate ranks. The mode of life, the whole ritual of his civilization, tendered to foster in the Southerner an individuality and independence of character to which the idea of subordination to authority was entirely foreign. He had come to war to fight, and could see no sense in any such " tomfoolery " as saluting his officer, lately " Tom " or " Jack," and his associate on terms of equality, especially when the elevation to the title had been, as it was in

A MILITIA COMPANY IN LOUISIANA AT DRILL
BEFORE ITS ARMORY
1861

During its half-century of oblivion, damage came to this unique photograph of a militia company in Louisiana hopefully drilling in front of its armory as the war began.   In many sections, the notions of the hastily organized companies in regard to military discipline and etiquette were crude in the extreme.   A certain Virginia regiment, for the first time in its service, held a dress-parade.   At the stage of the ceremony when the first-sergeants of the respective companies announce the result of the evening roll-call, one reported thus: "All present in the Rifles, except Captain Jones, who is not feeling well this evening, but hopes to be feeling better to-morrow."   Of like tenor was the response of a militia field-officer in the late autumn of 1861, when challenged by a sentry who demanded: "Who comes there?"   "We kem from over the river, gwine the grand rounds," was the response of him who presumptuously sported the insignia of a colonel.   From such raw material was developed the magnificent Confederate army which supplied the "matchless infantry" of Lee.

the lower grades, at least, procured by the exercise of his own suffrage. For the officers of the volunteers up to and including company commands, were purely elective, and were distinguished more by personal popularity or local prominence than by any consideration of fitness for the position under the use of actual service, yet to be applied. In view of this circumstance, it is fortunate that the early contestants were enlisted generally for the period of one year, that being estimated at the outset as the probable duration of the war.

When the time came for reenlistment " for three years or the war," the experience of that first year had begun to bear fruit, and the reelection showed better discrimination as to the quality of the officers chosen. The soldier had begun to learn his trade and to recognize that the " good fellow " or the county magistrate was by no means therefore the best officer, when it got down to the real business in hand. But all this required time, a test not even yet grasped by the American people, who are prone to confound good raw—excessively " raw "—material with an efficient fighting force, and to ignore the waste of blood and treasure pending the conversion of one into the other.

Naturally, the evolving of an army from this crude personnel, and its organization into an effective body capable of being handled in the field, were matters requiring time and much consideration of the peculiar conditions of the situation—a problem further complicated by the fact that an overwhelming proportion of the officers of the force were quite as devoid of any military experience as the men they commanded, or of any right appreciation of their shortcomings in this regard—all were untrained. The political aspect had to be taken into account—the popular sentiment underlying and sustaining the enterprise. A very large percentage of the force, amounting to a majority perhaps, had been but little in sympathy with secession in the beginning; had only given in their adherence to the movement when actually at the parting

A LIEUTENANT OF THE FOURTH GEORGIA, IN 1861

The ornateness of the uniform of Lieutenant R. A. Mizell, Company A, Fourth Georgia Regiment, would be sufficient proof that his ambrotype was taken early in the war. The epaulets, the towering shako, and the three rows of buttons are all more indicative of pomp and glory than of actual work. Two years later, even the buttons became so rare that the soldiers of the Army of Northern Virginia were driven to sew one or two tough berries on their tunics to serve as fastenings. The war career of this hopeful and earnest-looking young soldier was traced through a clue afforded by the letters "S. R." visible on his shako. This suggested "Southern Rifles," which was found to be the original title of Company A, Fourth Georgia Regiment. From its muster roll it was learned that Robert A. Mizell enlisted as a private April 26, 1861. He was promoted to second-lieutenant in April, 1862. He was wounded in the Wilderness, and at Winchester, Va.; resigned, but re-enlisted in Company A, Second Kentucky Cavalry, of Morgan's command.

of the ways and constrained to make a choice between staying in the Union their ancestors had helped to establish and to which they were bound by the traditions of a lifetime, and taking arms against their fellow countrymen whose institutions and political creed accorded with their own.

It is to be remembered that Virginia steadfastly declined in its conversion to sever its connection with the Government of which it had formed so large and so significant a part from its formation, until called upon to furnish its quota of troops for the army of invasion, and the final decision was made with full recognition of what the choice implied, of the devastation and bitter misery to be visited upon the territory thus predestined to become the main battle-ground of the contending forces.

And so those wiser in the ways of war had, perforce, to proceed cautiously, to feel their way in the undertaking of welding these heterogeneous elements into a tempered weapon capable of dealing effective and intelligently directed blows, when the time should arrive for confronting the formidable adversary assembling his forces just across the border. The primary policy of the Confederate Government of attempting to defend its entire frontier, mistaken as it was soon proved to be, in the purely military sense, was possibly influenced in large degree by this consideration.

The deficiency of transportation may have also wielded its influence; indeed, the entire staff administration was, for quite a year or more, scarcely organized, and any movement of even a small body of troops could only be effected by the impressment of teams and wagons from the adjacent country, if leading away from the railway lines, and these last were neither numerous nor very efficient in the South at that period.

Yet, in spite of the many incongruities and deficiencies already indicated, the Southern volunteer was perhaps more prompt to acquire the ways of war than was his Northern opponent. The latter indisputably outclassed him in point of

SOUTH CAROLINA SOLDIERS IN '61

A group of Charleston Zouave Cadets—militia organized before the war, hence among the few that had swords and guns to start with in '61. The Zouave Cadets, under command of Captain C. E. Chichester, formed part of the First Regiment of Rifles, Fourth Brigade, South Carolina, at the outset of the war. The Fourth Brigade was the largest organized body of State militia. It was commanded by Brigadier-General James Simons, was well-organized, well-drilled and armed, and was in active service from December 27, 1860, to May, 1861. Some of its companies continued in service until the Confederate regiments, battalions, and batteries were organized and finally absorbed all the effective material of the brigade. One of the first duties of these companies was to guard some of the prisoners from New York regiments who were captured at the first battle of Bull Run, sent to Charleston harbor, and incarcerated at Castle Pinckney.

material, and was, in general, more amenable to discipline, for reasons heretofore stated—having been recruited, in large part, in the cities and large industrial centers. The Northern soldier had already formed the habit of subordination. The company or regimental commander simply replaced the general manager or the "boss"—it was merely a new job, and in one case as in the other what the superior said "went." The country-bred Southerner, on the other hand, was accustomed to the exercise of almost absolute authority over his slaves, few or many, according to his estate. But the simple and more primitive habit of his rural mode of life stood him in good stead when he came into the field. A gun was by no means an unfamiliar implement in his hands; he had known its use from boyhood and could usually hit what he aimed at. And in the mounted service his efficiency in action was in no wise impaired by preoccupation with his mount. He could no more remember when he learned to ride than when he learned to walk, and had graduated from the "school of the trooper" long before he brought himself and his best saddle-horse into the field.

It was in this arm of the service peculiarly that the Southerner, at the outset, held a long lead in advance of his adversary. As has been already stated, there were many organized bodies of horse in existence before the beginning of hostilities, and finer cavalry material has rarely, if ever, been assembled. The service had naturally tended to attract, for the most part, young men of wealth, leisure, and intelligence, forming a species of *corps d'élite*, and the equine part of the force could boast the best blood of Virginia and Kentucky stables. A few battlefields served to make good all deficiencies of equipment, so that by the time the war was well under way there was no distinction between the opposing forces in this respect: arms, saddlery, accouterment, down to blankets, haversacks, and canteens—all bore the stamp of some United States arsenal— "requisition on the spot," without process of Ordnance or

SUPPER WITH SOLDIERS OF THE NINTH MISSISSIPPI—1861

Ignorance of military conventionalities was of course the rule among Confederate volunteers of '61. In the matter of meals especially many amusing instances arose. There was the reply of a soldier of Dreux's Louisiana battalion of Magruder's division, when that force was holding the lines of Yorktown. "Prince John," who was noted for "putting on side," had bespoken dinner for himself and staff at a nearby farmhouse. Meanwhile the "full private" put in a petition to be fed. The good lady of the house, who was no respector of official rank, so long as one wore a gray jacket, and confident of the abundance of her provision, readily acceded to his request. When the somewhat belated staff entered the dining-room, the general was scandalized to find a bob-tail private already putting away the good cheer upon which he considered he held a prior claim. "This dinner was engaged, sir," he said haughtily, in his peculiar lisp. "That's all right," rejoined the private. "Sit down; there's plenty for all of us, I daresay." "Perhaps, young man, you don't know whom you are talking to," said the general, with increased hauteur. "I haven't the honor, but that doesn't matter," was the reply; "sit right down and help yourself." "I'm General Magruder, sir—your commanding officer." "Don't worry about that, general," said the imperturbable youngster; "I used to be particular who I ate with before this war, but now I don't care, so long as the victuals are clean." The Ninth Mississippi men in this photograph appear equally careless in preparing their evening meal. When it came to fighting, however, they could hold up their heads with the "smartest" European troops. Not long after this photograph, their regiment was especially mentioned for conspicuous gallantry at the attack of Price and Van Dorn on Corinth, October 3–4, 1862. The soldiers awaiting their evening meal above, from left to right, are James Pequio, Kinlock Falconer, and John Fennel.

Quartermaster's Department. The discriminating eye could discern from a glance at its equipment whether or not a regiment or brigade had been so engaged. It might, indeed, without straining the point unduly, be asserted that long before the close of the war the Federal Government had fitted out *both* armies.

The artillery arm was less fortunate, and for obvious reasons. This branch of the service is not so readily improvised as either of the other fighting forces. From start to finish it was under handicap by reason of its lack of trained officers, no less than from the marked inferiority of its material, ordnance, and ammunition. The batteries of the regular establishment were, of course, all in the United States service, commanded and served by trained gunners, and were easily distributed among the volunteer brigades by way of "stiffening" to the latter. This disparity was fully recognized by the Confederates and had its influence in the selection of more than one battle-ground, in order that it might be neutralized by local conditions, yet the service was very popular in the Southern army, and it was pervaded by a strong *esprit de corps*.

The young men of the cities and towns very generally chose it for enlistment; thus, New Orleans sent a battalion of five batteries, fully equipped, into the field—the famous "Washington Artillery"—besides some other batteries, and the city of Richmond, which furnished but one regiment of infantry and a few separate companies, contributed no less than eight or ten full batteries. Few of the minor towns but claimed at least one. The grade of intelligence of the personnel was rather exceptionally high, so that in the school of war, already referred to, these came in time to attain quite a respectable degree of efficiency, especially after the abolition of the system under which each battery was attached to an infantry brigade, subject to the orders of its commander, and the battery units became organized into battalions and corps commanded by officers of their own arm.

MOTLEY CONFEDERATE UNIFORMS—COMPANY B, NINTH MISSISSIPPI, IN '61

"Falstaff's regiment could hardly have exhibited a more motley appearance than did ours at 'dress parade,' at which the feature of 'dress' was progressively and conspicuously absent." This reminiscence is furnished by Allen C. Redwood, of the Fifty-fifth Virginia, from whom other contributions appear in the following pages. "There was no official attempt in the beginning to do more than to arm the troops and to provide the purely warlike accouterments of cartridge-box and belts and haversacks. Canteens and the like were provided quite as a matter of course, and in default of blankets and waterproof coverings, requisition was made upon the household stock of the individual and duly honored—bed-quilts and homespun 'spreads' were freely contributed, and buggy lap-robes and pianos and tables were despoiled of their oilcloth covers to fend the rain from the men gone from the homes to do battle for the cause, which was even dearer to the women left behind, who were steadfast to the end." These conditions applied also in States farther south, as the Mississippi photograph above witnesses. Standing at the left is James Cunningham; on the camp-stool is Thomas W. Falconer, and to his left are James Sims and John I. Smith.

Some of the early organizations were quite erratic; for a while, "legions" were a good deal in favor—mixed bodies comprising the several arms of the service under one command. These were speedily abandoned as unwieldy and inoperative. They probably had their origin in tradition, dating back to the days of Marion and Sumter and "Light Horse Harry" Lee, and may possibly have been effective in the partisan operations of that period. Otherwise, the regiments hurried to the front were thrown together into brigades in the hap-chance order of their arrival; gradually those hailing from the same State were brigaded together as far as practicable, an arrangement significant in its recognition of the State feeling, of the issue pending between the sections. This feature was not generally prevalent in the Federal ranks. As a result, the unit of the brigade persistently maintained its prominence in the estimation of the Confederate soldier throughout the whole term of his service; when vaunting his prowess he was apt to speak of his "brigade"; with his antagonist it was usually the "corps." The rivalry between the respective States had probably no small influence in stimulating his zeal; the men from Georgia or the Carolinas could not hold back when the Alabamans or Texans on right or left were going ahead. It was but the repetition of Butler's rallying cry at Cherabusco, "Palmettos! stand your ground; *remember where you came from!*" when Bee, at Manassas, pointing to the Virginians, "standing like a stone wall," restored his wavering line.

The Confederate soldier of the ranks may be said to have been *sui generis*. In the mass he was almost devoid of military spirit, as the term is popularly applied, and quite indifferent—antagonistic, even—to the "pomp and circumstance of glorious war." As to devotion to his flag, he had scarcely time to cultivate the sentiment which figured so largely in the patriotic fervor of his opponents. No one of the "motley many" national ensigns ever entirely received his approval.

TWO MEMBERS OF THE McCLELLAN ZOUAVES IN 1861

The host of ornately uniformed and armed companies which sprang up at the outset of the war was ultimately merged into the gray monotone of the respective regiments into which they were incorporated. The Confederate soldier on the left is Ellis Green, of the McClellan Zouaves, and his companion on the right belonged to the same company. The photographs were taken at Charleston, S. C., and the spruce appearance and spotless uniforms make it unnecessary to add that they were taken early in the war. The Southern volunteer was perhaps more prompt to acquire the ways of war than was his Northern opponent. The latter was more amenable to discipline, having been recruited, in large part, in the cities and large industrial centers. He had already formed the habit of subordination. The country-bred Southerner, on the other hand, was accustomed to the exercise of almost absolute authority over his slaves, but the simple and more primitive habits of his rural mode of life stood him in good stead when he came into the field.

The original " Stars and Bars " he regarded as a sort of off-spring of the discarded " gridiron "—of this abandonment he often expressed himself in terms of regret, by the way—and its successors he was wont to describe irreverently as " shirt-tails." He did, in time, come to develop respect and affection for his battle-flag, the little red square charged with the star-studded blue saltire, but even that his eminently prac-tical mind conceived mainly as a convenient object upon which to dress up a line of battle or to serve as a rallying-point in the event of that line being broken. It was essentially his, the soldier's flag, and was never at any stage the national flag; its traditions were all of his own creation and he had baptized it with his blood. In the main, he regarded his service in the light of an unpleasant duty, and he went at it much as he would have undertaken any other disagreeable job.

General Lord Wolseley—then Colonel Wolseley—relates an interview he had with General Lee, during a visit to the headquarters of the latter, just after the Maryland campaign of 1862. Having intimated a desire to see the troops of whose performance he had heard so much, General Lee took him for a ride through the lines, and upon their return remarked to his distinguished guest:

" Well, Colonel, you have seen my army—how does it impress you, on the whole? "

" They seem a hardy, serviceable looking lot of fellows," Wolseley replied, " but, to be quite frank, General, I must say that one misses the smartness which we in Europe are accus-tomed to associate with a military establishment—but perhaps it would not be reasonable to look for that so soon after the hard campaign they had just gone through."

" Ho! " replied " Marse Robert," " my men don't show to advantage in camp, and to tell the truth, I am a little ashamed to show them to visitors. But, sir, you should see them when they are fighting—then I would not mind if the whole world were looking on! "

PART I
SOLDIER LIFE

———

THE CONFEDERATE
IN THE FIELD

———

WASHING DISHES
REAL SOLDIERING FOR
A CONFEDERATE OF 1863

WHERE UNIFORMS WERE LACKING, BUT RESOLUTION WAS FIRM

The Confederates who stood in this well-formed line saw active service from the earliest period of the war. The day that Florida seceded from the Union, First-Lieutenant Adam J. Slemmer withdrew with Company G of the First United States Artillery from the shore to Fort Pickens, on the western extremity of Santa Rosa Island. Colonel W. H. Chase was in command of the Southerners and demanded the surrender of Fort Pickens January 13, 1861. It is recorded that his voice shook and his eyes filled with tears when he attempted to read his formal demand for the surrender; he realized, with all true and far-sighted Americans, how terrible a

A CONFEDERATE DRILL IN FORT McREE, PENSACOLA HARBOR

blow was impending in the form of fratricidal strife. Lieutenant Slemmer refused the demand. Colonel Chase had an insufficient force at the time to take the fort by storm. November 22d and 23d, the United States vessels *Niagara* and *Richmond*, together with Fort Pickens and the adjoining batteries, bombarded the Confederate lines. Although Fort McRee was so badly damaged that General Bragg thought of abandoning it, the garrison held firm, and the plan of the Union commanders to "take and destroy it" did not succeed. Forts McRee and Barrancas were bombarded again by the Union warships and batteries January 1, 1862.

THE CONFEDERATE IN THE FIELD

By Allen C. Redwood

Fifty-fifth Virginia Regiment, Confederate States Army

A QUESTION which is often asked of the survivor of the Civil War, when recounting the " battles, sieges, and fortunes he has passed," is, " How does it feel to be in battle? " If he is in the habit of taking account of his sensations and impressions the answer is not so simple as might appear at first sight.

Much of the ground disputed by the contending forces in our Civil War was quite unlike the popular conception of a battlefield, derived from descriptions of European campaigns or from portrayals of the same, usually fanciful. The choice of a battle-ground in actual warfare is not determined by its fitness for the display of imposing lines, as at a review. As often as not, the consideration of concealment of those lines has much to do with the selection, or else there is some highway which it is important to hold or to possess, or again, some vulnerable point of the foe invites attack, in which case the actual *terrain* is such as may happen, and the disposition cf the forces is made to conform as far as possible thereto.

The first engagement in which the writer took a modest part had been entirely foreseen, yet its development refuted all preconceived ideas of what a battle was like. It was the beginning of the series which resulted in frustrating McClellan's campaign on the Peninsula and raising the siege of Richmond, in 1862. We had been holding the left of the Confederate line on the Meadow Bridge road, picketing the bridges spanning a fork of the Chickahominy at that point—a Union picket-post being at the crossing of another branch, about a hundred yards distant, and in plain view from our outpost.

CONFEDERATES AT DRILL—NOT "SMART" BUT FIGHTERS

"One misses the smartness which we in Europe are accustomed to associate with military establishments." The sight of this Confederate officer in his shirt-sleeves, and of his determined-looking company behind, recalls this remark, made by General Lord Wolseley, then Colonel Wolseley and later Governor-General of Canada, after inspecting Lee's army in the lower Shenandoah Valley just after the Maryland campaign of 1862—the year after the Florida photograph above was taken. The look of the men, gaunt and hollow-eyed, worn with marching and lack of proper food, until they did not carry an ounce of superfluous flesh; powdered thick with dust until their clothing and accouterment were all one uniform dirty gray, except where the commingled grime and sweat had streaked and crusted the skin on face and head; the jaded, unkempt horses and dull, mud-bespattered gun-carriages and caissons of the artillery; even trivial details; the nauseating flavor of the unsalted provisions, the pungent smell of the road-dust which filled the nostrils—all these impressions came thronging back across the intervening years which have transformed the beardless young soldier into the grizzled veteran who still "lags superfluous on the stage," and who recalls these things that have passed. And he glories in "Marse Robert's" reply: "No, my men don't show to advantage in camp, and to tell the truth I am a little ashamed to show them to visitors. But, sir," he resumed, his face flushing and his eyes kindling, as sometimes happened when stirred from his habitual poise, "you should see them when they are fighting—then I would not mind if the whole world were looking on!"

At the date of the opening of the battle, June 26, 1862, it was the turn of the regiment for this duty, our company holding the advanced post at the bridges. But we had supposed that we were to receive an attack from the foe, being ignorant of the fact that the Federal force on the north bank was " in the air," owing to the retention of McDowell's corps, before which we had retired from Fredericksburg, and which was to have joined and extended this flank on the Rappahannock. Thus, when the advance began, we were the first to cross the river. For some distance the road was a corduroy through the swamp, which our company traversed at double-quick and without opposition until we came into the open and approached the small hamlet of Mechanicsville, at the intersection of a road leading to Richmond and the Old Cold Harbor road, running almost parallel with the Chickahominy.

Thus far we had seen no Federals except the picket, which had promptly retired before our advance. Nor was the country about us in any way distinctive—just an ordinary eastern Virginia landscape of fields, farmhouses, and commonplace woods, and seeming peaceful enough in the light of a summer's afternoon. Before opening this vista the column, marching in fours, was halted in a shallow cut of the road, and some one ahead called back an order to " clear the road for the artillery! " A wild scramble up the banks ensued, under the apprehension that we were about to be raked by McClellan's guns. But the real intent was to advance a section of our brigade battery traveling in our rear, to " feel " a thin belt of timber intervening between us and the village. This was our first scare; number two was soon to follow.

Meanwhile, we had formed line on the right of the road and approached the wooded camp-site in which, as we supposed, the foe was concealed and awaiting us. When almost up to it, some excited soldier discharged his musket; at once, and without orders, the entire right wing of the regiment blazed away at the numerous collection of tent-poles and cracker-

THE CONFEDERATE SOLDIER AT WORK

The photograph of this garrison at a "sand battery" on the Gulf Coast gives a view of the Confederate at work that will be treasured by veterans. Every one of them knows how eminently unsatisfactory an occupation is war for the private in the ranks. He is ordered, he knows not whither, he knows not why, and, likely as not, has to stay there to die. "I wondered if they were deliberately planning my death," recalled an old soldier who was invariably chosen for the skirmish line. "First, we had to go out there to see if anyone could be induced to shoot at us; and if they did, and we got back alive, we had to take our places in the ranks and go forward with the other fellows, taking an equal risk with them after the other fellows were entirely through shooting at us individually. Somehow it didn't seem quite fair."

boxes, reminders of its late occupation. At that time there probably was not a Federal soldier nearer than the further side of Beaver Dam Creek, nearly a mile distant. But we were to hear from them before long.

Having passed through the straggling little village we were halted again just beyond, in a dip of the ground through which coursed a small rivulet, and some of us took the opportunity to fill canteens. It was while waiting there that we received the first hostile shots from the guns beyond the creek. They soon got our range and it began to look like real war at last.

It was at this point that, for the first time, I saw a man killed in battle. We were standing to arms awaiting orders to advance; another regiment of the brigade was supporting us a short distance in the rear—the Sixtieth Virginia, under Colonel Starke, who was killed later while commanding a Louisiana brigade at Sharpsburg, in September, 1862. A shell plowed the crest of the elevation in front, and our line made a profound obeisance as it passed over; it seemed as if it must clear us but about reach the Sixtieth, and as I ducked I glanced back that way and witnessed its effect in their ranks. The body of a stalwart young fellow suddenly disappeared, and on the ground where he had stood was a confused mass of quivering limbs which presently lay still—the same shell, as I learned afterward, carried away the top of a man's head in our own regiment.

Another took effect soon after, as we were moving out by the left flank, knocking over several men and killing one of them. By this time the fire had grown quite brisk, and we lost more men as we lay in the open field before entering some woods still more to the left, where the regiment commenced firing, against an imaginary foe, I have cause to believe. Yet, these same skittish troops, under fire for the first time, just four days later charged and captured a regular battery of 12-pounder guns and were complimented on the field by

THE WORK OF WAR WITH COASTWISE GARRISON—INSIDE SUMTER, 1864

The soldiers of the Army of Northern Virginia, with the Confederate troops who struggled over the Western mountains and swamps, were wont to allude to coast "garrison" duty as an easy berth, but this Confederate photograph of the interior of Fort Sumter, taken in 1864, does not indicate any degree of superfluous ease and convenience. The garrison drawn up in the background, in front of the ruined barracks, could point to the devastation wrought by the bombardment, visible in the foreground and on the parapets, with just pride. In spite of the hundreds of shells that crashed into the fort from the belching guns of the Federal fleets, the Stars and Bars still floated defiant throughout the four years of the war. The Southern heart may well glow with pride at the thought of the little fort.

General Longstreet—such progress had they made within that brief period in the " school of the soldier."

We are coming to the period in this narration when we might fairly claim to have been soldiers indeed; when the disjointed fragments had at last been welded together into an army. We had been " shooted over " and even " blooded "; had heard the screech of shell and the hiss of minie balls, and had learned to discount their deadliness in some measure; had learned how to make ourselves snug and comfortable in camp, even though our wagons still might be miles in the rear; had learned to cook without utensils and to improvise a shelter without tents or, failing that, to take the weather as it came and say no more about it. We knew that a march meant much fatigue —agony, even—and accepted both as a matter of course and part of the work on which we were engaged. Blistered feet, we had come to learn, were indeed serious, and as a corollary, that it was wise to get a foot-bath, and to put on dry socks upon going into camp for the night, even if one were tired out, and felt more disposed just to lie down and rest. There was to-morrow's march to be considered, and we had come to recognize that to-day's exertion was by no means exceptional.

We knew how to make a fire which would last all night; that it was well to start out before daylight with just a bite, if no more, rather than upon an empty stomach, and to confine the consumption of water while on the road to what was in the canteen, though that might be lukewarm, instead of going out of ranks at a spring or well—the canteen's contents were just as *wet*—and one was not tempted to drink too much when overheated, and most important of all, he did not have to overfatigue himself in trying to catch up with his command in a road full of other troops, who had " troubles of their own " and were by no means disposed to get out of the way.

The soldier could find water in a perfectly unfamiliar country just by the lay of the land, and by a kind of prescience almost amounting to instinct, and, at a glance, could estimate

THE CHANGE FROM THEORY TO PRACTICE

Wall-tents, such as appear in this photograph of 1861, were not seen for long in the Confederate army. At the beginning, no less than three wagons conveyed the *impedimenta* of a company of the Fifty-fifth Virginia—one having been provided by private subscription to transport the knapsacks! The rest of the transportation was in proportion. The regimental train, as it left the Rappahannock, would have sufficed amply for the use of at least a brigade. But a few months later, just after the "Seven Days," all this was changed and the soldiers began for the first time to realize what actual soldiering meant and to find out how very few were the articles one needed in his kit when he had to transport them on his person. An inkling of this had been gained before, however, when the brigade retained as an outpost at Fredericksburg, after Johnston's army went to Yorktown, evacuated that position before the advance of McDowell's Corps, which was moving overland to join McClellan north of the Chickahominy and complete the investment of Richmond on that side. This movement relegated to the rear the capacious mess-chests and wall-tents which had hitherto been regarded as requisite or necessary paraphernalia for field service. The soldiers in the field were permitted to retain only the "flies" belonging to the tents.

the merits or demerits of a camp-site, at the end of a day's march. Also, we had grown weather-wise in forecasting the final events to which all the preliminaries tended, from indications whose significance the experience of service enabled us to read with a fair approach to certainty, however these might vary, as they did, with the outward conditions—accidents of locality, the immediate object in view, and the like.

Many of the early engagements, from the point of view of the man in the ranks and the officers of the lower grades, seemed quite impromptu. Of one of the most stupendous of these—that of Gettysburg—a Confederate officer of high grade has said, "We accidentally stumbled into this fight."

It seemed so to the writer, then serving in Heth's division of the Third Army Corps, and which opened the engagement on the morning of July 1, 1863. Usually we knew there must be trouble ahead, but not always how imminent it might be. The column would be marching as it had been doing for perhaps some days preceding, the fatigue, heat, dust, and general discomfort being far more insistent upon the thought of the men than any consideration of its military objective. Perhaps the pace may have been rather more hurried than usual for some miles, and a halt, for any reason, was most welcome to the foot-sore troops, who promptly proceeded to profit by every minute of it—lying down on the dusty grass by the roadside, easing knapsack straps and belts, and perhaps snatching the opportunity for a short smoke (for which there had been no breath to spare previously) or for a moistening of parched throats from the canteen.

This might be of longer or shorter duration, often it was aggravatingly cut up into a series of advances or stops, more fatiguing than the regular marching swing. Getting up and down is rather tiresome when one is carrying the regular campaigning kit of a soldier and when muscles have been taxed until there is no spring left in them—quite another affair from the same process when fresh and unencumbered. It is then that

WALL–TENTS

COMPARATIVE COMFORT ON THE CONFEDERATE COAST

Although most comforts had disappeared from the Army of Northern Virginia by 1862, as well as from the armies in the West, the port garrisons like those around Charleston were able to keep their wall-tents. So great is the "luxury" among this mess of the Washington Light Infantry in garrison at Charleston, that they even have initials painted upon their water-bucket; and, wonder of wonders! there hangs a towel. One who inquired of a veteran as to the opportunities for toilet-making was answered thus: "On the march we generally had water enough to wash our hands and faces, but sometimes, especially when there was brisk skirmishing every day, the men didn't get a chance to wash their bodies for weeks together. It was fun in a country comparatively free from the enemy to see a column strike a river. Hundreds of the boys would be stripped in an instant, and the river banks would reëcho with their shouts and splashing. It was only on garrison duty or in winter-quarters that the supreme luxury, laundry from home, could ever be attained." The men in this photograph from left to right are Sergeant W. A. Courtney, Privates H. B. Olney, V. W. Adams, and Sergeant R. A. Blum. The organization still existed, half a century after the scene above.

the voice of a man with a " grouch " is heard in the land. There is sure to be one in every company, and his incessant jeremiads by no means tend to alleviate the discomforts of his fellows, and so receive small sympathy from them.

A mounted orderly comes riding back, picking his way through the recumbent ranks, and pretending indifference to the rough chaffing prescribed by custom in the infantry as the appropriate greeting for the man on horseback—good-natured on the whole, even if a little tinged with envy—or some general officer with his staff is seen going forward at a brisk trot through the fields bordering the road, or maybe a battery of guns directing its course toward some eminence. It becomes apparent that the check ahead is not due to such ordinary causes as a stalled wagon or caisson or to the delay occasioned by some stream to be forded; the objective aspect of the situation begins to assert itself; the thought of present personal discomfort gives place to that of prospective peril, and a certain nervous tension pervades the ranks.

Soldiers are but human, and the veterans who have been in battle before know what is implied in the work ahead and that some—and it may be one as well as another—will probably not answer at next roll-call. The " eagerness for the fray " of which we read so often, rarely survives the first battle; in all that follows, it is conspicuously absent, however the men may have gained in steadiness and have acquired self-possession under fire.

The troops in front are moving now, filing off to right or left, to take their allotted position in the line, or possibly beginning a flank movement; there may be no fight to-day after all—these things have happened before, without anything serious coming of it. The hostile force may be only a small one and we daresay will not give battle, but retire on its main body. For, in the field we live merely from day to day anyhow and " sufficient unto the day is the evil thereof." We are not in the confidence of the powers that be and know nothing of their

CONFEDERATES IN CAMP

This photograph of Confederate troops in camp was taken at Camp Moore, Louisiana, in 1861. The man writing the letter home on the box is Emil Vaquin, and Arthur Roman is the man completing the washing. Thomas Russel is gleaning the latest news from the paper, and Amos Russel is grinding coffee. The fifth man is Octave Babin. Names of French extraction, these, appropriate to Louisiana. The soldiers are facing their period of "breaking-in." A veteran of the eastern army describes this transition period: "Our breaking-in was rather rough—it was the beginning of a prolonged spell of wet, raw weather, which is so often mentioned in McClellan's reports of his operations on the Peninsula—and, with little notion of how to adapt ourselves to the situation, we suffered much discomfort at first. After the experience of a few months and with half the equipage we then possessed, we would have been entirely comfortable, by campaigning standards. As yet we were drawing the full army ration, including the minor items of coffee, sugar, rice, and beans, and were abundantly supplied with the necessary utensils for their preparation whenever we were in contact with our wagons, but we simply did not know how to use this bountiful provision and had yet to learn that the situation was not exceptional or ephemeral but would be just the same in the future months of war, and must be met and faced in permanent fashion—that it was 'all in the day's work,' and that any departure from these hard times, as they then seemed, would be in the direction of 'worse a-comin'.'"

machinations, however intimately these may concern our fortunes. We only know that we have " no orders " as yet.

This condition of affairs may continue for hours or for minutes. Meanwhile, the best thing to do is to make ourselves as comfortable as possible—the philosophy of the seasoned soldier, in all circumstances—and take the chance of being permitted to remain so, and we shall be all the better prepared for the work if it *does* come. But, hello! look yonder! the battery-men, who have been lounging about, are standing to their pieces now, and immediately become busy executing mysterious movements about the same, in the methodical fashion distinctive of their arm. Those about the nearest gun suddenly break away to right and left. A dense white stream of smoke leaps from the muzzle, and the crashing report strikes our ears a few seconds later, as the gunners step forward again, lay hold of handspike and spokes, and run the gun back into position. Another shot and another, and yet another, and the smoke thickens and we discern only vaguely the movements at the cannon —but the war-music has begun and we know the battle has opened.

From somewhere in front comes another and fainter report, and possibly in mid-air above our battery a round cloud jumps into view, snowy white against the blue sky; another remote, jarring growl, followed by a fluttering sound but too familiar to our ears and growing louder each moment, and a spurt of earth is projected into the air not far from the road we occupy. One finds the foe does not propose that the argument shall be all on one side and is rising " to a point of information."

Evidently it is this road which is the object of their curiosity; just now we also are interested, but in the sense of wishing we were somewhere else before their aim shall have become more accurate with practice—we don't like the talk to be too one-sided either, and they are beyond the range of our ordnance, while the ground in front which conceals from view what is beyond affords slight protection. Ah! there is a staff-

"IMPEDIMENTA" DID NOT HARASS THE CONFEDERATES

AN UNUSUALLY LUXURIOUS CAMP

This is an unusually luxurious Confederate camp for the second year of the war.   The photograph was taken by Scheier of Nashville, Tenn., and the scene is indicated as on the Harding road.   The shining muskets stacked in front of the tents contrast with the soldiers' nondescript costumes.   The boxes and barrels have rather the appearance of plunder than that of a steady supply from the commissary department.   Conspicuous are the skillet on the barrel-head, and the shirt hung up to dry.   The Confederate soldier traveled light.   Indeed, a long train would have impeded, perhaps frustrated, the swift movements which were so great an element of his strength.   The old Romans rightly termed their baggage "*impedimenta*," when put upon their mettle.   However, the size of their wagon-train was seldom a cause of anxiety to the Confederates.   Jackson's "Foot Cavalry" could always outstrip the wagons, and the size of the Union wagon-train was apt to interest them more frequently.   For the rank and file of the Army of Northern Virginia, there were no more tents after the middle of the war.   The camping site was almost always in the woods, as giving ready access to fuel and being as near as possible to some stream of water.   Each company selected ground in the rear of its stacks of arms, but beyond that there was little semblance of order in the arrangement.   The consideration of level ground, free from stubs or roots, usually determined the selection.

officer talking in an animated tone to the brigade commander, motioning with his hand, while the other closely studies a folding map which has just been handed to him and which he presently returns, nodding the while to signify that he understands what he is expected to do. "Attention!"—but we are already on our feet in advance of the order, and most willingly leave the road, now growing momentarily more insalubrious, following the head of the column through fields of stubble or fallow or standing corn, the blades of which cut and the pollen irritates the moist skin. Or it may be through dense woodland, where nothing is visible a few yards distant, in which furious fighting may occur and many men fall with the opposing lines in close contact, yet entirely concealed from each other, the position of either being only conjectured by the smoke and the direction of the firing, as the bullets from the opposite side come rapping against the tree trunks and cutting twigs and leaves overhead.

Before this stage is reached, however, there may be numerous changes of direction, countermarching and the like to attain the position; long lines of battle require a good deal of space for their deployment, and in the woods, especially, it is not easy to determine in advance just how much ground any command will occupy. In each case, however, at some stage, the troops are in line, and we may suppose them there, awaiting the attack or about to deliver it, as may be.

It is perhaps the most ominous moment of all when the command is heard, "Load at will—load!" followed by the ringing of rammers in the barrels and the clicking of gun-locks—neither of which sounds, with the arms of to-day, has any significance, but it was otherwise when we loaded "in nine times," as the manual prescribed. The modern soldier fails utterly to grasp the meaning of biting cartridges; a cartridge to him is essentially a brass shell with the fulminate enclosed in its base, requiring only to be taken from his belt and put in the chamber of his rifle—nowadays, indeed, they go in in

FIELD AND FOREST—TWO CONTRASTING BUT FAMOUS SCENES OF CONFLICT

The two photographs are eloquent of the two distinct styles of warfare that Captain Redwood contrasts. Over the wide fields near Gettysburg, across the trampled stubble where lie the bodies of Confederates fallen in the battle, ten, fifteen, twenty thousand men could be maneuvered intelligently. But in the dense woodland conflicts were waged blindly, in total ignorance of the strength and location of the foe—yet sanguinary, as the photograph of the battlefield of the Wilderness below attests.

"clips" of five. But we veterans managed to fight through the big war with the old muzzle-loaders, and they seem to have done some execution, too. It has "a strange, quick jar upon the ear," the dry metallic snapping running along the line when it came to "prime," and each man realized that when next heard it will be with no uncertain sound and closely followed by the command, "Fire!"

Once engaged, the soldier's attention is too much taken up with delivering his fire effectively to give heed to much else —it is hard work and hot work, in the literal, no less than in the figurative, sense, and extremely dirty work withal. The lips become caked with powder-grime from biting the twist of car-tridges, and after one or two rounds the hands are blackened and smeared from handling the rammer; the sweat streams down and has to be cleared from the eyes in order to see the sights of the rifle, and the grime is transferred from hands to face.

Think you of a gang of coal-heavers who have just fin-ished putting in a winter's supply ordered by some provident householder in midsummer, and you get a fair impression of troops at the end of a day's fighting. The line soon loses all semblance of regular formation; the companies have become merely groups of men, loading and firing and taking advan-tage of any accident of ground—natural depression, tree, rock, or even a pile of fence rails that will give protection. But if the soldier is about where he belongs—to right or left of the regimental colors, according to the normal place of his com-pany in line—he feels reasonably sure of resuming formation whenever the command may come to "cease firing" and to "dress on colors" preparatory to an advance or a charge. If the latter, though the move next may begin in perfect order, it is almost immediately lost.

The charge delivered by our brigade at Frayser's Farm —to which allusion has been made earlier in this chapter— was, as seen by a Federal general who was captured there, "in V-shape, without order and in perfect recklessness." This

WHERE THE COURAGE TO FIGHT IN THE DARK WAS NEEDED

Old soldiers say that it takes more courage to fight with an unseen foe than it does to sweep in long lines through the open fields to the mouths of the roaring batteries. A veteran cavalryman has stated that he thought a cavalry charge took less bravery than any other kind of action. There is the dash, the emulation, the "thunder of the captains and the shouting" all stimulating the participant to supreme effort. Such are the famous European battles of song and story— usually waged in open fields; but the American soldier soon became an adept at fighting an unseen enemy. These dense woodlands of the Wilder-

ness are not the European idea of a battlefield, but the ghastly ruins of the human frame, and the trees clipped and broken by the fearful hail of shot and shell, attest that here was a battle where they fought in the darkness of the woods, instead of on the open plain. These photographs convey wonderful mute tributes to the courage of every American participant, from the South or from the North. The forest-trees are pitted and scored and hacked and gnawed by the galling fire of musketry—in some instances, entirely felled from this cause alone, for the country afforded but little scope for the employment of artillery by either side. The underbrush, withered and reddened by the summer's sun, lies at all angles as the bullets have cut it down along the battlefield.

formation was in no wise intentional, the apex of the V in question being simply the brigade commander, General Field, who personally conducted the attack upon the battery and the slope of the sides, as the individual prowess of his followers might determine. Even more characteristic of a Confederate infantry onset was the description of an officer of high rank on that side, " A tumultuous rush of men, each aligning on himself, and yelling like a demon, on his own hook." The " yell " which has become historical, was merely another expression of the individuality of the Southern soldier, though as its moral force came to be recognized, it was rather fostered officially, and grew into an institution—it was the peculiar slogan of the Gray people. A gallant, accomplished staff-officer of General Meade's household, in a recent work on the battle of the Wilderness, pays the thrilling yell this tribute, " I never heard that yell that the country in the rear did not become intensely interesting!" And more than one Federal soldier has borne similar testimony.

This allusion recalls to mind a visit of two days' duration, made to that historic field in the summer of 1910, after an interval of forty-six years, which served to illustrate forcibly what has already been recorded in these recollections as to the absence of distinction in the features of a battle-ground *per se*. When last seen the blighting breath of war had but lately passed over those dense and tangled woodlands and the signs of strife, deadly and determined, were manifest everywhere. The forest trees were pitted and scored and hacked and gnawed by the galling fire of musketry, in some instances, entirely felled from this cause alone, for the country afforded but little scope for the employment of artillery by either side. The underbrush, withered and reddened by the summer's sun, lay at all angles as the bullets had cut it down, as if some one had gone over the ground with a *machete* and given each little bush or sapling a stroke. In all directions, one came upon the rude breastworks hastily thrown up, of earth, logs, rails—anything that might serve to stop a bullet. They had failed to stop a

[176]

IN THE WILDERNESS

In these photographs reappears the dreadful Wilderness as it looked in 1864—the shambles in the thickets, with the forest trees pitted and scarred and hacked and gnawed by the galling musketry fire, where the dead still outnumbered the living, where the woods bordering the Orange Plank Road were thickly strewn with the bodies of Hancock's men who had so furiously assailed Hill and Longstreet on that line. The underbrush, withered and reddened by the summer's sun, lay at all angles as the bullets had cut it down, as if someone had gone over the ground with a *machete* and given each little bush or sapling a stroke. In all

directions one came upon the rude breastworks, hastily thrown up, of earth, logs, rails—anything that might serve to stop a bullet. But nearly half a century later, a visitor could find here the deep significance of peace; as Captain Redwood records in his accompanying reminiscence: "The bark has closed over the bullet scars on the trees; a new growth has sprung up to replace that leveled by the musketry; goodly trees, even, are standing upon the diminished earthworks. The others have long since rotted into mould. The traveler might easily pass along that quaint road, so hotly contested, with never a suspicion of what befell there—'grim-visaged war has smoothed his wrinkled front' indeed."

THE ORANGE PLANK ROAD

AS IT LOOKED IN 1864

"THE GRIM HARVEST" OF THE WILDERNESS—SOLDIERS' GRAVES
AFTER THE BATTLE

good many, and all the failures were not recorded upon the natural growth.

In this sparsely settled region, but lately so populous, the dead occupants still outnumbered the living. The woods bordering the Orange plank road were thickly strewn with the mouldering bodies of Hancock's men who had furiously assailed Hill and Longstreet on that line. Here gallant old Webb, for whom " taps " have sounded, led his staunch brigade against Gregg's Texans and Low's Alabamans, almost up to the works, and the trefoil badges—the " clover-leaves " on the cap-fronts of the fallen covered the ground on the edge of the Widow Tapp's field where Lee attempted to lead the Texans' charge, and the men refused to go forward until he consented to go back. Cattle were quietly browsing the herbage in a little grass glade at this point, their pasture the aftermath of the grim harvest reaped there on that May morning long ago.

To-day scarcely a trace remains of all that. In the intervening years beneficent Nature has been silently but unremittingly at work effacing the marks of man's devastation of her domain. The bark has closed over the bullet-scars on the trees, so that diligent search is required to detect them now; a new growth has sprung up to replace that leveled by the musketry; goodly trees, even, are standing upon the diminished earthworks. The others have long since rotted into mold. The traveler might easily pass along that quaint road, so hotly contested, with never a suspicion of what befell there—" grim visaged war has smoothed his wrinkled front," indeed.

The war is definitely over. In its time it ravaged our fair land almost beyond recognition, put our young manhood to the uttermost proof, and left in its track many deeper and more poignant wounds than those in the Wilderness woods, but it ended at last. And time has been closing over the scars ever since and new growth springing into life all the while. Who was right; who was wrong?—the God above us " who doth all things aright " alone knows surely.

PART I
SOLDIER LIFE

THE SCHOOL OF THE SOLDIER

VETERANS ALREADY IN '61

These drummer-boys of the Eighth Regiment of the National Guard of the State of New York were photographed in the '50s, wearing their Mexican War uniforms. The boys of this regiment went to the front in these same uniforms and marched throughout the war.

THE SCHOOL OF THE SOLDIER

By Fenwick Y. Hedley

Brevet Captain United States Volunteers, and Adjutant, Thirty-second Illinois Infantry

THE American volunteer of 1861–65 never before had his like, or ever will again. He was of only the third generation from the Revolutionary War, and the first after the Mexican War, and he had personal acquaintance with men who had fought in each. Besides, a consideration of much meaning, he was brought up in a day when school declamation was practised, and once a week he had spoken or heard Patrick Henry's "Give me liberty or give me death," Webster's "Reply to Hayne," "The Battle of Buena Vista," "The Charge of the Light Brigade," "The boy stood on the burning deck," and the like. So it was, when Lincoln called him, he responded with a heart intensely patriotic and aflame with military ardor, and he proved marvelously adaptable as a soldier.

At the outset and occasionally afterward, many young men went into service in companies and regiments of militia. A few were well drilled, the greater number indifferently. These were but a sprinkling in the great mass of volunteers, who were without such experience, and came fresh from farms, workshops, stores, and schools. But most of them had been members of the uniformed clubs in the exciting political campaign of 1861, and were fairly proficient in ordinary marching movements and handling torchsticks in semi-military fashion, which proved of advantage to them in entering upon a soldier's life.

Usually for a few weeks before taking the field, the embryo soldiers lay in camps of instruction. Probably in every regiment were some veterans who had seen service in the Mexican

A TIME–STAINED PHOTOGRAPH OF THE 'FIFTIES

OFFICERS AND NON–COMMISSIONED OFFICERS

COMPANY "F," EIGHTH NEW YORK

These officers of the Eighth New York are garbed in the same uniforms that they wore to the Mexican War. This and the hotly contested political campaign of 1861 served as the two great "drill-masters" of the Federal recruits at the outset of the war. A few of them were indifferently drilled through their connection with regiments of militia, but these were but a sprinkling in the great mass that thronged from the farms, the workshops, and the schools.   Most of these had marched as members of the uniformed clubs in the exciting political campaign of 1861, and were fairly proficient in ordinary movements and in handling torch-sticks instead of rifles.   Probably in every quota there were some men who had seen service in the Mexican War or in the militia.   They had become accustomed to military systems now obsolete, but their training enabled them to speedily put off the old and put on the new, and they often proved highly capable drill-masters.

War or in the militia. They had been accustomed to military systems now obsolete, but their training enabled them to speedily put off the old and put on the new, and they proved fairly capable drillmasters.

It was days, often weeks, before uniforms were provided, and entire battalions performed their evolutions in their civilian clothes, of all cuts and hues. Longer were they without arms. The sentries, or camp guards, walked their beats day or night with clubs. At the regimental headquarters were a score or two of " condemned " muskets which were utilized all day long by alternating squads of non-commissioned officers, practising the manual of arms in preparation for instructing the men.

Now armed and equipped, the men were industriously drilled, by squads, by companies, and by battalions, six to eight hours a day. There were awkwardness and blundering; sergeants would march their platoons, and captains, their companies, by the right instead of by the left flank, or *vice versa,* to the destruction of a column or square, necessitating re-formation and repetition of the movement, sometimes again and again. But, on the whole, the men progressed well, and soon performed ordinary evolutions with creditable approach to soldierlike exactness.

The greatest stress was laid upon the use of the musket, and this was the young soldier's severest experience. To begin with, the arms were old muzzle-loaders—muskets of Mexican War days, altered from flint-lock to percussion, or obsolete Austrian or Belgian guns, heavy and clumsy. The manual of arms, as laid down in the text-book of the time, Hardee's " School of the Soldier," was complicated and wearisome. In particular, the operation of loading and firing involved numerous counted " motions "—handling the cartridge (from the cartridge-box), biting off its end, inserting it in the gun-barrel, drawing the ramrod, ramming the cartridge home, returning the ramrod, and placing the percussion cap upon the

"THE SCHOOL OF THE SOLDIER"—BAYONET DRILL OF THE FORTIETH MASSACHUSETTS, 1863

The center photograph shows one of the lessons that had to be learned by the soldiers of both sides. This mock battery at Seabrook Point, South Carolina—logs of wood to represent guns—was Federal; but the Confederates, at Centerville, Port Hudson, and elsewhere, used "dummy" guns effectively. Before the soldiers met these problems, however, they had to conquer the manual of arms, and were diligently drilled in firing, by file and by company, to the right oblique, to the left oblique, and to the rear. But most awkward and wearisome of all was the bayonet experience, as shown in the upper photograph of the Forti-

"WHEN IS A GUN NOT A GUN?"—WHEN IT IS A DUMMY, LIKE THESE AT SEABROOK POINT, S. C., 1862

eth Massachusetts Infantry at bayonet drill. The men were drilled in open order so as to admit of free movement and give the instructing officer an opportunity to see the performance and action of each individual man, and correct his mistakes. Less arduous than bayonet drill was morning guard-mount. The men detailed to this duty were assembled about nine o'clock, drilled in a few of the movements of the manual of arms, and inspected by the officer of the day, distinguished by a scarf across the shoulder. Then they were marched out to relieve the guards on duty, and their full tour of this duty was twenty-four hours.

GUARD–MOUNT OF A SMART REGIMENT—THE ONE HUNDRED AND SIXTY-FOURTH NEW YORK gun-nipple. This feat (or series of feats) required much practice. The musket was to rest upon the ground, immediately in front of the soldier, and exactly perpendicular. Its excessive length made it impossible for a short man to draw and return his ramrod in precise manner, and, in either act, he frequently interfered with the man upon his right, breaking the symmetry of the movement, and provoking language forbidden by the "Articles of War."

Further, the men were diligently drilled in firing—by file and by company, to the front, to the right oblique, to the left oblique, and to the rear. But most awkward and wearisome of all was the bayonet exercise, requiring acrobatic agility, while the great length of the musket and fixed bayonet rendered the weapon almost impracticable except in the hands of one above the average stature. As a matter of fact, all of the accomplishments thus particularized—methods of loading and firing, and bayonet exercise—fell into disuse with entrance upon actual field-service, as having no practical worth.

With such preparation and such equipment, the soldiers marched to their first battle. The experience of a single regiment was that of thousands. The drums sound the "long roll," or the bugle "the assembly," and companies form and march to the regimental color-line. A few moments later the regiment marches forward until the first scattering fire of the foe is received. Sometimes the antagonists are visible; often but few are seen, but their presence is known by the outburst of flame and smoke from a fringe of forest. The regiment forms in line of battle, and at the word of command from the colonel, passed from company to company, opens fire. No thought now of manual of arms, but only of celerity of movement and rapidity of fire. Shouted a gallant officer who at home (as he was in the field, the war through) an exemplary Christian gentleman, "Load as fast as you can, and give them the devil!" The battle is now on in earnest, and the discharge of thousands of muskets becomes a roar. The range is not more than two hundred

THE VOLUNTEER'S TEACHERS—CLASS OF 1860, UNITED STATES MILITARY ACADEMY
IN THE FIELD, 1862

The men who founded the United States Military Academy in 1802 little thought that, three-score years later, hundreds of the best-trained military men in America would go forth from its portals to take up the sword against one another.   Nine of the forty-one men who were graduated from West Point in 1860 joined the Confederate army.   The men of this class and that of 1861 became the drill-masters, and in many cases the famous leaders, of the Federal and Confederate armies.   The cadet who stood third at graduation in 1860 was Horace Porter.   He became second-lieutenant, lieutenant-colonel three years later, and brigadier-general at the close of the war.   He received the Congressional medal of honor for gallantry at Chickamauga, and later gained great honor as ambassador to France.   Two other members, James H. Wilson and Wesley Merritt, fought their way to the top as cavalry leaders.   Both again were found at the front in the Spanish-American War.   The former was chief of the Cavalry Bureau in 1864 and commanded the assault and capture of Selma and Montgomery, Ala.   He was major-general of volunteers in the Spanish-American War, commanded the column of British and American troops in the advance on Peking, and represented the United States army at the coronation of King Edward VII of England.   General Wesley Merritt earned six successive promotions for gallantry as a cavalry leader—at Gettysburg, Yellow Tavern, Hawe's Shop, Five Forks, and other engagements—and was one of the three Union leaders to arrange for the surrender at Appomattox.   He participated in several Indian campaigns, commanded the American troops in the Philippines, and was summoned from there to the aid of the American Peace Commission, in session in Paris.

yards—sufficient for antiquated weapons carrying a nearly three-quarter-inch ball and three buckshot.

It may be here remarked that early in 1862 practically all the obsolete muskets were replaced with Springfield or Enfield rifles, the former of American, the latter of English make, and the best of their day. They were shorter and lighter than the discarded arms, well balanced, and of greater efficiency, carrying an elongated ball of the minie pattern, caliber .58, with a range of a thousand yards.

At times the regiment shifts its position, to right or left, sometimes diminishing the distance. During much of the time the men experience heavy artillery as well as musketry fire. At the outset a lad threw away a pack of cards, saying, " I don't know they would bring me any bad luck, but I wouldn't want to be killed and have them found in my pocket, and mother hear of it." He lived the war through, but never again so disburdened himself.

A grape-shot tore off the end of a lad's gun as he was capping it. He finished the operation, discharged his weapon, and recovered it for reloading, to find that, while the ragged muzzle would receive the powder, it would not admit the ball. "Don't that beat the devil," he exclaimed—his very first use of language he was taught to abhor. On the instant he had grasped another gun from the hands of a comrade by his side.

A youth, in a regiment which had lost nearly half its men, his ammunition exhausted, fell back into a ravine where the wounded had crawled, to replenish from their cartridge boxes. Returning, he saw so few of his comrades that he thought the regiment gone, and started for the rear. He came face to face with the colonel, who called out, " Where are you going? " " To find the regiment! " " Well, go to the front! All that are left are there," said the colonel. " All right," responded the lad, and he again went into action.

The first battle was a great commencement which graduated both heroes and cowards. A few, under the first fire,

THE "BEEF-KILLERS" OF THE ARMY

OFFICERS' "STRIKERS" AT HEADQUARTERS

WASHDAY IN WINTER-QUARTERS

RUSHING UP A CAMP

The recruit soon learned that slaughtering cattle, cooking, cleaning and wa. hing accouterments, chopping wood, and laundry work all come within the province of the soldier.   The upper left-hand photograph was taken at Yorktown in May, 1862.   In the upper right-hand view we see cooking, washing, and the vigorous polishing of a scabbard.   Enlisted men who were discovered to be efficient artisans were taken from the ranks and transferred to the repair department.   A group of these "veterans" is shown in the lowest photograph.

MECHANICS OF THE FIRST DIVISION, NINTH ARMY CORPS, NEAR PETERSBURG, 1864

ran away, and are only known on their company rolls as deserters. An elbow comrade of the lad whose gun was shot away, as told of above, ran from the field, and died the next day, from sheer fright. Men were known to fire their muskets into the ground, or skyward. In various battles scores of muskets were found to contain a half-dozen or more charges, the soldier having loaded his gun again and again without discharging it, and many a tree in Southern forests held a ramrod which had been fired into it by some nervous soldier. A great majority of those who had demonstrated their worthlessness, soon left the service, usually under a surgeon's certificate of disability, for they were generally so lacking in pride as to be unconformable to health-preserving habits. There were, however, some who fell short at first, but eventually proved themselves good soldiers, and the great majority of volunteers were pluck personified.

A soldier who saw the war through from beginning to end has said that he knew only two men who actually enjoyed a battle. The majority held to their place in the line from duty and pride. Except among the sharpshooters, charged with such a duty as picking off artillerists or signalmen, few soldiers have knowledge that they ever actually killed a man in battle, and are well satisfied with their ignorance.

More than thirty years after the war, an Illinoisan went into the heart of Arkansas to bury a favorite sister. After the funeral service, in personal conversation with the attending minister, Northerner and Southerner discovered that, in one of the fiercest battles of the first war year, their respective regiments had fought each other all day long; that they were similarly engaged in the severest battle of the Atlanta campaign, and finally in the last battle in North Carolina, in 1865; also that, in the first of these, as determined by landmarks recognized by each, the two men had probably been firing directly at each other. These past incidents, with the pathos of the present meeting, cemented a lasting friendship.

BOYS WHO MADE
GOOD SOLDIERS

"Jimmy" Dugan was a bugler-boy in the band at Carlisle barracks, the cavalry depot in Pennsylvania, as the Civil War opened. One who knew him writes: "He was about three feet six high, could ride anything on four legs, sound all the calls, and marched behind the band at guard-mounting at the regulation twenty-eight-inch step at the risk of splitting himself in two." "Jimmy" was heard of later when the serious work began, and, like many another daring youngster in the field-music contingent, did his duty under fire.

BOYS OF THE WAR DAYS

By Charles King
Brigadier-General, United States Volunteers

TIME and again of late years Grand Army men have made this criticism of the organized militia, "They look like mere boys." But it is a singular fact that, man for man, the militia of to-day are older than were the "old boys" when they entered service for the Civil War. In point of fact, the war was fought to a finish by a grand army of boys. Of 2,778,304 Union soldiers enlisted, over two million were not twenty-two years of age—1,151,438 were not even nineteen.*

So long as the recruit appeared to be eighteen years old and could pass a not very rigid physical examination, he was accepted without question; but it happened, in the early days of the war, that young lads came eagerly forward, begging to be taken—lads who looked less than eighteen and could be accepted only on bringing proof, or swearing that they were eighteen. It has since been shown that over eight hundred thousand lads of seventeen or less were found in the ranks of the Union army, that over two hundred thousand were no more than sixteen, that there were even one hundred thousand on the Union rolls who were no more than fifteen.

Boys of sixteen or less could be enlisted as "musicians." Every company was entitled to two field musicians; that made twenty to the average war-time regiment. There were 1981 regiments—infantry, cavalry, and artillery—organized during the war, and in addition there were separate companies sufficient in number to make nearly seventy more, or two thousand and fifty regiments. This would account for over forty thousand

*Abercrombie, Paper before Military Order of the Loyal Legion, Illinois Commandery.

A YOUNG OFFICER OF THE CONFEDERACY—WILLIAM H. STEWART

The subject of this war-time portrait, William H. Stewart, might well have been a college lad from his looks, but he was actually in command of Confederate troops throughout the entire war. His case is typical. He was born in Norfolk County, Virginia, of fighting stock; his grandfather, Alexander Stewart, had been a soldier of 1812, and his great-grandfather, Charles Stewart, member of a Virginia regiment (the Eleventh) during the Revolution. It was no uncommon thing to find regularly enlisted men of eighteen, seventeen, or even sixteen. And numerous officers won distinction, though even younger than Stewart. His first command, at the age of twenty-one, was the lieutenancy of the Wise Light Dragoons, two years before the war. After hostilities began, he soon won the confidence of his superiors in spite of his boyish face. During the Antietam advance, September, 1862, he was left in command of the force at Bristoe's Station. In the Wilderness campaign he commanded a regiment in General R. H. Anderson's division. In the battle of the Wilderness, May 6th, he took part in the flank movement which General Longstreet planned to precede his own assault on the Federal lines. Colonel Stewart served also at Spotsylvania and Cold Harbor, and helped to repel the assaults on the Petersburg entrenchments. On the evacuation of Petersburg the next April, he marched with the advance guard to Amelia Court House, and took part in the battle of Sailor's Creek on April 6th. Thus, like many another youth of the South, Colonel Stewart did not give up as long as there was any army with which to fight.

boy musicians. Here, at least, the supply far exceeded the demand; there were mere lads of twelve to fourteen all over the land vainly seeking means of enlistment. There were three hundred boys of thirteen or under who actually succeeded in being mustered into the Federal military service.

Many of the fine regiments that took the field early in 1861 had famous drum-and-fife corps made up entirely of boys. In those days, too, each regiment had two or more "markers," who, with the adjutant and sergeant-major, established the alignment on battalion drill or parade, and these were generally mere lads who carried a light staff and fluttering guidon instead of the rifle. There were little scamps of buglers in some of the old regular cavalry regiments and field-batteries, who sometimes had to be hoisted into the saddle, but once there could stick to the pigskin like monkeys, and with reckless daring followed at the heels of the squadron leader in many a wild saber charge.

There were others, too, that were so short-legged they could not take the service stride of twenty-eight inches and were put to other duties. One of the most famous of these was little Johnny Clem, who at the age of eleven went out as drummer in the Twenty-second Michigan, and before long was made a mounted orderly with the staff of Major-General George H. Thomas and decorated with a pair of chevrons and the title of lance-sergeant.

Another Western boy who saw stirring service, though never formally enlisted, was the eldest son of General Grant, a year older than little Clem, when he rode with his father through the Jackson campaign and the siege of Vicksburg. There were other sons who rode with commanding generals, as did young George Meade at Gettysburg, as did the sons of Generals Humphreys, Abercrombie, and Heintzelman, as did "Win" and Sam Sumner, both generals in their own right to-day, as did Francis Vinton Greene, who had to be locked up to keep him from following his gallant father into the

ADELBERT AMES AS BRIGADIER–GENERAL WITH HIS STAFF

"THE FIRST OF THE BOY GENERALS"

Surrounded by his staff, some of whom are older than he, sits Adelbert Ames (third from the left), a brigadier-general at twenty-eight. He graduated fifth in his class at West Point on May 6, 1861, and was assigned to the artillery service. It was while serving as first-lieutenant in the Fifth Artillery that he distinguished himself at Bull Run and was brevetted major for gallant and meritorious service. He remained upon the field in command of a section of Griffin's battery, directing its fire after being severely wounded, and refusing to leave the field until too weak to sit upon the caisson, where he had been placed by the men of this command. For this he was awarded a medal of honor. About a year later he again distinguished himself, at the battle of Malvern Hill. He then became colonel of the Twentieth Maine Infantry, from his native State, and on the twentieth of May, 1863, was made brigadier-general of volunteers. He had a distinguished part in the first day's battle at Gettysburg, July 1, 1863, and in the capture of Fort Fisher, North Carolina, January 15, 1865. For this he was promoted to major-general of volunteers. In the class of '61 with Ames at West Point was Judson Kilpatrick, who

JUDSON KILPATRICK
AS
BRIGADIER–GENERAL

stood seventeenth, and who became a general at twenty-seven. He, too, was assigned to the artillery, but after a short transfer to the infantry, in the fall of 1861, was made lieutenant-colonel of the Second New York Cavalry, rising to the rank of brigadier-general of volunteers on June 18, 1865. It was in the cavalry service that he became a picturesque figure, distinguishing himself at the battle of Aldie, in the third day's battle at Gettysburg, and in the engagement at Resaca, Georgia. In June, 1865, he was made major-general of volunteers and later brevetted major-general in the United States Army.

The third of these youthful leaders, a general at twenty-seven, was Wesley Merritt. He graduated from West Point the year before Kilpatrick and Ames. He was made brigadier-general of volunteers on June 29, 1863, distinguished himself two days later at Gettysburg, but won his chief fame as one of Sheridan's leaders of cavalry. He was conspicuous at Yellow Tavern and at Hawe's Shop, was made major-general of volunteers for gallant service in the battles of Winchester and Fisher's Hill, and brigadier-general in the United States Army for Five Forks. The boy generals won more than their share of glory on the grim "foughten field."

MAJOR–GENERAL WESLEY MERRITT AND STAFF

thick of the fray at Gettysburg, but "lived to fight another day" and win his own double stars at Manila.

And while the regulations forbade carrying the musket before reaching one's eighteenth birthday, they were oddly silent as to the age at which one might wield the sword, and so it resulted that boys of sixteen and seventeen were found at the front wearing the shoulder-straps of lieutenants, and some of them becoming famous in an army of famous men.

Two instances were those of two of the foremost major-generals of later years—Henry W. Lawton, of Indiana, and Arthur MacArthur, of Wisconsin. Lawton, tall, sinewy, and strong, was chosen first sergeant, promoted lieutenant, and was commanding a regiment as lieutenant-colonel at the close of the war and when barely twenty. MacArthur's case was even more remarkable. Too young to enlist, and crowded out of the chance of entering West Point in 1861, he received the appointment of adjutant of the Twenty-fourth Wisconsin when barely seventeen, was promoted major and lieutenant-colonel while still eighteen, and commanded his regiment, though thrice wounded, in the bloody battles of Resaca and Franklin. The "gallant boy colonel," as he was styled by General Stanley in his report, entered the regular army after the war, and in 1909, full of honors, reached the retiring age (sixty-four) as the last of its lieutenant-generals.

The East, too, had boy colonels, but not so young as Mac-Arthur. The first, probably, was brave, soldierly little Ellsworth, who went out at the head of the Fire Zouaves in the spring of 1861, and was shot dead at Alexandria, after tearing down the Confederate flag. As a rule, however, the regiments, East and West, came to the front headed by grave, earnest men over forty years of age. Barlow, Sixty-first New York, looked like a beardless boy even in 1864 when he was commanding a division. The McCooks, coming from a famous family, were colonels almost from the start—Alexander, of the First Ohio, later major-general and corps commander;

BOYS WHO
FOUGHT AND PLAYED
WITH MEN

The boys in the lower photograph have qualified as men; they are playing cards with the grown-up soldiers in the quiet of camp life, during the winter of 1862-3. They are the two drummers or "field musicians," to which each company was entitled. Many stories were told of drummer-boys' bravery. A poem popular during the war centered around an incident at Vicksburg. A general assault was made on the town on May 19, 1863, but repulsed with severe loss. During its progress a boy came limping back from the front and stopped in front of General Sherman, while the blood formed a little

A DRUMMER IN "FULL DRESS"

pool by his foot. Unmindful of his own condition, he shouted, "Let our soldiers have some more cartridges, sir—caliber fifty-four," and trudged off to the rear. Another poem is based on an incident in the first year of the war. A drummer-boy had beat his *rat-tat-too* for the soldiers until he had been struck on the ankle by a flying bullet. He would not fall out, but, mounted on the shoulders of a grown comrade, he continued to beat his drum as the company charged to victory, and at the end of the day's fighting he rode to camp sitting in front on the general's horse, sound asleep. The drummer-boy was the inspiration of many a soldierly deed and ballad both North and South. The little chaps in the photograph are not as long as the guns of their comrades.

DRUMMER–BOYS OFF DUTY—PLAYING CARDS IN CAMP, WINTER OF '62

Dan, of the Fifty-second Ohio; Edward, of the Second Indiana Cavalry; and gallant "Bob," of the Ninth Ohio, named brigadier-general before he was killed in August, 1862.

With the close of the second twelve months of the war came the first of the little crop of "boy generals," as they were called, nearly all of them young graduates of West Point. The first of the "boy generals" was Adelbert Ames, of the class of '61, colonel of the Twentieth Maine, closely followed by Judson Kilpatrick, colonel of the Second New York Cavalry, and by Wesley Merritt, whose star was given him just before Gettysburg, when only twenty-seven.

With Merritt, too, came Custer, only twenty-three when he donned the silver stars, and first charged at the head of the Wolverine Brigade on Stuart's gray squadrons at the far right flank at Gettysburg. A few months later and James H. Wilson, Emory Upton, and Ranald Mackenzie, all young, gifted, and most soldierly West Pointers, were also promoted to the stars, as surely would have been gallant Patrick O'Rorke, but for the bullet that laid him low at Gettysburg. That battle was the only one missed by another boy colonel, who proved so fine a soldier that New York captured him from his company in the Twenty-second Massachusetts and made him lieutenant-colonel of their own Sixty-first. Severe wounds kept him out of Gettysburg, but May, 1864, found him among the new brigadiers. Major-general when only twenty-six, he gave thirty-eight years more to the service of his country, and then, as lieutenant-general, Nelson A. Miles passed to the retired list when apparently in the prime of life.

The South chose her greatest generals from men who were beyond middle life—Lee, Jackson, Sidney Johnston, Joseph E. Johnston, Bragg, Beauregard, and Hardee. Longstreet and A. P. Hill were younger. Hood and Stuart were barely thirty. The North found its most successful leaders, save Sherman and Thomas, among those who were about forty or younger.

PART I
SOLDIER LIFE

MARCHING AND FORAGING
EAST AND WEST

A WESTERN BAND—FIELD—MUSIC
OF THE FIRST INDIANA HEAVY
ARTILLERY AT BATON ROUGE

GRANT'S SOLDIERS DIGGING POTATOES—ON THE MARCH TO COLD HARBOR, MAY 28, 1864

These boys of the Sixth Corps have cast aside their heavy accouterments, blankets, pieces of shelter-tent, and rubber blankets, and set cheerfully to digging potatoes from a roadside "garden patch." One week later their corps will form part of the blue line that will rush toward the Confederate works—then stagger to cover, with ten thousand men killed, wounded, or missing in a period computed less than fifteen minutes. When Grant found that he had been out-generaled by Lee on the North Anna River, he immediately executed a flank movement past Lee's right, his weakest point. The Sixth Corps and the Second Corps, together with Sheridan's cavalry, were used in the flank movement and secured a more favorable position thirty-five miles nearer Richmond. It was while Sedgwick's

FORAGING A WEEK BEFORE THE BLOODIEST ASSAULT OF THE WAR

Sixth Corps was passing over the canvas pontoon-bridges across the Pamunkey at Hanovertown, May 28, 1864, that this photograph was taken. When the foragers in the foreground have exhausted this particular potato-field, one of the wagons of the quartermaster's train now crossing on the pontoon will halt and take aboard the prize, carrying it forward to the next regular halt, when the potatoes will be duly distributed. Not alone potatoes, but wheat and melons and turnips, or any other class of eatables apparent to the soldiers' eye above ground, were thus ruthlessly appropriated. This incongruous episode formed one of the many anomalies of the life of the soldier on the march. Especially when he was approaching an enemy, he relaxed and endeavored to secure as much comfort as possible.

THE BUSY ENGINEERS STOP TO EAT

This is the camp of an engineer or pontonier company. The pontoons resting on their wagon bases are ready to be launched. But before work comes a pause for an important ceremony—dinner. In the eyes of the rank and file the company cook was more important than most officers. The soldiers in the upper photograph are located near the headquarters' wagons, while the cook himself is standing proudly near the center, "monarch of all he surveys." To his left is seen one of the beeves that is soon to be sacrificed to the soldiers' appetites. Of the two lower photographs on the left-hand page, one shows cooks of the Army of the Potomac in the winter

PREPARING A MEAL IN WINTER–QUARTERS

COOKING OUT–OF–DOORS

THE COMPANY COOK WITH HIS OUTFIT "IN ACTION"—BEEF ON THE HOOF AT HAND

of 1864, snug in their winter-quarters, and the next illustrates cooking in progress outdoors. The two lower photographs on the right-hand page draw a contrast between dining in a permanent camp and on the march. On the left is a mess of some of the officers of the Ninety-third New York Infantry, dining very much at ease, with their folding tables and their colored servants, at Bealton, Virginia, the month after Gettysburg. But in the last photograph a soldier is cowering apprehensively over the fire at Culpeper, Virginia, in August, 1862, while the baffled Army of Virginia under Pope was retreating before Lee's victorious northward sweep.

OFFICERS' LUXURY AT BEALTON—AUGUST, 1863

A MOUTHFUL DURING POPE'S RETREAT

MARCHES OF THE FEDERAL ARMIES

By Fenwick Y. Hedley
*Brevet Captain, United States Volunteers, and Adjutant, Thirty-second
Illinois Infantry*

IT was said of Napoleon that he "overran Europe with the
bivouac." It was the bivouac that sapped the spirit and
snapped the sinews of the Confederacy. No other war in history presents marches marked with such unique and romantic
experiences as those of the Federal armies in the Civil War.

It is worth while to note one march which has received little attention from annalists—one of much importance at
the moment, in the meaning it gave to the word "discipline,"
and, also, in the direction it gave to the fortunes of the man
who was destined to direct all the armies of the Union.

Early in the opening war-year, 1861, an embryo Illinois
regiment was on the verge of dissolution. It was made up of
as good flesh and blood and spirit as ever followed the drum.
But the colonel was a politician without military training, and
under him the men refused to serve. There was no red tape
to cut, for there had been no muster-in for service. So the re-
jected colonel was sent his way, and a plain, modest man,
Ulysses S. Grant by name, was put in his place.

Colonel Grant was ordered to Missouri. He declined railroad transportation. Said he, "I thought it would be good
preparation for the troops to march there." He marched his
men from Camp Yates, at Springfield, to Quincy, on the Mississippi River, about one hundred miles, expecting to go as
much further, when an emergency order from the War Department required him to take cars and hasten to another field.
So early in the war, such a march was phenomenal. It was

THE CIVIL WAR SOLDIER AS HE REALLY LOOKED AND MARCHED

There is nothing to suggest military brilliancy about this squad. Attitudes are as prosaic as uniforms are unpicturesque. The only man standing with military correctness is the officer at the left-hand end. But this was the material out of which was developed the soldier who could average sixteen miles a day for weeks on end, and do, on occasion, his thirty miles through Virginia mud and his forty miles over a hard Pennsylvania highway. Sixteen miles a day does not seem far to a single pedestrian, but marching with a regiment bears but little relation to a solitary stroll along a sunny road. It is a far different matter to trudge along carrying a heavy burden, choked by the dust kicked up by hundreds of men tramping along in front, and sweltering in the sun—or trudge still more drearily along in a pelting rain which added pounds to a soaked and clinging uniform, and caused the soldiers to slip and stagger in the mud.

"RIGHT SHOULDER SHIFT"—COLUMN OF FOURS—THE TWENTY-SECOND NEW YORK ON THE ROAD

midsummer, and the men, fresh from school, workshop, and farm, suffered severely. From the day Grant assumed command of the Twenty-first Illinois, it gave as good an account of itself as did any in the service.

In the East, throughout the war, the principal military movements were restricted to a comparatively small territory —the region about the Confederate capital, Richmond, and the approaches thereto. The chief exception was the Gettysburg campaign, in 1863, involving a march of somewhat more than two hundred miles. The famous marches in this part of the country were forced ones, short in duration, but involving intense fatigue and hardship, and often compelling troops to go into battle without much-needed rest. In the hasty concentration at Gettysburg there were some very noteworthy performances by Meade's army. The Sixth Corps started from Manchester, Maryland, at dark, on July 1st. "Without halting," says General Wright, "except for a few moments each hour to breathe the men, and one halt of about half an hour to enable the men to make coffee, the corps was pushed on to Gettysburg, where it arrived about 4 P.M. after a march variously estimated at from thirty-two to thirty-five miles."

Early in the afternoon of May 4, 1864, Grant telegraphed Burnside to bring the Ninth Corps immediately to the Wilderness. The divisions were stationed along the Orange and Alexandria Railroad, but by the morning of the 6th all were on the battlefield. Some of the troops had marched over thirty miles. General Grant says, "Considering that a large proportion, probably two-thirds, of the corps was composed of new troops, unaccustomed to marches, and carrying the accouterments of a soldier, this was a remarkable march." For hardships and exhaustion few marches exceeded the race from the North Anna to the Pamunkey in May, 1864. Hundreds of men dropped dead from lack of proper precaution in the intense heat.

In the West, unlike the East, the principal Union armies were almost constantly in motion, and on long extended lines.

OVER THE CUMBERLAND MOUNTAINS ON THE MARCH TO CHATTANOOGA—SEPTEMBER, 1863

A FOURTH ARMY CORPS DIVISION AT SHAM BATTLE NEAR MISSIONARY RIDGE, 1863

The peculiarity of the drill in the Western armies was their long swinging stride. The regulation army step was twenty-eight inches, and the men in the East were held rigidly to this requirement. But the Westerners swung forward with a long sweep of the leg which enabled them to cover great distances at a rapid pace. In November, 1863, Sherman marched his Fifteenth Corps four hundred miles over almost impassable roads from Memphis to Chattanooga; yet his sturdy soldier boys were ready to go into action next day.

A SENTRY ON THE RAMPARTS AT KNOXVILLE, TENNESSEE, 1864

Their field operations, from beginning to end, extended through seven States—Kentucky, Tennessee, Mississippi, Alabama, Georgia, South Carolina, and North Carolina, in all of which they fought important battles. Some of their divisions and brigades operated in Missouri, Arkansas, Louisiana, and Texas.

Operations in the West opened early in 1861, with St. Louis and the Ohio River as primary bases. By the summer of 1862, armies under Halleck in Missouri, under Grant in Tennessee, and under Buell in Kentucky had pushed their way hundreds of miles southward. These operations involved much marching, but, in view of later experiences, were not marked with such peculiar incidents as to claim attention here.

In September, 1862, occurred a march which alarmed the North much as did Lee's invasion of Pennsylvania the following year. General Don Carlos Buell's troops occupied points in Tennessee. The Confederates, under General Bragg, so threatened his rear that he was obliged to abandon his position. Then ensued a veritable foot-race between the two armies, on practically parallel roads, with Louisville as the goal. Buell reached the city just in advance of his opponent —both armies footsore and jaded from constant marching and frequent skirmishing.

An early march, and one well worthy of remark, was that ordered and directed by General Grant, in the fall of 1862. The objective point was the rear of Vicksburg. His army moved in two columns—one from La Grange, Tennessee, under his own personal command; the other from Memphis, Tennessee, under General Sherman. Their advance reached the neighborhood of Grenada, Mississippi, having marched a distance of one hundred miles. Further progress was stayed by the capture of Holly Springs, Mississippi, in their rear, with all its ammunition stores and commissary supplies, by the Confederate general, Forrest. As a consequence, a retrograde march was inevitable.

PROTECTING THE REAR FOR THE MARCH TO THE SEA—A TYPICAL ARMY SCENE—1864

The armed guard indicates that the pick-and-shovel detail is made up of delinquent soldiers serving petty sentences. It seems strange that the throwing up of entrenchments about a city should form an essential part of marching, but so it was in the case of the greatest march of the Civil War, which covered a total distance of a thousand miles in less than six months. Sherman did not dare to leave Atlanta with his 62,000 veterans until his rear was properly fortified against the attacks of Hood. The upper photograph shows some of Sherman's men digging the inner line of entrenchments at Decatur, Alabama, a task in vivid contrast to the comfortable quarters of the officers at the Decatur Hotel shown in the cut below. Their military appear-

OFFICERS' QUARTERS AT DECATUR HOTEL, 1864

PONTOON–BRIDGE AT DECATUR

ance suffers somewhat from their occupation, but digging was often more important than fighting, for the soldier. Having despatched Thomas to Nashville, and having left strongly entrenched garrisons at Allatoona and Resaca, as well as at Decatur, Sherman launched his army from Atlanta, November 15, 1864. He cherished the hope that Hood would attack one of the fortified places he had left behind, and that is precisely what occurred. Hood and Beauregard believed that Sherman's army was doomed, and turned toward Tennessee. Sherman believed that his march would be the culminating blow to the Confederacy. The lower photograph shows the pontoon-bridge built by Sherman at Decatur at the time his army marched swiftly to the relief of Chattanooga.

While southward bound, the Union troops found just sufficient opposition by the Confederates under General Pemberton to keep them engaged, without impeding their progress. The conditions were now changed. They were greatly harassed, and at times were obliged to march with the utmost speed to avoid being cut off at an intersecting road in their rear. Their unusual and protracted privations were experiences such as had been heretofore unknown. They had set out in the lightest marching order known at that time. Wagon trains were reduced to carry only ammunition and indispensable food. No tents were carried except a few for officers.

When Grant advanced upon Vicksburg in May, 1863, the army again " marched light," and it has been said that the general's only baggage was a package of cigars and a toothbrush. Vicksburg surrendered on July 4th, and the same day, without entering the city, a large portion of the army marched rapidly away to attack General Johnston, at Jackson. The distance was little more than fifty miles, but never did troops suffer more severely. It was a forced march, under an intense, burning sun; the dust was stifling, and the only water was that from sluggish brooks and fetid ponds.

In November, 1863, General Sherman marched his Fifteenth Corps from Memphis to Chattanooga, a distance of nearly four hundred miles, over almost impassable roads. When he arrived his men were in a most exhausted condition, yet they were ready to go into action the next day.

Following almost immediately after the march above mentioned, Sherman moved his men from Chattanooga to the relief of Burnside at Knoxville. The distance was not great, about one hundred and twenty-five miles, but the troops were utterly worn out by their forced march in the intensely cold mountain atmosphere.

In February, 1864, General Sherman marched a force of twenty thousand men from Memphis and Vicksburg to Meridian, Mississippi, a distance of one hundred and fifty miles.

ON THE MARCH—WATER FOR THE OUTER AND INNER MAN

It was a hot and dusty tramp after Spotsylvania in May, 1864, as Grant strove to outflank Lee. When Grant's men reached the North Anna River, they found that the bridge had been burned. Ignorant of the fighting before them at Cold Harbor, where ten thousand men were to be shot down in a few minutes, they enjoyed a refreshing swim and bath. The lower photograph will bring memories to every veteran of the Virginia campaigns—the eager rush of the men on the march for the deep dark well of the Virginia plantations. This one has been covered and a guard placed over it to prevent waste of water; for a well soon runs dry when an army commences to drink.

The troops moved in light marching order. The expedition entailed severe labor upon the men in the destruction of the arsenal and supply depots at Meridian, and the practical demolition of the railroad almost the entire distance.

Sherman's "march to the sea" is unique among marches. The army had good training for its undertaking. Its commander had led it from Chattanooga to the capture of Atlanta, and had followed the Confederate general, Hood, northward. Shortly after Sherman abandoned the pursuit of Hood, he detached Stanley's Fourth Corps and Schofield's Twenty-third Corps to the assistance of Thomas, in Tennessee. This march of nearly three hundred miles was one of the most arduous of the war, though lacking in the picturesqueness of that to the sea; it included the severe battle of Franklin, and had victorious ending at Nashville.

Sherman's army marched from Atlanta and vicinity on November 15, 1864. The men set forward, lifting their voices in jubilant song. As to their destination, they neither knew nor cared. That they were heading south was told them by the stars, and their confidence in their leader was unbounded.

It was a remarkable body of men—an army of veterans who had seen three years of constant field-service. Through battle, disease, and death, nearly every regiment had been greatly reduced. He was a fortunate colonel who could muster three hundred of the thousand men he brought into service. Thirty men made more than an average company; there were those which numbered less than a score. It was also an army of youngsters. Most of the older men and the big men had been worn down and sent home.

To each company was allowed a pack-mule for cooking utensils (frying-pans and coffee-pots), but frequently these were dispensed with, each soldier doing his own cooking after even more primitive fashion than in his earlier campaigns. All dispensable items of the army ration had been stricken out, the supply being limited to hard bread, bacon, coffee, sugar, and

THE EXTREMITIES OF THE THOUSAND—MILE FEDERAL LINE ON THE MISSISSIPPI

It was from Cairo that the Federals in 1862 cautiously began to operate with large forces in Confederate territory. And it was in New Orleans, the same spring, that the Federal Military Department of the Gulf established its headquarters. Farragut had forced the forts, and the city had fallen. The lower photograph shows the old St. Charles Hotel at New Or-

Cairo, Ills. Inundated 1862.

CAIRO, WHEN THE ADVANCE BEGAN

leans, a thousand miles from Cairo. The orderlies on the porch and the flag floating in front of the delicate "banquettes" of the building, the iron tracery that came over from France, show that the city has passed into Union hands and become the headquarters of the Military Department of the Gulf. The flag can be dimly descried opposite the corner of the building just below the roof. There was evidently enough wind to make it flap in the breeze.

THE ST. CHARLES HOTEL, NEW ORLEANS, HEADQUARTERS OF THE FEDERAL MILITARY DEPARTMENT OF THE GULF salt. A three days' supply of bread and bacon was issued at intervals to last the soldier ten days, the "foragers," of whom more anon, being his dependence for all else. Coffee, the greatest of all necessities to the soldier, was liberally provided, and the supply seldom failed. The soldier's personal effects were generally limited to his blanket, a pair of socks, and a piece of shelter tent, though many discarded the latter with contempt. In addition to his gun and cartridge-box with its forty rounds, the soldier carried his haversack, which with his food contained one hundred and sixty rounds of cartridges. After every occasion calling for expenditure of ammunition, his first concern was to restock, so as constantly to have two hundred rounds upon his person.

The train with each corps had been reduced to the lowest possible number of wagons. Nothing was transported but ammunition, commissary supplies, and grain for the animals —the latter only to be used when the country would not afford animal subsistence. In addition, to each regiment was allowed a single wagon to carry ammunition, a single tent-fly to shelter the field-desks of the adjutant and quartermaster, a small mess-kit for the officers in common, and an ordinary valise for each of them. In case of necessity (not an uncommon occurrence on account of crippled horses and bad roads), some or all of these personal belongings were thrown out and destroyed.

The army marched in four columns, usually ten to fifteen miles apart, on practically parallel roads. The skirmishers and flankers of each corps extended right and left until they met those of the next corps, thus giving a frontage of forty to fifty miles. As a consequence, the widely dispersed forces were soon ready for handling as a unit. At a river, two or more corps met, to utilize a pontoon train in common.

The day's itinerary was much the same throughout the march. Soon after daybreak the bugle sounded the reveille, and the men rolled their blankets and prepared their meal. An

[212]

COMMISSARY DEPARTMENT AT ARMY OF THE POTOMAC HEADQUARTERS, APRIL, 1864

The big barracks of a mess-hall with such food as would make a soldier grumble in times of peace, would have seemed a veritable Mecca to a soldier of 1864 in camp or on the march. The accompanying photographs show how the commissary department of the Army of the Potomac supplied the individual soldier with meat and water. Above is displayed a commissary at the front in full swing

WAITING FOR SUPPER
ON A CHILLY AUTUMN
EVENING OF '63

with a sentry to guard its precious stores. Below, soldiers can be seen filling their water cart at a well, and waiting while an attaché of the commissary department cuts off rounds of beef and issues portions to the various messes. The photograph in the center shows the final result, witnessed by the savory-looking steam blown from the kettle on top of the charred timbers.

THE SOLDIERS' WATER CART

SERVING OUT RATIONS

hour later, at the call of the assembly, they fell in, and soon took up the line of march, reaching the end for the day in the middle of the afternoon or early evening. The rear brigade awaited the movement of the wagon train and fell in behind. It frequently did not reach the halting-place until midnight, and sometimes much later. The average distance covered daily was something more than sixteen miles.

The men marched " at will," with little semblance of military order, yet each knew his place. Good-natured badinage, songs, school-day recitations, discussions as to destination— these served to pass the time. Seldom was halt made for a noon-time meal, the men eating as they marched. At an occasional halt, some gathered over their cards; some put a few stitches in a dilapidated garment; some beat the sand and dust out of their shoes, and nursed their blistered, travel-worn feet. The evening was pleasantly passed around the camp-fire.

But a day seldom passed without its trials. Frequently a Confederate force appeared in front; the cavalry advance was driven back, while a regiment or brigade, and a few pieces of artillery, moved rapidly to the front. A half-hour later the foe had vanished; a grave or two was dug beneath the shadow of the trees; an ambulance received a few wounded men, and the march was resumed.

Again, the rain fell in torrents the day long, and, sometimes, for days. The men marched in soaked clothing. The roads were quagmires, and thousands of men labored for hours tearing down fences and felling saplings to make a corduroy road, over which the artillery and wagon trains might pass.

At another time the march lay across or near a railway which could be of much use to the Confederates. The soldiers lined up along its length and, lifting the ends of the ties, literally overturned the iron way. The ties were piled together and fired; the iron rails were thrown upon them, and, after they were well heated in the middle, they were wrapped around trees, or twisted with cant-hooks.

[214]

PICKETS SEVEN HUNDRED MILES APART

The two picket stations shown in these photographs illustrate the extended area over which the Federal soldiers marched out to picket duty. European wars, with the exception of Napoleon's Russian campaign, have rarely involved such widely separated points simultaneously. Picketing was considered by the soldiers a pleasant detail. It relieved them of all other camp requirements, such as drills and parades. The soldiers in the photographs are lolling at ease with no apparent apprehension of any enemy, but it must not be assumed from their relaxation that they are not vigilant. Beyond these little camps

VIRGINIA—FEDERAL PICKET STATION NEAR BULL RUN, 1862

GEORGIA—PICKETS JUST BEFORE THE BATTLE OF ATLANTA, JULY 22, 1864

regular sentinels are on duty with keenly observant eyes. When their tour of duty has been completed they will be relieved by some of the men who are so much at ease. The pickets retreated before any advance in face of the Confederates, and rejoined the main body of troops. In the Atlanta photograph, the "reserve post" is slightly in the rear of the outer line of pickets. Judging from the rough earthworks, the dilapidated house, and the smashed window-frame in the foreground, there has evidently been fighting at this point. Nearly all of the men have on high-crowned hats, which afforded better protection against the sun than the forage cap.

General Sherman reduced foraging to a system in the West, and, more especially during his rapid and extended marches, foraging became a necessary means of subsistence for men and animals. As the general expressed it, " No army could carry food and forage for a march of three hundred miles, and there being no civil authorities to respond to requisition, this source of supply was indispensable to success."

In preparing for his march to the sea, he issued specific instructions for foraging " liberally upon the country," and these were reasonable in the interest of his men, and humane as regarding the people who were to be foraged upon. Each brigade commander was to send out a foraging party under a discreet commissioned officer, to gather in from the region adjacent to the route traveled whatever might serve as subsistence for man and beast, also wagons, horses, and mules for conveying the supplies to the troops; the animals were then to be utilized in the artillery and wagon trains to replace those worn out. Entering dwelling-houses was forbidden. With each family was to be left a reasonable portion of food, and discrimination was to be made in favor of the poor. As a matter of fact, few soldiers saw or heard of these regulations until after the march was ended. But, with the remarkable adaptability of the American soldier, they became on the instant " a law unto themselves," and in spirit and deed carried out the provisions of their commander, of which they had not heard. These foraging parties numbered twenty-five to fifty men each. They set out usually before the troops broke camp, and extended their expeditions three to five miles on either flank. They brought in their supplies in every manner of vehicle— wagons, carts, and carriages, drawn indiscriminately by horses, mules, oxen, or cows, strung together with harness, rope, or chains; a complete set of harness was seldom found.

The supplies thus obtained were turned over to the brigade commissary for issue in the regular way to the various regiments. The result was general dissatisfaction. At no time

PREPARATIONS FOR THE MARCH TO THE SEA—ATLANTA, 1864

The soldiers sprawling on the freight-cars are one of the bodies of troops that Sherman was shifting—changing garrisons, and establishing guards, in preparation for his famous march to the sea. Below appears a wagon-train leaving Atlanta; but comparatively few wagons accompanied the troops on this movement. Everything possible was discarded and sent back over Sherman's strong line of communications. The soldier's personal effects were generally limited to his blanket, a pair of socks, and a piece of shelter-tent, although many discarded even the latter. Nothing was transported but ammunition, absolutely necessary commissary supplies, and grain for the animals. All invalids and those incapacitated for hard marching were sent back, and the average company was less than thirty men.

ONE OF SHERMAN'S WAGON-TRAINS

was there a sufficiency for all. The men provided a remedy.
Probably every regiment in the army sent out its independent
foragers—a class known in history as "Sherman's Bummers,"
and there were no more venturesome men. They had no official
being, but were known to all, from commanding general down,
and their conduct was overlooked unless flagrant.

The forager or "bummer" at first was usually afoot;
sometimes he rode a horse or mule which had been "condemned" and turned out of the wagon train. His search at
the first farm was for a fresh mount; with this, success was
assured. The forager frequently found a willing ally in the
plantation negro, who would guide him to a swamp where animals had been taken, or to a spot where provisions had been
buried. In some instances what appeared to be a grave was
pointed out, which would yield treasures of preserves, choice
beverages, and jewelry.

Nearly all the inhabitants had gone farther into the interior, taking with them what of their possessions they could;
in such cases, the deserted buildings were utterly despoiled.
The few people who remained were old men, women, and children. To these the forager was usually respectful, even sympathetic, and in some instances he laid the foundations for a
personal friendship which exists to this day. But with all
his good nature, the forager was diplomatic, and he so skilfully
directed his conversation that he frequently acquired knowledge
of sources of supply at the next plantation, and even of movements of the Confederate soldiery, which was esteemed of value
at headquarters.

If the foragers were fortunate, the meal of their squad or
company was incomparable—turkeys, chickens, smoked meats,
sweet potatoes, preserves, sorghum, and not infrequently a jug
or keg of whisky. The cellars of some abandoned mansions
yielded even richer store—cobwebbed wine-bottles dating back
to the '30's.

Thus lived Sherman's army for eighteen days on its march

AT CHATTANOOGA, WHERE THE MARCH BEGAN—TROOPS AT THE "INDIAN MOUND"

SCENES AT THE BEGINNING, MIDDLE, AND END OF SHERMAN'S MARCH TO THE SEA

In these three photographs appear sturdy Western troops at the beginning, middle, and end of Sherman's march to the sea. Between Chattanooga and Atlanta he was busy strengthening the rear. At Atlanta he gathered his resources and made his final depositions for the great march. His was a remarkable body of men, the majority veterans who had seen three years of constant field service, yet in considerable proportion not yet old

HALF-WAY—SHERMAN'S MEN RESTING AT ATLANTA

enough to vote. Many of the staff and company officers were as young as the men in the ranks. The army marched in four columns usually ten to fifteen miles apart, and the skirmishes and flankers of the various corps extended over a frontage of forty or fifty miles. The day's itinerary was much the same throughout—reveille soon after daybreak, breakfast, assembly, and "forward march." The end of the day's march was reached in the middle of the afternoon or early evening, and the average distance was something more than sixteen miles. The sea was finally sighted at Savannah, Georgia, on the 10th of December.

THE SEA AT LAST—FEDERAL TROOPS IN FORT McALLISTER JUST AFTER ITS CAPTURE through Georgia. But this season of feasting was followed by a dismal fortnight of almost famine on the outskirts of Savannah, before entrance to the city was obtained. In the subsequent march through the Carolinas, foraging was resumed as in the interior of Georgia, but, except in a few favored localities, the provisions were neither so plentiful nor so choice.

The forager experienced a startling transformation in April of 1865. The war was over. Sherman's men were marching from Raleigh, North Carolina, for the national capital to be disbanded. The citizens no longer fled at their approach, but flocked to the road to see them pass. Among them were scores of Lee's or Johnston's men, still clad in their "butternut" uniforms. The forager's occupation was gone, and he was now in his place in the ranks, and he stepped out, now and again, to buy eatables, paying out "Uncle Sam's greenbacks."

Sherman's last two campaigns may be called a march in three acts. The march to the sea began at Atlanta and ended at Savannah, a distance of three hundred miles, consuming eighteen days. After a period of rest began the march through the Carolinas, ending at Goldsboro, four hundred and twenty-five miles, in the words of Sherman, "concluding one of the longest and most important marches ever made by an organized army," and culminating in the close of hostilities with the surrender of General Johnston.

After a few days the march to Washington was begun, a further distance of three hundred and fifty miles, and May 24, 1865, the troops marched down Pennsylvania Avenue in presence of applauding thousands, then to be at once disbanded and never to assemble again.

The total distance marched between Atlanta and Washington, in less than six months, was about one thousand miles. General Sherman claimed for his army, in its various marches, beginning at Vicksburg and ending at Washington, a total of twenty-eight hundred miles, including the many detours.

PART I
SOLDIER LIFE

WITH THE
VETERAN
ARMIES

THE

WELL–DISCIPLINED

"REGULARS"—A SCENE OF APRIL 3, 1864

MEN WHO DEMONSTRATED THE VALUE OF TRAINING AT GAINES' MILL

They stand up very straight, these regulars who formed the tiny nucleus of the vast Union armies. Even in the distance they bear the stamp of the trained soldier. At Bull Run the disciplined soldiers showed a solid front amid the throng of fugitives. At Gaines' Mill, again, they kept together against an overwhelming advance. It was not long, however, before the American volunteers on both sides were drilled and disciplined, furnishing to Grant and Lee the finest soldiery that ever trod the field of battle. There were surprisingly few regulars when '61 came. The United States regular army could furnish only six regiments of cavalry, sixty batteries of artillery, a battalion of engineers, and nineteen regiments of infantry.

THE

ELEVENTH "U. S."

IN THEIR TRIM CAMP AT ALEXANDRIA

THE AMERICAN VOLUNTEERS, HOWEVER, SOON ACQUIRED THE SOLDIERLY BEARING

Of the 3,559 organizations in all branches of the service in the Union armies, the States furnished 3,473. The Eleventh Infantry in the regular army was organized at Fort Independence, Boston Harbor, by direction of the President, May 4, 1861, and confirmed by Act of Congress, July 29, 1861. It fought throughout the war with the Army of the Potomac. This photograph was taken at Alexandria, Va., a month before the Wilderness. The regiment participated in every important battle of the Army of the Potomac, and was on provost duty at Richmond, Va., from May to October, 1865. The regiment lost during service eight officers, 117 enlisted men killed and mortally wounded, and two officers and eighty-six enlisted men by disease.

VETERANS IN CAMP—THE 114TH PENNSYLVANIA AT BRANDY STATION, WINTER OF 1863

A vivid illustration of the daily camp life of the Army of the Potomac in the winter of 1863–64 is supplied by these two photographs of the same scene a few moments apart.   On the left-hand page the men are playing cards, loafing, strolling about, and two of them are engaged in a boxing match.   On the right the horse in the foreground is dragging a man seated on a barrel over the snow on a sled, another man is fetching water, and the groups in front of the huts are reading newspapers.   In the lower photograph the card-playing,

BELOW, THE SAME AS IT HAD SHIFTED A FEW MOMENTS LATER

lounging, and boxing continue, the horses have been ridden, led, and driven out of the picture, and the man with the bucket has turned away. During the war Pennsylvania furnished to the service twenty-eight regiments, three battalions and twenty-two companies of cavalry, five regiments, two battalions, and three companies of heavy artillery, one battalion and twenty-nine batteries of light artillery, a company of engineers, one of sharpshooters, and 258 regiments, five battalions, and twenty-five companies of infantry.

WITH THE VETERAN ARMIES

By Charles King
Brigadier-General, United States Volunteers

IT was a fine, enthusiastic army that General McClellan finally marched forward on Manassas in the early spring of 1862. So far as dress and " style " were concerned it far surpassed that with which, two years later, General Grant crossed the Rapidan southward, and, unlike all preceding commanders in that field, took no backward step until he had crushed his foe.

But in point of discipline, efficiency, and experience—the essentials of modern military craft—it is doubtful if the world contained, man for man, anything to equal the two armies confronting each other in May, 1864, the matchless soldiery of Grant and Lee. Three years had they marched and maneuvered, fenced and fought—three tremendous years—and now it seemed as though every man realized that this would be the final struggle, that the question of the supremacy of the Union or of the South was to be settled forever.

Beautiful and bright had been the colors that fluttered over each proud battalion as it took the road for Manassas—gay and vivid the uniforms of the " foreign legions " and the Zouaves, spick and span the blue battalions, all with gleaming belts and brasses, many with white gloves, and some even with white gaiters. In spite of the clerical cut of his uniform, the average officer had a soldierly look about him, enhanced by a trimly buttoned coat well set off by the crimson sash. Those were the days of the dandy, encouraged by the example of many a general like McClellan, Porter, " Phil " Kearny, and Hooker, who believed in fine accouterments and glittering

HOOKER—HANDSOME IN PERSON AND EQUIPMENT

General Joseph Hooker, whose photograph appears above, was one of many able generals, such as McClellan, Porter, "Phil" Kearny, and others, who believed in fine accouterments and glittering trappings. These leaders used the costliest of housings and horse equipments, and expected their staff officers to follow suit. The latter were nothing loth; much money was spent at the outset of the war in giving the army as trig and smart an appearance as a European host. But there were no military roads in the United States, and the pageantry of a European army is not adapted to the swamps and morasses, the mountain heights, and rocky roads over which the war was fought. By the end of the second year the red sash which set off the trimly buttoned coat had turned to purple or disappeared entirely, and in many instances the coat was gone as well. The costly shoulder-straps of gold embroidery had given place to metal substitutes, and the "hundred-dollar housings" of the grand review in the fall of 1861 were left in the swamps or lost in battle.

trappings, used the finest of housings and horse equipments, and expected their staff officers to follow suit. Those were the days when each regiment still had its band, some of them strong in numbers and splendid in effect, when each band still had its spectacular drum-major, and some few of them even a prettily dressed *vivandière*. By common consent, the glittering epaulet had been abandoned, but the plumed felt hat, the yellow sash and gantlets still decked the martial persons of the corps, division, and brigade commanders, and the regimental officers in many an instance made the most of the regulations as to uniform.

Much of the picturesque remained with the army when McClellan floated it around to the Peninsula and lost priceless weeks at Yorktown. But the few *vivandières* seemed to wilt after Williamsburg. Many a bandsman balked at having to care for the wounded under fire. Quite a few chaplains decided that their calling was with the hospitals at the rear rather than with the fighters at the front. Then the humid heat of a Chickahominy June had taken the starch out of the last collar, and utterly killed the buttoned-up coat. Officers and men by thousands shed the stiff and cumbersome garment, marched and fought in their flannel shirt-sleeves until they could get the uncouth but unbothersome "blouse." Regiments that long had paraded in leggings or gaiters kicked themselves loose and left the relics strung out from Mechanicsville to Malvern. When next they came trudging out toward Manassas, to join John Pope and his hard-hammered army, many men had learned the trick of rolling the trousers snug at the ankle, and hauling the gray woolen sock, legging-wise, round them. *There* was a fashion that endured to the last, and spread westward and southward to the ends of the lines.

But with the second summer of the war the hooked standing collar and buttoned-up coat were almost gone. Men had learned wisdom, and wore the blue blouse and gray-flannel shirt—open at the throat in warm weather, snug-fastened in

ONE FOREIGN UNIFORM RETAINED THROUGHOUT THE WAR—A "RUSH HAWKINS'
ZOUAVE" AT GENERAL GILLMORE'S HEADQUARTERS, 1863

The vivid sunlight in this photograph makes the grass and roof look almost like snow, but the place is Folly
Island before Charleston in July, 1863. In the foreground to the left stands one of Rush Hawkins' Zouaves,
from the Ninth New York Infantry. He adheres to his foreign uniform, although most of the white gaiters
and other fancy trappings of the Union army had disappeared early in '62. But his regiment did good service.
It fought at South Mountain, at Antietam, and Fredericksburg, with much scouting and several forced
marches before it was mustered out May 20, 1863. The three-years men, after they were assigned to the
Third New York Infantry, which was ordered to Folly Island in July, 1863, retained their uniforms when in
entire companies. The scene is the headquarters of General Quincy Adams Gillmore, who was promoted to
lieutenant-colonel April 11, 1862, for gallant and meritorious service in the capture of Fort Pulaski, Ga.,
and to colonel, March 30, 1863, for gallant and meritorious service in the battle of Somerset, Ky. He
became major-general of volunteers in July, 1863. Note the black shadows cast by the soldier and the tree.

cold—and so lived and marched in comfort. Almost every-thing that was conspicuous or glittering had disappeared from the dress of horse or man. The army that came back from Fair Oaks and Gaines' Mill plodded on through the heart of Maryland in quest of Lee, bronzed, bearded in many cases, but destitute of ornament of any kind. The red sash had turned to purple or faded away entirely; the costly shoulder-straps of gold embroidery, so speedily ruined by dust and rain, had given place to creations of metal, warranted to keep their shape, nor rust or fade—no matter what the weather.

Officers who proudly bestrode "hundred-dollar housings" at the grand review in the fall of 1861, had left them in the swamps or lost them in battle, and were now using the cavalry blanket instead of the shabrack, and the raw hogshide, rough stitched to wooden saddle-tree, instead of the stuffed seat of the Jenifer—and speedily learning that what they lost in style they gained in comfort. So, too, had the polished brass or steel stirrup given way to the black-hooded, broad-stepped, wooden frame wherein the foot kept warm and dry whatever the weather.

Only generals were wearing, with the second and third years, the heavily frogged and braided overcoats of dark blue. Capes, ponchos, and cavalry surtouts were the choice of the line-officer, and the men of the ranks had no choice. By the time they had finished the second summer of the war, had later crossed the icy Rappahannock and vainly stormed the heights at Fredericksburg, and later still had followed "Fight-ing Joe" to Chancellorsville—and back—the pomps and vani-ties of soldier life had become things of the remote past; they had settled down to the stern realities of campaigning. It was a seasoned, a veteran army that marched to Gettysburg and for the first time fairly drove the Southern lines from the field. Long before this the treasured colors were stained, faded, rent, and torn. Some had been riven to shreds in the storm of shot and shell along the Chickahominy, in front of the

UNION SOLDIERS AT WORK TO PRESERVE THEIR HEALTH

The soldier in the field had to learn to take care of his health between battles as well as to save his skin while the bullets were flying. In these two photographs, separated by only a few moments, Union men appear at the work of sanitation. Huts are being erected and ditches dug for drainage near the headquarters of General George W. Getty, Sixth Army Corps. In the upper photograph the man with the wheelbarrow is just starting away from the tent with a load. In the lower, he has reached the unfinished hut. The men standing upright in the upper picture have bent to their work and the sentry has paced a little farther along on his beat.

unfinished railway at Second Bull Run, in the cornfields of the Antietam, on the frozen slopes of Marye's Hill, or among the murky woods of Chancellorsville. Now, in many a regiment, by the spring of 1864, half the original names had gone from the muster-rolls, the fearful cost of such battling as had been theirs—theirs, the home-loving lads who came flocking in the flush of youth and the fervor of patriotism to offer their brave lives at the earliest call, in 1861.

It was a veteran army of campaigners with which Meade, Hancock, and Reynolds, those three gallant Pennsylvanians, overthrew at Gettysburg the hard-fighting army of the South —Reynolds laying down his life in the fierce grapple of the first day—veterans, yet more than half of them beardless boys. Few people to-day who see the bent forms and snowy heads of our few remaining " comrades " of the Civil War, begin to know, and fewer still can realize, the real facts as to the ages of our volunteers. It is something worthy of being recorded here and remembered for all time, that the " old boys," as they love to speak of themselves, were young boys, very young, when first they raised their ungloved right hands to swear allegiance to the flag, and obedience to the officers appointed over them.

It is something to be inscribed on the tablets of memory —the fact that over one million of the soldiers who fought for the preservation of the Union were but eighteen years of age or less at date of enlistment—that over two millions were not over twenty-one. It is a matter of record that of a total of 1,012,273 enlistments statistically examined it was found that only 46,626 were twenty-five years of age—only 16,070 were forty-four. It is something for mothers to know to-day that three hundred boys of thirteen years or less (twenty-five were but ten or under) were actually accepted and enlisted, generally as drummers or fifers, but, all the same, regularly enrolled and sworn in by the recruiting officers of the United States. Many a time those little fellows were

[232]

MILITARY MUSIC OF THE BEGINNING

Many of the Union regiments started the war with complete and magnificent bands, but when active campaigning began they proved too great a luxury. Every man was needed then to fight. It was the bandsman's duty during an engagement to attend to the wounded on the field, a painful and dangerous task which discour-

aged many a musician. The topmost photograph shows one of the bands that remained in permanent headquarters, in camp near Arlington, Virginia. In the next appears the field music of the 164th New York. In the next photograph the post musicians of Fortress Monroe stand imposingly beneath their bearskins. The bottom picture shows a band at winter headquarters—Camp Stoneman, near Washington.

under heavy fire. Many a time they were cheered for deeds of bravery and devotion.

But with the coming of the spring of 1864 such a thing as a boyish face was hard to find among them. Young faces there were by hundreds, but the boyish look was gone. The days of battle and peril, the scenes of bloodshed and carnage, the sounds of agony or warning—all had left indelible impress. Eyes that have looked three years upon death in every horrible shape, upon gaping wounds and battle-torn bodies, lose gradually and never regain the laughing light of youth. The correspondents of the press filled many a column with description of the boy-faced generals—men like Barlow, Merritt, and curly-haired Custer; but a closer study of the young faces thus pictured would have told a very different story—a story of hours of anxious thought and planning, of long nights of care and vigil, of thrilling days of headlong battle wherein a single error in word or action might instantly bring on disaster.

In both East and West, by this time, there were regiments commanded by lads barely twenty years of age, brave boys who, having been leaders among their schoolfellows, on enlistment had been elected or appointed lieutenants at seventeen, and who within two years had shown in many a battle such self-control, such self-confidence, such capacity for command that they rose by leaps and bounds to the head of their regiments. Of such were the boy colonels of the Western armies—Lawton of Indiana, MacArthur of Wisconsin. There were but few young colonels in the camps of the Army of the Potomac, as the buds began to burst and the sap to bubble in the groves along the swirling Rappahannock—the last springtide in which those scarred and ravaged shores were ever to hear the old familiar thunder of shotted cannon, or the rallying cries of the battling Blue and Gray.

Three winters had the men of McClellan, of Hooker, and of Meade dwelt in their guarded lines south of the Potomac, three winters in which the lightest hearted of their number

FIELD MUSIC

The fife and drum corps became the chief dependence of the regimental commanders for music as the fighting wore on. They remained with the army to the end, and sounded all the "calls." They served under the surgeon. A cheerful bit of music is an inspiring thing to a tired column of soldiers on a long day's march or before a danger-

EVENING MUSIC AT PLEASONTON'S HEADQUARTERS, AUBURN, 1863

THE MUSIC THAT STAYED WITH THE SOLDIERS—TALTY'S FIFERS AND DRUMMERS

ous foe. General Sheridan recognized the value of this stimulus to the men, and General Horace Porter records that as late as March 30, 1865, he encountered one of Sheridan's bands under heavy fire at Five Forks, playing "Nellie Bly" as cheerfully as if it were furnishing music for a country picnic. The top photograph shows one of the cavalry bands at Auburn, in the fall of 1863. The frayed trousers of the band below show hard service.

A BAND THAT HAD SEEN SERVICE, NEAR FAIRFAX, 1863

must have matured ten years. What sights had they seen, what miles had they marched, what furious battles had they fought, yet to what end? In spite of all their struggles and all their sacrifices, here they lay along the same familiar slopes and fields, with the same turbid stream still barring the southward way. Once had the grand Army of the Potomac, led by McClellan, turned the opposing line, tried the water route, marched up the Peninsula, and after a few weeks of fighting, drifted back again. Twice had the gallant Army of Northern Virginia, led by Robert E. Lee, turned the opposing lines, tramped up to the Cumberland valley, and after the stirring days of Antietam and Gettysburg, fallen back, fearfully crippled, yet defiant. Now, nearly two to one in point of numbers, and with a silent, simple-mannered Westerner in command of a great array made up mainly of Eastern men, the Army of the Potomac was to begin its final essay. In size it was about what it had been when it set forth in the spring of 1862. In discipline, in experience, in knowledge of the war-game, it was immeasurably greater.

The winter had been long and dull. The novelty had long since worn off; the camps and cantonments had been made as snug and comfortable as so many homes; rations were abundant and fairly good; the sutler shops were full of tempting provender; the paymaster's visits had been regular; currency, in greenbacks, "shinplasters," and postal notes was plentiful. Drills, except for recruits, were well-nigh done away with. Reviews and parades were few and far between. Guard and sentry, patrol and picket, were about the only duties ordered, so time hung heavily on the hands of all. Writing home was one relaxation; cards, checkers, or dice supplied another, but in almost every regiment after nightfall and before tattoo, men gathered together and talked of those they had lost, of those that remained in high command, and sang or crooned their soldier songs. Across the Rapidan—where all day long silent, statuesque, yet undeniably shabby, sat in saddle those gray

DRUMMER–BOYS OF THE WAR DAYS

IDENTIFIED BY COMRADES HALF A CENTURY LATER

The rub-a-dub-dub of the drums and the tootle-te-toot of the fifes inspired the Union armies long after there remained in the service but a few of the bands which marched to the front in '61.   All the calls from "reveille" to "taps," "assembly," breakfast call, sick call, were rendered by the brave little boys who were as ready to go under fire as the stoutest hearted veteran.   Many a time a boy would drop his drum or fife to grab up the gun of a wounded soldier and go in on the firing-line.   Fifty years afterward, members of this group were recognized by one of their companions during the war.   The one standing immediately below the right-hand star in the flag, beating the long roll on his drum, is Newton Peters.   He enlisted at fifteen, in the fall of 1861, and served throughout the four years, not being mustered out until June 29, 1865.   The boy standing in the front line at his left is Samuel Scott, aged sixteen when he entered the army as a drummer in August of 1862.   He, too, was faithful to the end, receiving his discharge on June 1, 1865.   The leader, standing forward with staff in his right hand, is Patrick Yard, who served from November 14, 1861, to July 1, 1865, having been principal musician or drum-major from July 1, 1862.   These are only a few of the forty thousand boy musicians who succeeded in securing enlistment in the Union armies, and followed the flag.

vedettes—the widely dispersed army of Lee had been under-
going a great religious revival, until they entered upon their
final and fateful campaign with fervent hope and prayer and
self-devotion.

Along the north bank, the spirit of the Union host, as
compared with the lightsome heart of 1861, had become tinged
with sadness. It was manifest in their songs. The joyous,
spirited, or frolicsome lays of the earlier months of the war had
been well nigh forgotten. Men no longer chorused " Cheer
Boys Cheer," or " Gay and Happy," for the songs of 1864
were pitched in mournful, minor chord. The soldiers sang
of home and mother and of comrades gone before—" Just Before the Battle," " We Shall Meet, but We Shall Miss Him "
were in constant demand. Only rarely did the camps resound
with " The Battle Cry of Freedom " and " The Red, White,
and Blue." They had seen so much of the sadness, they had
thus far known so little of the joy of soldier life. In the West
it had been different. There they had humbled the foe at
Forts Henry and Donelson. They had fought him to a draw,
winning finally the field, if not the fight, at Shiloh and Stone's
River. Brilliantly led by Grant, they had triumphed at Jackson and Champion's Hill, and then besieged and captured
Vicksburg, setting free the Mississippi. They had suffered
fearful defeat at Chickamauga where, aided by Longstreet and
his fighting divisions from Virginia, their old antagonist,
Bragg, had been able to overwhelm the Union lines.

Yet within three months the Army of the Cumberland,
led by George H. Thomas, and under the eyes of Grant, had
taken the bit in their teeth, refused to wait longer for Sherman's columns to their left, or Hooker's divisions sweeping
from Lookout to their rear, and in one tumultuous rush had
carried the heights of Missionary Ridge, sweeping Bragg and
his veterans back across the scene of their September triumph,
winning glorious victory in sight of those who had declared
they could not fight at all. They of the West had more than

AN INTERLUDE OF WARFARE —SERENADING THE COLONEL

The colonel of the regiment is sitting upon a chair fronting the house, holding his baby on his lap. His family has joined him at his headquarters, which he is fortunate to have established in a comfortable farmhouse near Union Mills, Virginia, early in 1862. A veteran, examining this photograph, found it to represent a rare event in soldier life—the serenading of an officer by the regimental band. These organizations, which entered the service with the regiments of 1861 and 1862, did not retain their organization very long. Their duty during action was to care for the wounded on the field and carry them to the rear, but it was soon found that those with sufficient courage for this service were needed on the firing-line with muskets in their hands, and they either became soldiers in the ranks or were mustered out of service. Thereafter the regiments depended for music upon their own fife and drum corps and buglers, or upon brigade bands.

held their own, and now as the spring released them from their winter quarters along the Tennessee, they were eager to be marched onward to Atlanta, even to Mobile. They had with them still many of the leaders whom they had known from their formative period—notably Sherman, Thomas, McPherson, Stanley, and by them they enthusiastically swore.

They had lost Halleck, Pope, Grant, and Sheridan, as they proudly said, " sent to the East to teach them Western ways of winning battles," but Halleck and Pope had hardly succeeded, and Grant and Sheridan were yet to try. They had as yet lost no generals of high degree in battle, though they mourned Lytle, Sill, Terrill, W. H. L. Wallace, and " Bob " McCook, who had been beloved and honored. They were destined to see no more of two great leaders who had done much to make them the indomitable soldiers they became—Buell and Rosecrans. They had parted with Crittenden, McCook, and McClernand, corps commanders much in favor with the rank and file, though not so fortunate with those higher in authority. They were soon to be rejoined by Blair and Logan, generals in whom they gloried, and all the camps about Chattanooga were full of fight.

But here along the open fields in desolated Virginia there was far different retrospect; there was far less to cheer. With all its thorough organization, armament, equipment; with all its months of preparation, its acknowledged superiority in drill and its vaunted superiority in discipline, the Army of the Potomac had been humbled time and again, and it was not the fault of the rank and file—the sturdy soldiery that made up those famous *corps d'armée*. At First Bull Run they had been pitted from the very start against forces supposed to be beyond the Blue Ridge, and overthrown at the eleventh hour by arriving brigades that a militia general was to have held fast on the Shenandoah. At Ball's Bluff they had been slowly surrounded by concentrating battalions, no precaution having been taken for their extrication or

PASTIMES OF OFFICERS AND MEN

Occasionally in permanent camps, officers were able to receive visits from members of their families or friends. This photograph shows an earnest game of chess between Colonel (afterward Major-General) Martin T. McMahon, assistant adjutant-general of the Sixth Corps, Army of the Potomac, and a brother officer, in the spring of 1864 just preceding the Wilderness campaign. Colonel McMahon, who sits near

the tent-pole, is evidently studying his move with care. The young officer clasping the tent-pole is one of the colonel's military aides. Chess was also fashionable in the Confederate army, and it is recorded that General Lee frequently played chess with his aide, Colonel Charles Marshall, on a three-pronged pine stick surmounted by a pine slab upon which the squares had been roughly cut and the black ones inked in. Napoleon Bonaparte is said to have been another earnest student of chess.

A GAME OF CHESS AT COLONEL McMAHON'S CAMP

WHEN THE ARMY RELAXED

With the first break of spring the soldiers would seize the opportunity to decorate their winter huts with green branches, as this photograph shows. Care has been cast aside for the moment, and with their arms stacked on the parade ground the men are lounging comfortably in the soft spring air, while the more enterprising indulge in a game of cards. From the intentness of their comrades who are looking over their shoulders, it may be imagined that there is a little money at stake, as was frequently the case.

support. In front of Washington, long months they had been held inert by much less than half their number. At Yorktown, one hundred thousand strong, they had been halted by a lone division and held a fatal month. At Williamsburg they had been stopped by a much smaller force. At Fair Oaks their left had been crushed while the right and center were "refused."

At Gaines' Mill their right had been ruined while the center and left, under McClellan's own eye, had been held passive in front of a skeleton line. At Second Bull Run they had been hurled against an army secure behind embankments, while another, supposed to be miles away, circled their left flank and crushed it. At Antietam, bloodiest day of the story thus far, they had been sent in, a corps at a time, to try conclusions with an army in position, to the end that, when Lee slipped away with his battered divisions, even with superior numbers McClellan dare not follow. Twice within six months had Stuart, with a handful of light horsemen, ridden entirely around them, and with abundant cavalry had failed to stop him. In November they had mournfully parted with their idol of the year before, never to look again on "Little Mac," realizing that something must have been wrong, though it was not theirs to ask or to reason why. Obedient to Burnside's orders, they had stormed the heights of Fredericksburg in the face of Lee's veterans, laying down their lives in what they knew was hopeless battle.

Confident in their numbers, in their valor, in their comrades, and hopeful of their new and buoyant commander, they had crossed above Fredericksburg, while Sedgwick menaced from the north, and then, worst fate of all, had found themselves tricked and turned, their right wing sent whirling before "Stonewall" Jackson, whom Hooker and Howard had thought to be in full retreat for the mountains, their far superior force huddled in helpless confusion and then sent back, sore-hearted, to the camps from which they had come. They

THE THIRTEENTH NEW YORK ARTILLERY PLAYING FOOTBALL DURING THE
SIEGE OF PETERSBURG

THE BIRTH OF BASE-BALL

Some of the men who went home on furlough in 1862 returned to their regiments with tales of a marvelous new game which was spreading through the Northern States. In camp at White Oak Church near Falmouth, Va., Kearny's Jersey brigade and Bartlett's brigade played this "baseball," as it was known. Bartlett's boys won this historic ball-game.

BOXING AT THE CAMP OF THE THIRTEENTH NEW YORK AT CITY POINT, 1864

AN ARMY OF BOYS

It is hard to remember when one reads of the bloody battles, the manly sacrifices, the stern, exhausting work of the Union armies, that over one million of the soldiers who fought for the Union were not over twenty-one. It was an army of boys, and in camp they acted as such. They boxed and wrestled and played tricks on each other like boys in school.

A DIVERSION AT GENERAL O. B. WILCOX'S HEADQUARTERS, IN FRONT OF
PETERSBURG, AUGUST, 1864

had taken full measure of recompense for this humiliation in the three tremendous days at Gettysburg, had triumphed at last over the skilled and valiant foemen who for two long years had beaten them at every point, but even now they could not make it decisive, for, just as after Antietam, they had to look on while Lee and his legions were permitted to saunter easily back to the old lines along the Rapidan. They had served in succession five different masters. They had seen the stars of McDowell, McClellan, Pope, Burnside, and Hooker, one after another, effaced. They had seen such corps commanders as Sumner, Heintzelman, Keyes, Fitz John Porter, Sigel, Franklin, and Stoneman relieved and sent elsewhere. They had lost, killed in battle, such valiant generals as Philip Kearny, Stevens, Reno, Richardson, Mansfield, Whipple, Bayard, Berry, Weed, Zook, Vincent, and the great right arm of their latest and last commander—John F. Reynolds, head of the First Corps, since he would not be head of the army.

They had inflicted nothing like such loss upon the Army of Northern Virginia, for "Stonewall" Jackson had fallen, seriously wounded, before the rifles of his own men, bewildered in the thickets and darkness of Chancellorsville. They had been hard hit time and again—misled, misdirected, mishandled—yet through it all and in spite of all had maintained their high courage and dauntless spirit. Tried again and again in adversity and disaster, saddened, sobered, but resolute and indomitable, they asked only the chance to try it again under a leader who would *stay,* and that chance they were now to have—that test which was destined to be the most deadly and desperate of all; for though Meade was commander of the Army of the Potomac, Grant had come, supreme in command of all, and Grant had brought with him that black-eyed little division commander from the Army of the Cumberland whose men had broken loose and swept the field at Missionary Ridge. The cavalry corps of the Army of the Potomac was to take the field under, and soon to learn to swear by, Philip Sheridan.

WHEN WAR HAD LOST ITS GLAMOUR—PROVOST–MARSHAL'S OFFICE
IN ALEXANDRIA, 1863

The novelty had departed from "the pomp and pageantry of war" by the fall of 1863. The Army of the Potomac had lost its thousands on the Peninsula, at Cedar Mountain, at Second Bull Run, Antietam, Fredericksburg, Chancellorsville, and Gettysburg. The soldiers were sated with war; they had forgotten a host of things taught to them as essential in McClellan's training camps that first winter around Washington. The paraphernalia of war had become familiar, and they yearned for the now unfamiliar paraphernalia of peace. This photograph shows the provost-marshal's office in Alexandria, Virginia, in the fall of 1863. The provost-marshal's men had long since learned to perform their duties with all the languid dignity of a city policeman. Attached to the flag-pole is a sign which heralds the fact that Dick Parker's Music Hall is open every night. Two years before the soldiers might have disdained to seek such entertainment in the face of impending battles. Now war was commonplace, and the "gentle arts of peace" seemed strange and new.

And they had need of all their discipline and determination, for over against them, along the southern shores of the Rapidan, Lee's widely dispersed army was girding up its loins for the last supreme struggle, sustained and strengthened as never before. There had always been a devout and prayerful spirit among their chieftains, notably in Lee, Jackson, and " Jeb " Stuart.

And so as the soft springtide flooded with sunshine the Virginia woods and fields, and all the trees were blossoming, and the river banks were green, the note of preparation was sounding in the camps of Meade, from Culpeper over to Kelly's Ford, and one still May morning, long before the dawn —their only reveille the plaintive call of the whippoorwill— the Army of the Potomac stole from its blankets, soaked the smouldering fires, silently formed ranks and filed away southeastward, heading for the old familiar crossings of the Rapidan. Three strong corps were there, with Hancock, Warren, and Sedgwick as their commanders, while away toward the Potomac stood Burnside, leading still another.

It was the beginning of the end, for the strong and disciplined array that marched onward into the tangled Wilderness nearly doubled the number of Lee's tried and trusted soldiery. It was the last stand of the Confederacy along that historic line, but was a stand never to be forgotten. Away to the southwest were the cheerless camps of the Southern corps, led by grim, one-legged old Ewell (he had lost the other in front of the Western brigade at the opening fight of Second Bull Run), by courtly A. P. Hill, by Grant's old comrade in the army, now Lee's " best bower," Longstreet. It was an easy march for the Army of the Potomac—Sheridan's troopers picking the way. It was far longer and harder for those ragged fellows, the Army of Northern Virginia, but the Northerners reeled and fell by hundreds under the terrific blows of Longstreet, when, with the second day, he came crashing in through the tangled shrubbery. It cost the North

SHIFTING GROUPS BEFORE THE SUTLER'S TENT—1864

In the early days, when there were delays in paying the troops, the sutlers discounted their pay-checks at ruinous rates. Sometimes when the paymaster arrived the sutler would be on hand and absorb all the money due to some of the soldiers. Before the end of the war the term "sutler" came to have no very honorable meaning, and an overturned wagon filled with his stores found plenty of volunteers to send it on its way, somewhat lighter as to load. Sometimes, however, a popular and honest vendor of the store supplies contributed by his industry and daring to smooth the corners of a hard campaign and break the monotony of camp fare.

FIRST WISCONSIN LIGHT ARTILLERY AT BATON ROUGE, LOUISIANA, IN AUGUST, 1864

This and the facing page show the first light artillery sent to the Union armies from what were then far-Western States. This battery was commanded by Captain Jacob T. Foster, and consisted of six 20-pounder Parrott guns. On April 3, 1862, they accompanied an expedition under General Morgan to Cumberland Gap, hauling their heavy guns by hand over the steep passes of the mountains. After the retreat from Cumberland Gap they joined the forces of General Cox at Red House Landing, Virginia, and December 21, 1862, they proceeded down the Mississippi to take part in Sherman's movement against Vicksburg. On the first of January, 1863, Sherman withdrew the army and moved to Arkansas Post. During Grant's campaign in Mississippi the battery fired over twelve thousand rounds. Their guns were condemned at Vicksburg, being so badly worn as to be unserviceable. They were then furnished with 30-pounder Parrotts, and ordered with the Thirteenth Army Corps to the Department of the Gulf. In December the Wisconsin men were ordered to New Orleans, and assigned to a position in the defenses of that city. There they were equipped as horse artillery and armed with three-inch rifled guns. By this time they were seasoned artillerists; the report of a commission appointed to inspect the quarters of all troops in New Orleans closes thus: "A more self-sustaining, self-reliant body of men cannot be found in the United States army." On April 22, 1864, they went to the aid of Banks' columns on their retreat from the Red River expedition, and in August took part in an expedition to Clinton, Louisiana. The battery lost during service five enlisted men killed and mortally wounded, and one officer and twenty-two enlisted men by disease.

[248]

COMPANY I, FIRST OHIO LIGHT ARTILLERY, AT CHATTANOOGA, NOVEMBER, 1863

This company was organized at Cincinnati, Ohio, and mustered in December 3, 1861. This photograph shows it in charge of some hundred-pounder Parrott guns on Signal Hill at Chattanooga where it was encamped in November, 1863. The guns had just been placed and the battery was not yet finished. Company I served at Gainesville, Groveton, and Second Bull Run in August, 1862, fought at Chancellorsville and Gettysburg, and took part in the Chattanooga-Ringgold campaign, and remained on garrison duty at Chattanooga till April 23, 1864. Thereafter it took part in Sherman's Atlanta campaign, fought at Kenesaw Mountain and Jonesboro and in many lesser engagements, and was mustered out June 13, 1865. The battery lost during service one officer and thirteen enlisted men killed and mortally wounded, and fifteen enlisted men by disease. Ohio furnished to the Federal armies thirteen regiments, five battalions, and ten companies of cavalry, two regiments of heavy artillery, forty-two batteries of light artillery, ten companies of sharp-shooters, and 227 regiments, one battalion, and five companies of infantry—a grand total during the war of 313,180 soldiers out of a military population of 459,534 in 1860.

the lives of two great leaders—Hays and Wadsworth, and hosts of gallant officers and men, did that battle of the Wilderness. Fearful was the toll taken by Lee in his initial grapple of the last campaign, for no less than eighteen thousand men, killed, wounded, and missing, were lost to Grant. It would have cost very much more but for one potent fact that, in the hour of success, triumph, and victory, even as Lee's greatest corps commander had been stricken just the year before and almost within bugle-call of the very spot, Lee's next greatest corps commander, Longstreet, was here shot down and borne desperately wounded from the field.

And when another morning dawned, and through the misty light the wearied eyes of the Southern pickets descried long columns in the Union blue marching, apparently, away from the scene of their fearful struggle, away to the barrier river, the woods rang with frantic cheers of exultation. Small wonder they thought that Grant, too, had given it up and gone. They had yet to know him. They had barely time to spring to arms and dart away, full tilt by the right flank, on the eastward race for Spotsylvania, there once again to clinch in furious battle—to kill and maim almost as many of Grant's indomitable host as three days at Gettysburg had cost them, and still, with an added eighteen thousand shot out of his ranks, that grim, silent, stubborn leader forced his onward way. On to the North Anna, and another sharp encounter; on to Cold Harbor and the dread assault upon entrenched and sheltered lines, where in two hours' fighting the Southern army, suffering heavily in spite of its screen, none the less took ten times its loss out of the assailing lines, and still had to fall back, amazed at the persistence of the foe. Sixty-one thousand effectives in round numbers, could Lee muster at the first gun of the campaign. Fifty-five thousand effectives in round numbers at the last gun had they shot from the ranks of Grant—nearly their own weight in foes. But even Cold Harbor could not turn that inflexible Westerner from his purpose. With nearly half

FOURTEENTH IOWA VETERANS
AT LIBBY PRISON, RICHMOND, IN 1862, ON THEIR WAY TO FREEDOM

In the battle of Shiloh the Fourteenth Iowa Infantry formed part of that self-constituted forlorn hope which made the victory of April 7, 1862, possible. It held the center at the "Hornet's Nest," fighting the live-long day against fearful odds. Just as the sun was setting, Colonel William T. Shaw, seeing that he was surrounded and further resistance useless, surrendered the regiment. These officers and men were held as prisoners of war until October 12, 1862, when, moving by Richmond, Virginia, and Annapolis, Maryland, they went to Benton Barracks, Missouri, being released on parole, and were declared exchanged on the 19th of November. This photograph was taken while they were held at Richmond, opposite the cook-houses of Libby Prison. The third man from the left in the front row, standing with his hand grasping the lapel of his coat, is George Marion Smith, a descendant of General Marion of Revolutionary fame. It is through the courtesy of his son, N. H. Smith, that this photograph appears here. The Fourteenth Iowa Infantry was organized at Davenport and mustered in November 6, 1861. At Shiloh the men were already veterans of Forts Henry and Donelson. Those who were not captured fought in the battle of Corinth, and after the prisoners were exchanged they took part in the Red River expedition and several minor engagements. They were mustered out November 16, 1864, when the veterans and recruits were consolidated in two companies and assigned to duty in Springfield, Illinois, till August, 1865. These two companies were mustered out on August 8th. The regiment lost during service five officers and fifty-nine enlisted men killed and mortally wounded, and one officer and 138 enlisted men by disease. Iowa sent nine regiments of cavalry, four batteries of light artillery and fifty-one regiments of infantry to the Union armies, a grand total of 76,242 soldiers.

his army strewn from the Rapidan to the lines of Richmond, Grant flung his pontoons across the James, and marched to Petersburg.

And there at last he had to pause, refit, reorganize, for Sedgwick and Hancock were lost to him—Sedgwick killed at the head of the Sixth Corps, still mourning for their beloved " Uncle John "; Hancock disabled by wounds. New men, but good, were now leading the Second and Sixth corps— Humphreys, and Wright of the Engineers, while Warren still was heading the Fifth. And now came the details of Sherman's victorious march from Chattanooga to Atlanta, and later of the start to the sea. Here the waiting soldiers shouted loud acclaim of Thomas' great victory at Nashville, of the pursuit and ruin of the army under Hood. Here they had to lounge in camp and read with envy of Sheridan and the Sixth Corps playing havoc with Early in the Shenandoah, and now with occasional heavy fighting on the flanks, here they heard of Sherman at Savannah, and a little later of his marching northward to meet them.

And then it seemed as though the very earth were crumbling at Petersburg, the Government at Richmond. With Thomas, free now to march eastward up the Tennessee and through the Virginia mountains at the west; with Sherman coming steadily from the south, with Grant forever hammering from the east, and with formidable reserves always menacing at the north, what could be the future of that heroic, hardpounded army of Lee! Long since the last call had been made upon their devoted people. The aged and the immature were side by side in the thinned and starving ranks. Food and supplies were well nigh exhausted. The sturdy, hard-marching, hard-fighting Southern infantry had learned to live on parched corn; their comrades, the gaunt cavalry, on next to nothing. With the end of March, Sheridan came again, riding buoyantly down from the Shenandoah, singing trooper songs along the James River Canal, rounding the Richmond

SOLDIER LIFE UNDERGROUND—BOMB–PROOFS ON THE LINES IN FRONT OF PETERSBURG, 1864

There were places on the advanced line around Petersburg where it was almost certain death to look over the side of the trench. There pickets had to be changed at night. The constant hail of shot and shell made life underground, such as the soldiers in these photographs are leading, not only welcome but necessary. There are two distinct kinds of physical courage. The story is told of a burly camp-bully who threatened to thrash a wiry little veteran half his size for some trivial or fancied slight. "No," said the veteran, "I won't fight you now, but come out on picket where you can be alone after dark with me to-night." They crept out silently to relieve the picket in the outer trench that night, but a dislodged stone attracted the Confederates' attention and the shots whistled about their ears. "Oh!" whined the camp-bully, as he crouched in the bottom of the trench, "they're trying to kill me!" "Of course they are," replied the little veteran quietly: "They've been trying to kill me for the last six nights." But there was no fight left in the camp-bully when he was required to face bullets.

BOMB–PROOFS NEAR ATLANTA, GEORGIA

fortifications, and rejoining Grant at Petersburg. Within a week he bored a way into the dim, dripping forests about Dinwiddie, found and overwhelmed Pickett at Five Forks, and, with thirty thousand men, turned Lee's right and cut the South Side Railroad.

That meant the fall of Petersburg—the fall of Richmond. There was barely time to fire the last volleys over the third of Lee's great corps commanders, A. P. Hill; to send hurried warning to Jefferson Davis at Richmond; to summon Longstreet, and then began the seven days' struggle to escape the toils by which the army was enmeshed. There had been no Sheridan in command of the cavalry when the Southern army fell back from the Antietam in 1862, or from Gettysburg in 1863, but now, on their moving flanks, ever leaping ahead and dogging their advance, ever cutting in and out among the weary and straggling columns, lopping off a train here, a brigade there, but never for a moment, day or night, ceasing to worry and wear and tear, Sheridan and his troopers rode vengefully, and there was no "Jeb" Stuart to lead the Southern horse—Stuart had gone down before his great foeman in sight of the spires of Richmond, long months before—and at last, with their wagon-loads of waiting rations cut off and captured before the eyes of their advance, with every hour bringing tidings of new losses and disasters at the rear, worn out with hunger, fatigue, and loss of sleep, their clothing in shreds, their horses barely able to stagger, the men who never yet had failed "Marse Robert," as they loved to call him, found their further way blocked at Appomattox; the road to Lynchburg held by long lines of Union cavalry, screening the swift coming of longer lines of infantry in blue. And then their great-hearted leader bowed his head in submission to the inevitable.

"Not a drum was heard, not a funeral note" when the British buried Sir John Moore at Corunna. Not a shot was heard, not a single cheer, not a symptom of triumph or

WHEN TIME SEEMED LONG, BUT HOME WAS NEAR—ON DUTY AT FORT WHIPPLE IN JUNE, '65

The war is over and the great machine of the Union armies which has been whirring at breakneck speed for full four years is now moving more and more slowly. But it cannot be stopped all at once, and the men who form its component parts are going through motions now become mechanical. The scene is Fort Whipple, Va., part of the vast system of defenses erected for the protection of Washington. The time is June, 1865. With the sash across his breast stands the Officer of the Day, whose duty it is during his tour of twenty-four hours to inspect all portions of the camp and to see that proper order is preserved. Just at the moment when this picture was taken, the adjutant of the regiment was giving some information to the Officer of the Day from his general order book. It is safe to assume that the thoughts of the three other officers, as well as those of the sentry pacing to and fro, are all tinged with alluring pictures of home and the comforts that have been so long denied to them. The sturdy bugler below will need no urging to sound taps for the last time. He is a soldier of the 26th Michigan. It was his regiment that issued the paroles to Lee's soldiers at Appomattox. In a few weeks he may rest his eyes on the long undulations of the inland prairies. In his western home he will often find echoing in his memory the mournful dying notes of the bugle as it sounded "taps" and will recall the words soldiers have fitted to the music: "Go to sleep. Go to sleep. The day is done." One of the marvels of our war to the belligerent nations of Europe was that, having raised and trained such gigantic armies, we should disperse them so quietly when the fighting was over. There is an apocryphal story of a mad scheme to combine the armies of the North and South and proceed to intervene in Mexico.

A BUGLER OF THE 26TH MICHIGAN

rejoicing when the Army of the Potomac leaned at last upon their rifles, and from under the peaked visors of their worn forage-caps watched the sad surrender of the men of Lee. Four long years they had fought and toiled and suffered; four long years they had everywhere encountered those grim gray lines, and always at fearful cost; four long years had they been cut off from home and loved ones, to face at any moment death, desperate wounds, the prison stockade, hardship, and privation, all that the great Union might be maintained—that even these, their skilled and valiant opponents, might prosper in future peace and unity under the rescued and resistless flag. All the peril, privation, and suffering were ended now. All the joys of home-coming were soon and surely to be theirs. Glad, glorious thanksgiving welled in every heart and would have burst forth in shout and song and maddening cheers, but for the sight of the sorrow in those thinned and tattered ranks, the unutterable grief in the gaunt, haggard faces of these, their brethren, as they stacked in silence the battle-dinted arms and bent to kiss, as many did, the sacred remnants of the battle-flags that had waved in triumph time and again, only to be borne down at the last, when further struggle was hopeless, useless, impossible. It was but the remnant, too, of his once indomitable array that was left to Lee for the final rally at Appomattox. The South had fought until between the cradle and the grave there were no more left to muster—fought as never a people fought before, and suffered as few in the North-land ever yet knew or dreamed.

Without a sound of exultation, without a single cheer, we have said, yet there *was* a sound—the murmur of pity and sympathy along the serried lines in blue, as there slowly passed before their eyes the wearied column of disarmed, dejected soldiery, weak from wounds, from hardship, from hunger. There *was* a cheer—a sudden spontaneous outburst from the nearest division, when, almost the last of all, the little remnant of the old Stonewall brigade stacked the arms they had borne

THE 69TH NEW YORK AT MASS IN THE FIELD

CHAPLAINS OF THE NINTH ARMY CORPS—OCTOBER, 1864

Nearly every regiment that went into the Civil War from the Northern cities had a chaplain as a member of its staff. Many of these peaceful warriors kept on through the campaigns. They worked in the field-hospitals, often under fire on the field itself where the wounded lay. More than one was carried away by patriotic ardor and, grasping the musket and car-tridge-box of a wounded soldier, was seen to sally out on the firing-line, and bear himself as courageously as any veteran—after the battle returning to the duty of ministering to the wounded. And in several instances, chaplains asked for a command after a few months in the field. The church shown below was built by the Fiftieth New York Engineers at Petersburg.

SPIRE AND BAYONETS

FEDERAL VETERANS IN WEST AND EAST, 1863—TWO ENTIRE REGIMENTS IN LINE

These two photographs are unusual as showing each an entire regiment in line on parade. Here stands the type of soldier developed West and East by the far-flung Union armies. The Fifty-seventh Illinois were already veterans of Forts Donelson and Henry and the bloody field of Shiloh when this photograph was taken, and had seen hard service at the siege of Corinth. Their camp is near the Corinth battlefield, May, 1863. The Forty-fourth New York, known as the "People's Ellsworth Regiment," was a graduate of Bull Run, the Peninsula, Antietam, Second Bull Run, Fredericksburg, Chancellorsville, and Gettysburg. It took part in even

ABOVE, THE FIFTY–SEVENTH ILLINOIS; THE FORTY–FOURTH NEW YORK BELOW

more pitched battles than the Illinois regiment and its loss was proportionately larger. Both were known as "fighting regiments." The Fifty-seventh Illinois lost during service three officers and sixty-five enlisted men killed and mortally wounded, and four officers and 118 enlisted men by disease. The Forty-fourth New York lost four officers and 178 enlisted men killed and mortally wounded, and two officers and 145 enlisted men by disease. The long lines of soldiers shown in these photographs have already looked death in the face, and will do so again; the Westerners at Atlanta and Kenesaw, the New Yorkers in the Wilderness and before Petersburg.

on every field from First Bull Run, but the cheer was for the gallant fellows who had fought so bravely and so well. It was the tribute of innate chivalry to a conquered foe, and many an officer, listening a moment in mute appreciation, suddenly swung his cap on high and joined the cheer, or, too much moved to speak, unsheathed the sword that so long had flashed in defiance of the Southern cause, and in silence lowered the battle-worn blade in salute to Southern valor.

For that was the lesson learned by these men who had borne the brunt of so many a desperate battle; for this army was the finished product of four long years of the sternest discipline, the hardest fighting, the heaviest losses known to modern warfare. The beardless boys of the farm, school, and shop had been trained by the hand of masters in the art to the highest duties of the soldier of the Nation; and now, their stern task ended, their victory won, it was theirs to be the first to take this foeman by the hand, comfort him with food and drink, and words of soldier cheer and sympathy, and then, turning back from the trampled fields of Virginia, to march yet once again through the echoing avenues of Washington, to drape their colors and to droop their war-worn crests in mourning for their martyred, yet immortal President, to place their battle-flags under the dome of the Capitol of their States, and then, unobtrusively to melt away and become absorbed in the throng of their fellow citizens, conscious of duty faithfully performed, and intent now only on reverent observance of the last lesson of him who had been through all their patient, prayerful, heaven-inspired leader. "To bind up the Nation's wounds; to care for him who shall have borne the battle, and for his widow and his orphan—to do all which may achieve and cherish a just and lasting peace among ourselves, and with all nations."

THE SECRET SERVICE
OF THE
FEDERAL ARMIES

WILLIAM WILSON—A SCOUT
WITH THE ARMY OF THE POTOMAC

COPYRIGHT, 1911, PATRIOT PUB. CO.

THE FAMOUS ALLAN PINKERTON—THE MONTH OF THE BATTLE OF ANTIETAM

The name of Allan Pinkerton became one of the most famous in secret-service work, the world over. This keen-witted detective came to America from Scotland about twenty years before the opening of the Civil War. He was conducting a successful agency in Chicago when his friend, George B. McClellan, sent for him to be chief detective in the Department of the Ohio. Shortly after, he went to Washington and under General McClellan directed the secret-service operations in the Army of the Potomac, besides doing extensive detective work for the provost-marshal at the Capital. As a stanch admirer of McClellan, Pinkerton refused to continue in the military end of the service after the general's removal in November, 1862. He remained, however, in Government service, investigating cotton claims in New Orleans, with other detective work, until the close of the war, when he returned to his agency in Chicago.

[262]

AT THE TENT OF McCLELLAN'S CHIEF DETECTIVE, 1862

Only a handful of people, in North and South together, knew the identity of "Major Allen," as, cigar in hand, he sat before his tent in 1862. His real name was Allan Pinkerton. As the head of his famous detective agency, he had been known by General McClellan before the war. He was chosen as the head of "Little Mac's" secret service, and remained until McClellan himself retired in November, 1862, only a month after this picture was made. Directly behind "Major Allen" stands young Babcock (in the same costume that he wears with his beautiful horse in the frontispiece), between George H. Bangs and Augustus K. Littlefield, two operatives. The man seated at Pinkerton's right is William Moore, private secretary to Edwin M. Stanton, the Secretary of War, down from the Capital to consult Pinkerton.

A NEW SECRET SERVICE—THE "MILITARY INFORMATION BUREAU"

After Pinkerton's departure from the Army of the Potomac, the secret-service department was allowed to fall into hopeless neglect. All organization vanished. When General Hooker assumed command there was hardly a record or document of any kind at headquarters to give information of what the Confederates were doing. Hooker was as ignorant of what was going on just across the Rappahannock as if his opponents had been in China. With the energy that marked his entire course of organization, he put Colonel George H. Sharpe, of the 120th New York regiment, in charge of a special and separate bureau, known as Military Information. Sharpe was appointed deputy provost-marshal-general. From March 30, 1863, until the close of the war, the Bureau of Military Information, Army of the Potomac, had no other head. Gathering a staff of keen-witted men, chiefly from the ranks, Sharpe never let his com-

RESTING AFTER THE HARD WORK OF THE GETTYSBURG CAMPAIGN

manding general suffer for lack of proper information as to the strength and movements of Lee's army. The Confederate advance into Pennsylvania, in June, taxed the resources of the bureau greatly. Scouts and special agents, as well as signal-men, were kept in incessant action, locating and following the various detachments of the invading force. It was a difficult matter to estimate, from the numerous reports and accounts received daily, just what Lee was trying to do. The return to Virginia brought some relief to the secret-service men. In August, while Lee hastened back to the old line of the Rapidan, Colonel Sharpe lay at Bealeton, and here the army photographer took his picture, as above, on the extreme left. Next to him sits John C. Babcock; the right-hand figure is that of John McEntee, detailed from the 80th New York Infantry. These men were little known, but immensely useful.

THE FEDERAL SECRET SERVICE

By George H. Casamajor

THERE was one fact that became evident with startling emphasis to the American people the moment secession was established, and this was that it was not political ties alone that had held the Union together. Financial, commercial, and domestic bonds had, in seventy years, so stretched from North to South that to divide and disrupt the social organism was a much more difficult feat to accomplish than mere political separation upon a point of Constitutional interpretation. An unparalleled state of public confusion developed in the early months of 1861, which was all the worse because there was little or no uncertainty in the individual mind. Probably every citizen of the country capable of reason had reached conviction upon the points at issue.

Not only the Government at Washington but the whole world was astounded that the new Confederacy could bring at once into the field a military force superior in numbers to the standing army of the United States. Every department at the capital was disorganized by the defection of employees whose opinions and ties bound them to the cause of the South. Legislators in both houses, cabinet officers, and judges volunteered their services in the making of the new nation. Ministers and consuls hastened from foreign countries to enter its councils or fight for its existence. Army and navy officers left their posts and resigned their commissions for commands under another standard. The Episcopal bishop of Louisiana exchanged the surplice for the uniform and rode at the head of an army corps.

Opinion was positive, but it did not separate along

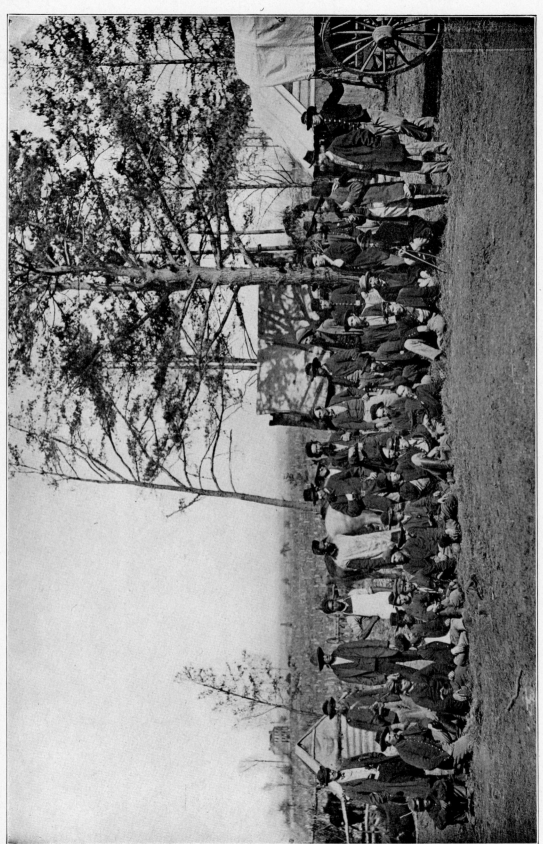

SCOUTS AND GUIDES IN THE ARMY OF THE POTOMAC

The individuals in the group were attached to the secret-service department of the Army of the Potomac when it was directed by Allan Pinkerton. Many of these men who were gathered for service on the Peninsula were known as Pamunkey Indians, relics of a small Virginia tribe which had intermarried considerably with the Negroes. They were very loyal to the Union, and their services were invaluable to McClellan during the spring and summer of 1862. After Pinkerton left the army, the whole secret-service department was reorganized by Colonel Sharpe, and he drew more largely from the ranks for the composition of his force. Whenever these men were captured they were hanged as spies.

geographic lines. Thousands in the North believed sincerely in the justice of the Southern cause. Business men dealing largely with the South realized that hostilities would reduce them to poverty. Northern men established in Southern territory, solicitous for their fortunes and their families, found that an oath of allegiance would mean the confiscation of their property and the ruin of their hopes. Political combinations and secret societies in the most loyal parts of the Union were aiding the new Government to establish itself on a firm basis. Individuals, for reasons more or less advantageous to themselves, were supplying men, money, materials of war, and supplies to the Confederacy.

This review of existing conditions is necessary to understand the full scope of the secret service which was necessary in order that the Federal Government might comprehend and grapple with the situation. Congress had not anticipated the emergency and made no provisions for it, but the Constitution gives the President extraordinary powers to suppress insurrection, and these were employed at once and with energy. Most important was the organization of that branch of the military service whose function it is to obtain information as to the adversary's resources and plans, and to prevent like news from reaching the opponents. But the work of fighting was only a portion of the task. All communication between the North and South was carefully watched. The statutes of the post-office were arbitrarily changed and its sacredness violated, in order to prevent its use as a means of conveying information. Passengers to and from foreign countries were subjected to new passport regulations. A trade blockade was instituted. The writ of habeas corpus was suspended in many places, and all persons who were believed to be aiding the South in any way were arrested by special civil and military agents and placed in military custody for examination. Most of this, it will be evident, had to be accomplished by means of detection known as " secret service."

IN THE HEART OF THE HOSTILE COUNTRY—MAY, 1862

As the secret-service men sit at Follen's house, near Cumberland Landing, all is ready for the advance to the Chickahominy and to Richmond. The scouts and guides are aware that there is hard and dangerous work before them. Their skilful leader, whom they know as Major Allen, sits apart from the group at the table, smoking his pipe and thinking hard. He must send his men into the Confederate lines to find out how strong is the opposing army. Probably some of them will never come back. The men were new to the work, and had not yet learned to approximate the numbers of large masses of troops. Thus it happened that Pinkerton greatly overestimated the size of the Army of Northern Virginia, and McClellan acted as if dealing with an overwhelming opponent. Had he discovered that he greatly outnumbered the Confederates, the war in the East might have been ended by the 1st of July, 1862.

The Federal Government was, in the beginning, lacking in any organized secret service. The Department of State, the Department of War, and the Department of the Navy each took a hand in early attempts to define the line between loyalty and disloyalty to the Union cause, but upon that of State fell the greater share of the effort. Secretary Seward engaged a force of detectives, and sent them to Canada and frontier places to intercept all communication between the British dominion and the South. He assigned other secret agents to the specific task of stopping the sale of shoes for the Confederate army. The police chiefs of Northern cities were requested to trail and arrest suspected persons. No newspaper editorial that might be construed as containing sentiments disloyal to the Union appeared in print but some one sent a copy to Washington, and, if necessary, the offending journal was suppressed.

The police commissioners of Baltimore were arrested, as was also a portion of the Maryland legislature. So active was the multifarious work of the secret service that the prisons at Forts Warren, Lafayette, and McHenry were soon overflowing with prisoners of state and war. Distracted wardens pleaded that there was no room for more, but it was not until the middle of February, 1862, that relief was afforded. By this time the Government felt that the extent of all forms of activity in the Southern cause within the existing Union were well understood and under control. The President was anxious to return to a more normal course of administration and issued an order for the release on parole of all political and state prisoners, except such detained as spies or otherwise inimicable to public safety. Henceforth, important arrests were made under the direction of the military authorities alone.

These, meanwhile, had not been idle, since detective work in regard to the plans and movements of the foe has always been one of the most important departments of warfare. The organization of the Federal military secret service involved no complicated machinery. In every military department the

PINKERTON ENTERTAINS VISITORS FROM WASHINGTON

DETECTIVE WORK FOR THE FEDERAL ADMINISTRATION

The proximity of the headquarters of the Army of the Potomac to the National Capital, after the battle of Antietam, drew many visitors from Washington during the pleasant October days of 1862. Naturally they spent some time with Allan Pinkerton, whom they knew as Major Allen, for he had come to be a prominent figure in the city. There he made his headquarters, and could be found when not in the field with the commanding-general. In the Capital city there was much work to do of a kind for which Pinkerton was already famous. When he arrived from

A CHARACTERISTIC POSE

Chicago shortly after the first battle of Bull Run, he brought his entire force with him and began to investigate people suspected of assisting the Confederate cause by sending information secretly to Richmond and the Southern armies in the field. He made a number of important arrests, both in Washington and in Baltimore, acting under orders from Provost-Marshal Andrew Porter, as well as General McClellan and the heads of the Departments of State and War. Several of his most skilful operatives, both men and women, were constantly traveling between Richmond and Washington, bringing valuable information of the plans of President Davis and his advisers, military and civil.

commander appointed a chief detective who gathered about him such a force of soldiers and civilians as he required to perform the work of espionage and investigation. These detectives were responsible to the heads of the military departments. Besides these the War Department employed special agents who reported directly to the secretary.

The imagination is apt to enwrap the character of the detective or spy in an atmosphere of mystery and excitement, against which these individuals are generally the first to protest. An aptitude for the work naturally implies an amount of fearlessness and daring which deadens the feeling of danger and affords real pleasure in situations involving great risk. We must picture the successful secret-service agent as keen-witted, observant, resourceful, and possessing a small degree of fear, yet realizing the danger and consequences of detection.

His work, difficult as it is to describe precisely, lay, in general, along three lines. In the first place, all suspected persons must be found, their sentiments investigated and ascertained. The members of the secret service obtained access to houses, clubs, and places of resort, sometimes in the guise of guests, sometimes as domestics, as the needs of the case seemed to warrant. As the well-known and time-honored shadow detectives, they tracked footsteps and noted every action. Agents, by one means or another, gained membership in hostile secret societies and reported their meetings, by which means many plans of the Southern leaders were ascertained. The most dangerous service was naturally that of entering the Confederate ranks for information as to the nature and strength of defenses and numbers of troops. Constant vigilance was maintained for the detection of the Confederate spies, the interception of mail-carriers, and the discovery of contraband goods. All spies, "contrabands," deserters, refugees, and prisoners of war found in or brought into Federal territory were subjected to a searching examination and reports upon their testimony forwarded to the various authorities.

"MAJOR" PAULINE CUSHMAN, THE FEDERAL SPY WHO BARELY ESCAPED HANGING

Pauline Cushman was a clever actress, and her art fitted her well to play the part of a spy. Although a native of New Orleans, she spent much of her girlhood in the North, and was so devoted to the Union that she risked her life in its secret service. The Federal Government employed her first in the hunt for Southern sympathizers and spies in Louisville, and the discovery of how they managed to convey information and supplies into the territory of the Confederacy. She performed the same work in Nashville. In May, 1863, as Rosecrans was getting ready to drive Bragg across the Tennessee River, Miss Cushman was sent into the Confederate lines to obtain information as to the strength and location of the Army of Tennessee. She was captured, tried by court-martial, and sentenced to be hanged. In the hasty evacuation of Shelbyville, in the last days of June, she was overlooked and managed to regain the Union lines. It was impossible to describe the joy of the soldiers when they found the brave spy, whom they had thought of as dead, once more in their midst. Her fame after this spread all over the land. The soldiers called her "Major" and she wore the accouterments of that rank. Her accurate knowledge of the roads of Tennessee, Georgia, Alabama, and Mississippi was of great value to the commander of the Army of the Cumberland.

As the conflict progressed the activities of the baser elements of society placed further burdens upon the secret service. Smuggling, horse-stealing, and an illicit trade in liquor with the army were only the lesser of the many crimes that inevitably arise from a state of war. Government employees and contractors conspired to perpetrate frauds. The practice of bounty-jumping assumed alarming proportions. Soldiers' discharges were forged and large sums collected upon them. Corrupt political organizations attempted to tamper with the soldiers' vote. The suppression of all this was added to the already heavy labors of the secret agents.

There were, from the very beginning, several strongly concentrated centers of suspicion, and of these probably the most important and dangerous was located within the higher social circles of the city of Washington itself. In the spring of 1861, the capital was filled with people suspected of supplying information to the Confederate authorities. These Southern men and women did not forget the cause which their friends and families in the home-land were preparing valiantly to defend. Aristocratic people still opened their doors to those high in office, and who could tell what fatal secrets might be dropped by the guests, or inadvertently imparted, to be sent to the leaders of the South? Nor were the activities confined entirely to homes. At office doors in the department buildings the secret agents watched and waited to learn some scrap of information; military maps and plans were often missing after the exit of some visitor.

Such vital information as this was constantly sent across the Potomac: "In a day or two, twelve hundred cavalry supported by four batteries of artillery will cross the river above to get behind Manassas and cut off railroad and other communications with our army whilst an attack is made in front. For God's sake heed this. It is positive." And again: "To-day I have it in my power to say that Kelley is to advance on Winchester. Stone and Banks are to cross and go to

GUERRILLA AND SCOUT—"TINKER DAVE" BEATTY WITH DR. HALE

General Crook, writing to General James A. Garfield, chief of staff, Army of the Cumberland, in March, 1863, asked, "Who is 'Tinker Dave' Beatty?" One would like to learn what Crook had heard about the tinker. There is no record that Garfield ever replied to the question, and perhaps he, too, knew very little of this famous character. David Beatty was the leader of an irregular band of guerrillas working in the Federal cause throughout middle Tennessee. The Confederate officers, to whom they gave constant trouble, refer to them as "bushwhackers" and "tories." Especially annoying were Beatty and his men to Captain John M. Hughs, commanding a small detachment from Bragg's army. Hughs attempted to stop Beatty's marauding expeditions. On September 8, 1863, he attacked Beatty, killing eight of his men and putting the rest to rout. Again on February 14, 1864, Hughs fell upon Beatty, who this time had a band of about one hundred. The Confederate troops killed seventeen and captured two of the band, and the remainder disappeared. Beatty continued his irregular activities from time to time. He often worked in connection with Dr. Jonathan P. Hale, who was the chief of scouts of the Army of the Cumberland under Rosecrans and Thomas. Both leaders valued Hale's services highly. He kept special watch on Morgan, Forrest, and Wheeler when they were in his neighborhood, making constant reports as to their strength and location.

Leesburg. Burnside's fleet is to engage the batteries on the Potomac, and McClellan and Company will move on Centreville and Manassas next week. This information comes from one of McClellan's aides."

In the secret-service work at Washington the famous name of Allan Pinkerton is conspicuous, but it is not on the records, as during his entire connection with the war he was known as E. J. Allen, and some years elapsed before his identity was revealed. Pinkerton, a Scotchman by birth, had emigrated to the United States about twenty years before, and had met with considerable success in the conduct of a detective agency in Chicago. He was summoned to grapple with the difficult situation in Washington as early as April, 1861. He was willing to lay aside his important business and put his services at the disposal of the Government. But just here he found his efforts hampered by department routine, and he soon left to become chief detective to General McClellan, then in charge of the Department of the Ohio.

When this secret service was well established, Pinkerton went to Washington, shortly after the first battle of Bull Run. He immediately pressed his entire staff of both sexes into the work, but even that was insufficient for the demands upon it. Applications came in on all sides and not the least of the problems was the selection of new members.

Pinkerton was in daily contact with and made reports to the President, Secretary of War, the provost-marshal-general and the general-in-chief of the armies. But his connection with the military concerns of the Government was brief. In November, 1862, McClellan, to whom Pinkerton was sincerely attached, was removed. Indignant at this treatment, the detective refused to continue longer at Washington. He was, however, afterward employed in claim investigations, and at the close of the war returned to Chicago.

Later on, when Hooker took command of the Army of the Potomac, Colonel George H. Sharpe was placed at the

In April, 1862, J. J. Andrews, a citizen of Kentucky and a spy in General Buell's employment, proposed seizing a locomotive on the Western and Atlantic Railroad at some point below Chattanooga and running it back to that place, cutting telegraph wires and burning bridges on the way.   General O. M.

Mitchel authorized the plan and twenty-two men volunteered to carry it out.   On the morning of April 12th, the train they were on stopped at Big Shanty station for breakfast.   The bridge-burners (who were in citizens' clothes) detached the locomotive and three box-cars and started at full speed for Chattanooga, but after a run of about a hundred miles their fuel was exhausted and their pursuers were in sight.   The whole party was captured.   Andrews was condemned as a spy and hanged at Atlanta, July 7th.   The others were confined at Chattanooga, Knoxville, and afterward at Atlanta, where seven were executed as spies.   Of the fourteen survivors, eight escaped from prison; and of these, six eventually reached the Union lines.   Six were removed to Richmond and confined in Castle Thunder until they were exchanged in 1863.   The Confederates attempted to destroy the locomotive when they evacuated Atlanta.

head of the Bureau of Military Information and supervised all its secret-service work until the close of the war. He brought the bureau to a state of great efficiency. Lieutenant H. B. Smith was chief detective of the Middle Department, which comprised Maryland, Delaware, and part of Virginia. His headquarters was at Baltimore, one of the most fertile fields for the work of the secret service. This city, of all that remained within the Union, was probably the most occupied in aiding and abetting the cause of the South.

Smith gathered about him a staff of about forty soldiers and civilians, and an immense amount of significant information as to the plans and movements of the citizens, some of them of great prominence, began to pour into the provost-marshal's office. Many schemes were frustrated and the offenders arrested. The numerous coves and bays of the Chesapeake offered secure harbors and secluded landing-places for contraband vessels. On one occasion, Smith and two of his assistants came upon a fleet of a dozen schooners riding at anchor in an isolated spot. The crews were unarmed and the three agents succeeded in capturing the entire lot of blockade-runners with their rich cargoes.

Spies and mail-carriers were constantly apprehended and their activities interrupted. Deserters were pursued and brought to justice. In March, 1865, one Lewis Payne was arrested in Baltimore on a criminal charge. Smith believed the man to be a spy, but a searching examination failed to procure any definite evidence. The cautious detective, however, made him take the oath of allegiance, and recommended his release on condition that he would go to some point north of Philadelphia and remain there until the close of the war. A month later Payne committed the attack on William H. Seward and others at the secretary's Washington home.

During the presidential campaign of 1864, certain party powers at Albany were striving for the election. They sent their political agents to various voting-agencies of the New

COLONEL SHARPE GETTING READY FOR THE LAST GRAND MOVE—1864

In the spring of 1864, the headquarters of the Army of the Potomac was near Brandy Station, Virginia. One of the busiest spots is shown in this picture—the headquarters of Colonel Sharpe, deputy provost-marshal-general, who was organizing his scouts and secret-service men for the coming campaign. It is April, and although no one knows yet what the new General-in-Chief purposes doing, he has announced his intention of making his headquarters with the Army of the Potomac. Many scouting parties have been sent southward beyond the Rapidan, where the Army of Northern Virginia lies entrenched. Sutlers and their employees have been ordered to leave the army. General Patrick, the provost-marshal-general, has recalled all permits granted citizens to remain within the lines; leaves of absence and furloughs have been revoked; army-lists have been called for. The secret-service men around Colonel Sharpe's quarters know that they will soon be off on their many dangerous missions, as the eyes and ears of the moving army.

York troops with instructions to forge the officers' affidavits that accompanied the votes and turn in illegal ballots for their candidate. The keen eye of Smith detected an unknown abbreviation of the word " Cavalry " on one of the signatures, and this led to the exposure of the plot and the arrest of three of the corrupt agents. The detective also did much work in western Maryland and West Virginia in observing and locating the homes of Mosby's famous raiders who were a source of great trouble to the Federal army.

Other missions often took Smith outside the boundaries of his department. In the guise of a New York merchant he took into custody in Washington a Confederate agent who was endeavoring to dispose of bonds and scrip. Many visits to New York and Philadelphia were made in connection with bounty-jumping and other frauds, and he once arrested in New York an agent of the Confederacy who was assisting in the smuggling of a valuable consignment of tobacco. All this was combined with various and hazardous trips south of the Potomac, when necessary, in search of information concerning the strength and position of Confederate defenses and troops. It all denotes a life of ceaseless activity, but it is very typical of the secret agents' work during the Civil War.

In addition to the various detective forces in the field, the War Department had its special agents directly under the control of the President and the Secretary of War. These, too, were employed in the multiform duties previously outlined. One of the most noted of the special agents, Colonel Lafayette C. Baker, was a New Yorker by birth who had removed to California, but was in the East when the conflict opened. He hastened to put his services at the command of the Union, and on account of his work on the Vigilance Committee in the stormy days of 1856, was engaged as a detective in the Department of State.

The authorities at Washington were most anxious to obtain information as to the Confederate force at Manassas.

LATER SCOUTS AND GUIDES
ARMY OF THE POTOMAC

As the Federal secret service developed under experience, a great change came over the personnel of its members. Less and less were civilians employed. Instead, capable scouts were drafted from the army. Much had been learned through the excellent results obtained by the Confederate scouts, who were chiefly the daring cavalrymen of Ashby, Morgan, Wheeler, and Forrest. In this picture appears a group of scouts and guides headed by Lieutenant Robert Klein, Third Indiana Cavalry, who spent some time with the Army of the Potomac. On the ground by his side is his young son. Many of the men here depicted were among the most noted of the army's secret-service men. Standing at the back are James Doughty, James Cammock, and Henry W. Dodd. On the ground are Dan Plue, W. J. Lee, — Wood, Sanford Magee, and John W. Landegon. Seated at the left is John Irving, and on the right is Daniel Cole, seen again on page 289.

Five men had been sent to Richmond; of these two had been killed, and the others were thought to be prisoners. In July, 1861, Baker started for the Confederate capital. He was promptly arrested but managed to convince both General Beauregard and President Davis that he belonged in Tennessee. So cleverly was the part played that he was sent North as a Confederate agent, and before the end of three weeks was able to give General Scott a vast amount of valuable information regarding Manassas, Fredericksburg, and Richmond, together with the plans of the Confederate leaders, and the scheme for blockade-running on the Potomac. After that he reported on suspected persons in Baltimore, and was sent to Niagara Falls to watch and arrest the Southern agents there.

When in February, 1862, the secret service came directly under the control of the War Department, Baker was employed as special agent. He was given a commission as colonel and organized the First District of Columbia Cavalry, a regiment chiefly employed in the defense and regulation of the National capital, although it saw some service in the field.

Baker's concerns were chiefly with matters that had little to do with the active conduct of the war. He took charge of all abandoned Confederate property; he investigated the fraudulent practices of contractors; he assisted the Treasury Department in unearthing counterfeiters; he was the terror of the bounty-jumper, and probably did more than anyone else to suppress the activities of that vicious citizen. His last notable achievement in the secret service was the pursuit and capture of the assassin of Abraham Lincoln.

Another valuable agent in the War Department was William P. Wood, superintendent of the Old Capitol Prison, at Washington. In pursuit of his duties Mr. Wood was in daily contact with the most important of the military prisoners who fell into the clutches of the Federal Government. He lost no opportunity of gaining any sort of information in regard to the workings of the Confederacy and the plans of its armies,

SECRET–SERVICE HEADQUARTERS IN THE LAST MONTHS OF THE WAR

During the winter of 1864–65, General Grant had his headquarters at City Point, Virginia, and the building occupied by the secret-service men is shown here, as well as a group of scouts who are as idle as the two armies in the Petersburg trenches. But a few weeks' work in the opening spring, as Grant maneuvers to starve Lee out of Petersburg, and the scouts' duties will be over. Sheridan will come, too, from the Shenandoah with his cavalry scouts, the finest body of information seekers developed by the war. General Grant was in a constant state of uneasiness during the winter, fearing that Lee would leave his strong lines around Petersburg and unite with Johnston. Consequently he depended on his secret-service men to keep him informed as to any signs of movement on the part of Lee.

and his reports to the Secretary were looked upon as among the most helpful that reached the department.

The maintenance of the secret service was a large item in the conduct of the war. The expenses of the provost-marshal's office at Washington alone, covering a period of nearly three years, were nearly $175,000 for detective service and incidental expense. This, of course, was only a small portion of the total outlay.

In dealing with the secret service the words "spies" and "scouts" are constantly used. A clear and definite distinction between the two is indeed difficult to make. By far the greater number of persons described as spies in an account of the war would be classed as scouts by a military man. To such a one the word "spy" would most often mean a person who was located permanently within the lines or territory of the opponent and applied himself to the collection of all information that would be valuable to his military chief. The latter communicated with his spies by means of his scouts, who took messages to and fro. The real spies seldom came out. Scouts were organized under a chief who directed their movements. Their duties were various—bearing despatches, locating the foe, and getting precise information about roads, bridges, and fords that would facilitate the march of the army. Thus many opportunities for genuine spy work came to the scout and hence the confusion in the use of the terms, which is increased by the fact that an arrested scout is usually referred to as a spy.

The use and number of Federal spies were greatly increased as the war went on and in the last year the system reached a high degree of efficiency, with spies constantly at work in all the Confederate armies and in all the cities of the South. In the very anonymity of these men lay a large part of their usefulness. The names of a few, who occupied high places or met with tragic ends, have been rescued from obscurity. Those of the remainder are not to be found on any rolls of honor. They remain among the unknown heroes of history.

THE SECRET SERVICE
OF THE
CONFEDERACY

UNCONSCIOUS ALLIES OF THE CONFEDERACY—
NEWSPAPER CORRESPONDENTS IN THE FIELD WITH
THE UNION ARMY, WHOSE MOVEMENTS WERE MANY
TIMES REVEALED BY NEWSPAPER DESPATCHES
SUPPLYING INFORMATION TO THE SOUTHERNERS.

THE CONFEDERATE SECRET SERVICE

By John W. Headley
Captain, Confederate States Army

THE Confederate States had no such secret-service organization as was developed and used by the Federal Government during the Civil War, and yet it is probably true
that, in the matter of obtaining needed military information,
the Confederacy was, on the whole, better served than was the
North. Of course, many uses of the Federal secret service
were not necessary in the South. The Government at Washington had to face at once the tremendous problem of sepa-
rating in the non-seceding States loyalty from disloyalty to
the idea that the Union formed under the Constitution was a
unit and could not be divided. Thousands of citizens in the
North not only denied the right of the Federal Government
to invade and coerce the South, but in this belief many stood
ready to aid the Confederate cause.

From such conditions as these the Southern States were
practically free. They contained nothing that the North
needed for the coming conflict, while the latter had much to
give. The prevention of assistance to the North was not one
of the problems of existence. So, while a certain class of spies
and detectives for the Union and the Confederacy operated
on both sides of the dividing line, the Confederacy needed none
of these in its own territory. Capable devotees of the South
readily volunteered for secret service within the Federal military lines or territory, while the United States Government
was compelled to organize and employ several classes of spies
and detectives all over the North, for the purpose of suppress-
ing bounty-jumpers, fraudulent discharges, trade in contra-

NANCY HART
THE CONFEDERATE GUIDE AND SPY

The women of the mountain districts of Virginia were as ready to do scout and spy work for the Confederate leaders as were their men-folk. Famous among these fearless girls who knew every inch of the regions in which they lived was Nancy Hart. So valuable was her work as a guide, so cleverly and often had she led Jackson's cavalry upon the Federal outposts in West Virginia, that the Northern Government offered a large reward for her capture. Lieutenant-Colonel Starr of the Ninth West Virginia finally caught her at Summerville in July, 1862. While in a temporary prison, she faced the camera for the first time in her life, displaying more alarm in front of the innocent contrivance than if it had been a body of Federal soldiery. She posed for an itinerant photographer, and her captors placed the hat decorated with a military feather upon her head. Nancy managed to get hold of her guard's musket, shot him dead, and escaped on Colonel Starr's horse to the nearest Confederate detachment. A few days later, July 25th, she led two hundred troopers under Major Bailey to Summerville. They reached the town at four in the morning, completely surprising two companies of the Ninth West Virginia. They fired three houses, captured Colonel Starr, Lieutenant Stivers and other officers, and a large number of the men, and disappeared immediately over the Sutton road. The Federals made no resistance.

band goods, and contract frauds, thus maintaining a large force which was prevented from doing any kind of secret service within the Southern lines or territory.

The personality, the adventures, and the exploits of the Confederate scouts and spies are seldom noted in the annals of the war, and yet these unknown patriots were often a controlling factor in the hostilities. Generals depended largely on the information they brought, in planning attack and in accepting or avoiding battle. It is indeed a notable fact that a Confederate army was never surprised in an important engagement of the war.

Apart from the military service in the field, the State Department at Richmond maintained a regular line of couriers at all periods between the capital and Maryland, and thus kept familiar with every phase of the war situation at Washington and in the North. The operations of these skilful secret agents gave constant employment to the detective force of the Federal Middle Department. One efficient means of securing information was through agents at Washington, Baltimore, New York, and other Northern points, who used the cipher and inserted personals in friendly newspapers, such as the New York *News, Express,* and *Day Book.* These journals were hurried through to Richmond. At the opening of the war many well-known people of Baltimore and Washington were as hostile to the Federal Government as were the inhabitants of Richmond and New Orleans, and these were of great service to the Southern armies.

Colonel Thomas Jordan, adjutant-general of the Confederate forces under General Beauregard at Manassas, made arrangements with several Southern sympathizers at Washington for the transmission of war information, which in almost every instance proved to be extremely accurate. On July 4, 1861, some Confederate pickets captured a Union soldier who was carrying on his person the returns of McDowell's army. "His statement of the strength and composition of

OLD CAPITOL PRISON, WASHINGTON, IN THE EARLY DAYS OF THE WAR

This historic building once the temporary Capitol of the United States, played a large part in the workings of the Federal secret service; its superintendent, William P. Wood, was a special secret agent of the War Department. It was used for the incarceration of many Confederate prisoners of war, suspects and political offenders. Mr. Wood frequently subjected his wards to searching examination. Information thus gained was immediately forwarded to the Secretary of War. Mrs. Greenhow, Belle Boyd, Mrs. Morris, M. T. Walworth, Josiah E. Bailey, Pliny Bryan, and other famous Confederate spies spent some time within its walls. The advantage gained by the Confederate secret agents was often nullified through the counter information secured by the Federal scouts. The photograph shows one of Colonel Sharpe's trusted men, a private of the Third Indiana Cavalry, who would often lead out a party of scouts to get information as to the location and strength of the various parts of the Army of Northern Virginia. These men would go forward until they discovered the line of Confederate pickets, and then use all their trained powers of observation to find out what was behind it. Citizens in the neighborhood were closely questioned, and all the information procurable was turned in to Colonel Sharpe.

DANIEL COLE, A FEDERAL SCOUT

that force," relates Beauregard, in "Battles and Leaders of the Civil War," "tallied so closely with that which had been acquired through my Washington agencies . . . that I could not doubt them. . . . I was almost as well advised of the strength of the hostile army in my front as its commander."

Not only that, but Beauregard had timely and accurate knowledge of McDowell's advance to Manassas. A former government clerk was sent to Mrs. Rose O'Neal Greenhow, at Washington, who was one of the trusted friends of the Confederacy and most loyal to its cause. She returned word in cipher immediately, "Order issued for McDowell to march upon Manassas to-night," and the vitally important despatch was in Beauregard's hands between eight and nine o'clock on that same night, July 16, 1861. Every outpost commander was immediately notified to fall back to the positions designated for this contingency, and Johnston in the Valley, who had likewise been informed by careful scouting parties that Patterson was making no move upon him, was able to exercise the option permitted by the Richmond authorities in favor of a swift march to Beauregard's assistance.

Thus "opportunely informed," the Confederate leader prepared for battle without orders or advice from Richmond. The whole of these momentous Confederate activities were carried out through the services of couriers, spies, and scouts. In the opening of the war, at least, the Confederate spy and scout system was far better developed than was the Federal.

As the war went on, each commanding general relied upon his own spies and the scouts of his cavalry leader. Colonel J. Stoddard Johnston was a nephew of Albert Sidney Johnston and served on General Bragg's staff from Stone's River to Chattanooga. All through this important campaign he had charge of the secret-service orders and reports. He has related how he always utilized soldiers of known intelligence, honor, and daring as spies, without extra compensation, and employed the cavalrymen of Wheeler, Morgan, and Forrest

BELLE BOYD—A FAMOUS SECRET AGENT OF THE CONFEDERACY

This ardent daughter of Virginia ran many hazards in her zeal to aid the Confederate cause. Back and forth she went from her home at Martinsburg, in the Valley, through the Federal lines, while Banks, Frémont, and Shields were trying in vain to crush "Stonewall" Jackson and relieve Washington from the bugbear of attack. Early in 1862 she was sent as a prisoner to Baltimore. However, General Dix, for lack of evidence, decided to send her home. This first adventure did not dampen her ardor or stop her activities. Since she was now well known to the Federals, her every movement was watched. In May she started to visit relatives in Richmond, but at Winchester happened to overhear some plans of General Shields. With this knowledge she rushed to General Ashby with information that assisted Jackson in planning his brilliant charge on Front Royal. On May 21st she was arrested at the Federal picket-line. A search showed that she had been entrusted with important letters to the Confederate army. About the 1st of August Miss Boyd was taken to Washington by order of the Secretary of War, incarcerated in the Old Capitol Prison and was afterward sent South.

as scouts.   It was the same with Lee and the commanders in the Trans-Mississippi Department.

In " Stonewall " Jackson's 1862 campaign against Banks, Fremont, and Shields in the Valley of Virginia, the Federal forces were defeated, within a month, in five battles by an army that aggregated one-fifth their total, though divided, numbers.   This great achievement must not be attributed entirely to the genius of Jackson and the valor of his army.   A part of the glory must be given to the unknown daring spies and faithful scouts of Ashby's cavalry, who were darting, day and night, in all directions.   Their unerring information enabled Jackson to strike and invariably escape.   On the other hand, the Federal generals had no such means of gathering information, and they seem never to have been protected from surprise or advised of Jackson's movements.

Among the most noted bands of Confederate scouts was one organized by General Cheatham, over which one Henry B. Shaw was put in command.   Shaw, who had been a clerk on a steamboat plying between Nashville and New Orleans, had an accurate knowledge of middle Tennessee, which in the summer of 1863 was in the hands of the Federal army, owing to Bragg's retreat from Tullahoma.   He assumed the disguise of an itinerant doctor while in the Federal lines, and called himself Dr. C. E. Coleman.   In the Confederate army he was known as Captain C. E. Coleman, commander of General Bragg's private scouts.   The scouts dressed as Confederate soldiers, so that in case of capture they would not be treated as spies.   Nevertheless, the information they carried was usually put into cipher.

Shaw was finally captured and sent to Johnson's Island. The command of the famous scouts devolved upon Alexander Gregg, who continued to sign despatches " C. E. Coleman," and the Federal authorities never knew that the original leader of the daring band was in safe-keeping in Sandusky Bay.

On April 7, 1864, President Davis, at Richmond, sent the

NEW YORK HERALD HEADQUARTERS IN THE FIELD, 1863

The Confederate secret service worked through the Northern newspapers to an extent little appreciated. Without any disloyalty on the part of the newspaper men, this was necessarily the case. The North swarmed with spies, special correspondents, paid agents, Southern sympathizers by the score, and "copperheads" innumerable. It followed that Richmond often knew pretty much everything worth knowing of the disposition and preparation of the Union forces, and even of their carefully guarded plans. The Northern newspaper correspondent with the armies incurred practically all the perils that fell upon the soldier himself, and the more enterprising and successful he became, the less he ingratiated himself with the commanding generals, whose plans he predicted and whose conduct he criticised in newspaper leaders. But it was necessary that the people at home, whose money was paying for the armies in the field, should be kept informed how those armies fared, and it is safe to contend that a great debt was due to the American war-correspondents. While they were a source of information to the South on occasions, they were also active and indefatigable allies of the Northern Government, in that they persuaded the people at home to submit to the extraordinarily heavy taxation necessary to support the large and costly armies and prosecute the war to the end.

following telegram to the Honorable Jacob Thompson, in Mississippi, " If your engagements permit you to accept service abroad for the next six months, please come here immediately." Thompson was a citizen of Oxford, Mississippi, and said to be one of the wealthiest men in the South. He was, besides, a lawyer and a statesman, had served in Congress, and in the cabinet of President Buchanan as Secretary of the Interior.

The reason of the sending for Thompson was that the Confederate Government had decided to inaugurate certain hostile movements in Northern territory. Clement C. Clay, Jr., of Alabama, was selected as Mr. Thompson's fellow commissioner to head the Department of the North. Both were among the foremost public men of the Confederacy. Their mission was one of great secrecy, and if one of their projects could be successfully accomplished there was no doubt, in the opinion of the Southern Government, that the war would be brought to a speedy conclusion. Negotiations looking toward peace were opened with men like Horace Greeley and Judge Black, but the correspondence with Greeley was made public, and the matter reached an untimely end.

There existed in the Northern States an essentially military organization known as the Sons of Liberty, whose principle was that the States were sovereign and that there was no authority in the central Government to coerce a seceding State. It was estimated that the total membership of this society was fully three hundred thousand, of whom eighty-five thousand resided in Illinois, fifty thousand in Indiana, and forty thousand in Ohio. The feeling was general among the members that it would be useless to hold the coming presidential election, since Mr. Lincoln held the power and would undoubtedly be reelected. Therefore it was planned to resort to force. Plans for a revolution and a new Confederacy were promoted, in all of which the Southern commissioners took a most active interest.

The grand commander of the Sons of Liberty was C. L.

VESPASIAN CHANCELLOR

ONE OF "JEB" STUART'S KEENEST SCOUTS

The scouts were the real eyes and ears of the army. From the very beginning of the war the Confederate cavalry was much used for scouting purposes, even at the time when Federal commanders were still chiefly dependent upon civilian spies, detectives, and deserters for information as to their opponents' strength and movements. They saw the folly of this, after much disastrous experience, and came to rely like the Confederates on keen-witted cavalrymen. The true scout must be an innate lover of adventure, with the sharpest of eyesight and undaunted courage. Such was Vespasian Chancellor, one of the most successful scouts in General J. E. B. Stuart's cavalry command. He was directly attached to the general's headquarters.

Vallandigham, a sympathizer with the South, who in 1863 had been expelled from Federal territory to the Confederacy. He managed, however, to make his way to Canada, and now resided at Windsor. The prominence of his attitude against the further prosecution of the war led to his receiving the Democratic gubernatorial nomination in Ohio, and, braving rearrest, he returned home in June, 1864, ostensibly to begin the campaign, but with a far deeper purpose in view.

In brief, Vallandigham purposed by a bold, vigorous, and concerted action, engineered by the Sons of Liberty, to detach the States of Illinois, Indiana, and Ohio from the Union, if the Confederate authorities would, at the same time, move sufficient forces into Kentucky and Missouri to hold those lukewarm Federal States. The five commonwealths would thereupon organize the Northwestern Confederacy upon the basis of State sovereignty, and the former Federal Union would now be in three parts, and compelled, perforce, to end the contest with the South. The date for the general uprising was several times postponed, but finally settled for the 16th of August. Confederate officers were sent to various cities to direct the movement. Escaped Confederate prisoners were enlisted in the cause. Thompson furnished funds for perfecting county organizations. Arms were purchased in New York and secreted in Chicago.

Peace meetings were announced in various cities to prepare the public mind for the coming revolution. The first one, held in Peoria, was a decided success, but the interest it aroused had barely subsided when the publication of the Greeley correspondence marked the new Confederacy as doomed to stillbirth. The peace party in the Union was won over to the idea of letting the ballot-box in the coming presidential election decide the question of war or peace. The Sons of Liberty, none too careful as to who were admitted to membership, inadvertently elected a number of Federal spies to their ranks. Prominent members were arrested. The garrison at Camp

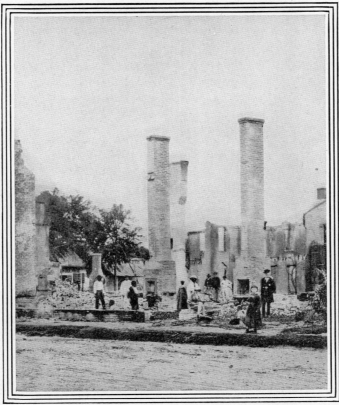

FEDERAL PRECAUTIONS AGAINST SURPRISE AS PHOTOGRAPHED BY A
SECRET–SERVICE ADVERSARY

The Confederates, kept out of their former stronghold at Baton Rouge, Louisiana, by the Union army of occupation, still obtained knowledge of the state of affairs there through Lytle, the photographer, who sent pictorial evidence of the Federal occupation in secrecy to the Southern leaders. The industrious and accommodating photographer, who was willing to photograph batteries, regiments, camps, headquarters, fortifications, every detail, in fact, of the Union army, did not limit himself to sending this exact knowledge through to the Confederate secret service. With flag and lantern he used to signal from the observation tower on the top of the ruins of the Baton Rouge capitol to Scott's Bluff, whence the messages were relayed to the Confederates at New Orleans. Here is pictured the wreckage of private houses torn down by Colonel Halbert E. Paine, in order that the Federal batteries might command the approaches to the town and prevent a surprise. In August, 1862, General Butler, fearing an attack on New Orleans, had decided to concentrate all the forces in his department there and ordered Colonel Paine to bring troops from Baton Rouge. The capital of Louisiana accordingly was evacuated, August 21st. Paine left the *Essex* and *Gunboat No. 7* in the Mississippi with instructions to bombard the city in case the Confederate army, then in the neighborhood, should make any attempt to enter. The citizens promised that Breckinridge's troops would not do so, and thus the town was spared.

Douglas, Chicago, was increased to seven thousand. The strength of the allies was deemed insufficient to contend with such a force, and the project was abandoned. The Confederates returned to Canada.

Before the prospects of the Northwestern Confederacy had begun to wane, Captain Charles H. Cole, one of Forrest's cavalrymen, confined as a prisoner on Johnson's Island in Sandusky Bay, made his escape. Reporting in Canada to Mr. Thompson, plans were made at once for the seizure of the United States gunboat *Michigan,* which was guarding Johnson's Island, and the release of the prisoners. The plot developed rapidly, and the services of Captain John Y. Beall of the Confederate navy were added in carrying out the scheme. The Confederates on the island were ready to overpower their guards as soon as the *Michigan* and her fourteen guns were in Beall's hands. The 19th of December was decided on for the date of the seizure. Cole, who had become very friendly with the *Michigan's* officers, was to go on board and give the signal for Beall and a boat-load of Confederates to approach and surprise the vessel. Beall, who had mustered some twenty Confederates at Windsor, was approaching Sandusky Bay in the steamer *Philo Parsons,* which he had seized, when seventeen of his men mutinied, and he was obliged to turn back. To make the failure complete, Cole fell under suspicion and was arrested even while waiting for Beall to appear.

The latter was arrested at the Suspension Bridge railway station, about the middle of December, while working on a plan to rescue seven captured Confederate generals, as they were being transferred from Johnson's Island to Fort Lafayette. He was hanged in New York, February 24, 1865, by order of a military court, for the seizure of the steamer *Philo Parsons.*

The active commissioners were also attempting to carry out an economic policy which had been suggested by Secretary of State Benjamin and developed by a Nashville banker, John

THE FIRST INDIANA HEAVY ARTILLERY AT BATON ROUGE

PHOTOGRAPHS THAT FURNISHED VALUABLE SECRET–SERVICE INFORMATION TO THE
CONFEDERATES

The clearest and most trustworthy evidence of an opponent's strength is of course an actual photograph. Such evidence, in spite of the early stage of the art and the difficulty of "running in" chemical supplies on "orders to trade," was supplied the Confederate leaders in the Southwest by Lytle, the Baton Rouge photographer—really a member of the Confederate secret service. Here are photographs of the First Indiana Heavy Artillery (formerly the Twenty-first Indiana Infantry), showing its strength and position on the arsenal grounds at Baton Rouge. As the Twenty-first Indiana, the regiment had been at Baton Rouge during the first Federal occupation, and after the fall of Port Hudson it returned there for garrison duty. Little did its officers suspect that the quiet man photographing the batteries at drill was about to convey the "information" beyond their lines to their opponents,

Porterfield by name. It was hoped thereby to work great damage to, and bring much distrust upon, the Federal finances. The Southern sympathizers in the North had, in obedience to request, converted much paper money into gold and withdrawn it from circulation. This, however, caused the price of gold to rise until it reached 290, which great figure naturally caused a change of policy. When the precious metal had fallen as low as 180, Mr. Porterfield went from Montreal, his temporary residence, to New York and began purchasing and exporting gold, selling it for sterling bills of exchange, and reconverting this into gold, the amount lost in trans-shipment being met out of the funds placed at his disposal by the commissioners. About two million dollars was thus exported, but before any perceptible disaster had been wrought upon the national finances, General Butler, in New York, arrested a former partner of Porterfield, and the latter prudently returned to Montreal.

About the 1st of September, Thompson's force of secret workers in the Southern cause had been joined by Colonel Robert M. Martin, who had been a brigade commander in Morgan's cavalry, and myself, who had served on Martin's staff. We had been detached for this service by the Secretary of War. We expected to take an active part in an attempt by the Sons of Liberty to inaugurate a revolution in New York city, to be made on the day of the presidential election, November 8th. Thompson sent Martin with seven selected Confederate officers, myself included, to report for duty to the leaders. Martin was in charge of the whole thing. The plot was exposed by Northern secret-service agents, and General Butler with ten thousand troops arrived, which so disconcerted the Sons of Liberty that the attempt was postponed. We remained in the city awaiting events, but the situation being chaotic we had nothing to do.

When Sherman burned Atlanta, November 15th, Martin proposed to fire New York city. This was agreed to by

HOW THE FEDERAL CAMP LAY BY THE ROAD OF APPROACH

A RECONNAISSANCE

BY MEANS OF THE CAMERA

Lytle, the Confederate secret agent at Baton Rouge, sent photographs of the Federal occupation from time to time to his generals. Thus they could determine just where the invading troops were located. The position of the large camps north of the State House, behind the penitentiary and near the Methodist Church, their relation to the avenues of approach, could be noted through the photographs. One of General Banks' first acts on assuming command of the Department of

THE CAMP NEAR THE PENITENTIARY

the Gulf had been to order the re-occupation of Baton Rouge. On December 17, 1862, General Grover arrived with forty-five hundred men. About five hundred Confederates who were in the town immediately departed, and Grover prepared for an attack which did not come. Baton Rouge suffered less than might have been expected during the war. Butler gave orders for its destruction in August, 1862, but on account of the many institutions it contained these were rescinded. The State House was burned December 28, 1862, but this was due to a defective flue and not to an incendiary's vandal torch.

THE CAMP IN FRONT OF THE METHODIST CHURCH

Thompson, and the project was finally undertaken by Martin and five others, including myself.

On the evening of November 25th, I went to my room in the Astor House, at twenty minutes after seven. I hung the bedclothes over the foot-board, piled chairs, drawers, and other material on the bed, stuffed newspapers into the heap, and poured a bottle of turpentine over the whole mass. I then opened a bottle of " Greek fire " and quickly spilled it on top. It blazed instantly. I locked the door and went downstairs. Leaving the key at the office, as usual, I passed out. I did likewise at the City Hotel, Everett House, and United States Hotel. At the same time Martin operated at the Hoffman House, Fifth Avenue, St. Denis, and others. Altogether our little band fired nineteen hotels. Captain Kennedy went to Barnum's Museum and broke a bottle on the stairway, creating a panic. Lieutenant Harrington did the same at the Metropolitan Theater, and Lieutenant Ashbrook at Niblo's Garden. I threw several bottles into barges of hay, and caused the only fires, for, strange to say, nothing serious resulted from any of the hotel fires. It was not discovered until the next day, at the Astor House, that my room had been set on fire. Our reliance on " Greek fire " was the cause of the failure. We found that it could not be depended upon as an agent for incendiary work. Kennedy was hanged in New York, March 25, 1865.

We left New York on the following Saturday over the Hudson River Railroad, spent Sunday at Albany, and arrived in Toronto on Monday afternoon.

Every Confederate plot in the North was fated to fail. The Federal secret service proved to be more than a match for the Sons of Liberty and the Confederates. Captain T. H. Hines, another daring officer of Morgan's command, had undertaken an even more extensive plot in Chicago for November 8th, election night. He had to assist him many escaped prisoners of war, Confederate soldiers, and members of the

THE FATE OF A CONFEDERATE SPY
BEFORE PETERSBURG
1864

The photograph gives an excellent idea of a military execution of a Confederate spy within the Federal lines.   The place was in front of Petersburg; the time August, 1864.   It is all terribly impressive: the double line of troops around the lonely gallows waiting for the unfortunate victim who is about to suffer an ignominious death.   Many devoted sons of the South met their fate by accepting duty in the secret service and performing the work of a spy.   The penalty of capture was certain death on the gallows, for the real spy wore civilian clothes and consequently could not claim the protection of the uniform.   Many men refused to do most kinds of secret-service work, scouting and gathering information, unless they were permitted to wear the insignia of their calling, but sometimes it was absolutely impossible to appear in uniform, and then the worst penalty was risked.   Many men, Federals and Southerners too, actuated by the most patriotic and self-denying motives, thus met death not only in shame, but also completely severed from all that was dear to them; for in their anonymity had lain the large part of their usefulness.   Their names will not be found on any roll of honor.   Their place is among the unknown heroes of history.

Sons of Liberty. The plot involved not only the overpowering of the little garrison at Camp Douglas, and the release of over eight thousand military prisoners, but the cutting of telegraph wires, the seizure of banks, the burning of the railroad stations, the appropriation of arms and ammunition within the city, in fact, the preparation for a general uprising in favor of terminating the war.

The Federal secret service, however, forestalled the conspirators' plans, and one hundred and six of them were arrested on November 7th. They were subsequently tried by a military court at Cincinnati, and many were sent to penitentiaries for terms ranging from three years to life.

Such were the last of the Confederate operations from Canada. The considerable force collected there gradually returned to the Confederacy. Martin and I left during the first week of February, 1865. We went from Toronto to Cincinnati and Louisville, where we attempted to kidnap the Vice President elect, Andrew Johnson, on his way to the inauguration. This failing, about ten o'clock on the morning of March 1st we went to a stable where Major Fossee of General Palmer's staff kept three fine horses. Two of these we seized, locked the surprised attendants in the stable and rode away to the South. We were at Lynchburg when Lee surrendered at Appomattox, eighteen miles away.

As we came to Salisbury, North Carolina, we met two gentlemen strolling alone in the outskirts. Martin recognized them as President Davis and Secretary of State Benjamin. We halted, and Mr. Benjamin remembered Martin. He enquired for Colonel Thompson. Continuing south, we fell in at Chester, South Carolina, with Morgan's old brigade under General Basil W. Duke, and marched in President Davis' escort as far as Washington, Georgia, where he left us all behind, and the Confederacy perished from the earth.

PART II
MILITARY
INFORMATION

THE
SIGNAL
SERVICE

CENTRAL STATION,
WASHINGTON,
SIGNALING
ACROSS THE
POTOMAC

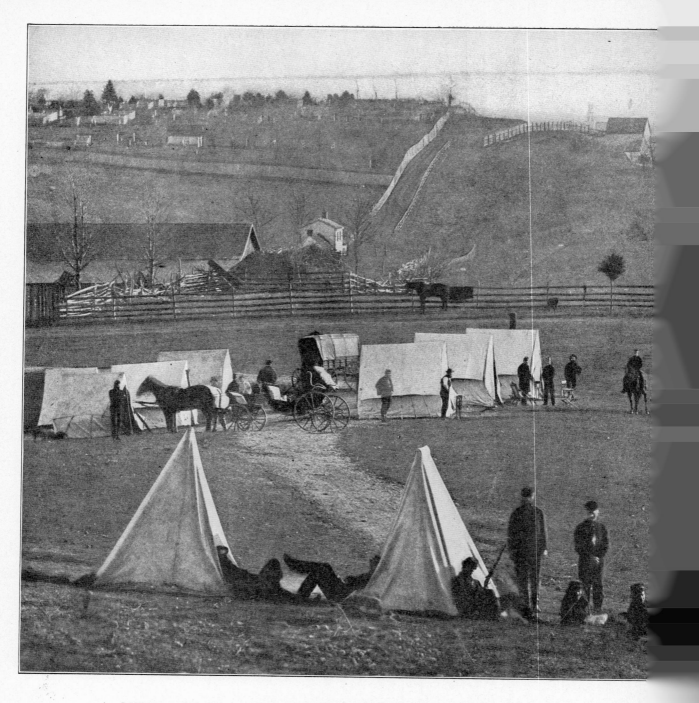

A QUIET EVENING, BEFORE THE DANGEROUS WORK BEGAN

Fashionable folks from Washington have come to the signal camp to look at what seems a strange new pastime of the soldiers, playing with little sticks and flags and entertaining themselves at night with fire-works. But now the shadows lengthen, and the visitors are mounting their horses and about to take their places in the waiting barouche to depart. In the foreground the signal-men are lounging comfortably, feet in the air, or drowsing against the sides of their tents. Their work is done, unless practice is ordered with the rockets and lights after the nightfall. A few months from now they will be in a place where the patronizing visitors will be loth to follow. With Confederate shells shrieking about them on the Peninsula,

SIGNAL CAMP OF INSTRUCTION, AT RED HILL, GEORGETOWN, 1861

the men with the flags will dip and wave and dip again, conveying sure information to "Little Mac" more speedily than the swiftest courier. Who would grudge them these few moments of peaceful comfort at twilight when he learns that the ratio of killed to wounded in the Signal Corps was one hundred and fifty per cent., as against the usual ratio of twenty per cent. in other branches of the service? Many found their fate in Confederate prisons. Sense of duty, necessity of exposure to fire, and importance of mission were conditions frequently incompatible with personal safety—and the Signal Corps paid the price. In no other corps can be found greater devotion to duty without reward.

[1—20]

EXPERTS OF THE UNITED STATES SIGNAL SERVICE
PHOTOGRAPHED IN 1861

General (then Major) Myer is distinguishable, leaning against the table on the right-hand page, by the double row of buttons on his field-officer's coat. The group comprises Lieutenant Samuel T. Cushing, Second United States Infantry, with seventeen officers selected for signal duty from the noted Pennsylvania Reserve Corps. Most of the enlisted men were from the same volunteer organization. It is interesting to examine the field paraphernalia with which the corps was provided. Every man has a collapsible telescope, or a powerful field-glass. Leaning against the table is a bunch of staffs, to which the flags were attached, for wig-wagging signals. One of the signal flags is lying in front of the group, and another is extended in the breeze behind. White flags with a red center were most frequent. In case of snow, a

CHIEF SIGNAL OFFICER A. J. MYER, WITH A GROUP OF HIS SUBORDINATES
AT RED HILL

black flag was used.   Against a variegated background the red color was seen farther.   In every important campaign and on every bloody ground, these men risked their lives at the forefront of the battle, speeding stirring orders of advance, warnings of impending danger, and sullen admissions of defeat.   They were on the advanced lines of Yorktown, and the saps and trenches at Charleston, Vicksburg, and Port Hudson, near the battle-lines at Chickamauga and Chancellorsville, before the fort-crowned crest of Fredericksburg, amid the frightful carnage of Antietam, on Kenesaw Mountain deciding the fate of Allatoona, in Sherman's march to the sea, and with Grant's victorious army at Appomattox and Richmond. They signaled to Porter clearing the central Mississippi River, and aided Farragut when forcing the passage of Mobile Bay.

"THREE"—SIGNALING FROM THE COBB'S HILL TOWER
BY THE APPOMATTOX—1864

In this second view of the Cobb's Hill signal tower, appearing in full length on the opposite page, the signal-man has dipped his flag forward in front of him—signifying "Three." Signal messages were sent by means of flags, torches, or lights, by combinations of three separate motions. With the flag or torch initially held upright, "one" was indicated by waving the flag to the left and returning it to an upright position; "two" by a similar motion to the right; and "three" by a wave or dip to the front. One or more figures constituted a letter of the alphabet, and a few combinations were used for phrases. Thus 11 indicated "A," 1221 "B," 212 "C," and so on. 12221 meant "Wait a moment"; 21112 "Are you ready?" And 3 meant the end of a word, 33 the end of a sentence, and 333 the end of a message. Where a letter was composed of several figures, the motions were made in rapid succession without any pause. Letters were separated by a very brief pause, and words or sentences were distinguished by one or more dip motions to the front; one, signifying the end of a word; two, the end of a sentence; and three, the end of a message. The tower shown in this photograph, 125 feet high, was first occupied June 14, 1864. It commanded a view of Petersburg, sections of the Petersburg and Richmond Railway, and extended reaches of the James and Appomattox Rivers. Its importance was such that the Confederates constructed a two-gun battery within a mile of it for its destruction, but it remained in use until the fall of Petersburg.

THE SIGNAL CORPS

By A. W. Greely
Major-General, United States Army

NO other arm of the military services during the Civil War excited a tithe of the curiosity and interest which surrounded the Signal Corps. To the onlooker, the messages of its waving flags, its winking lights and its rushing rockets were always mystic in their language, while their tenor was often fraught with thrilling import and productive of far-reaching effects.

The signal system, an American device, was tested first in border warfare against hostile Navajos; afterward the quick-witted soldiers of both the Federal and Confederate armies developed portable signaling to great advantage. The invention of a non-combatant, Surgeon A. J. Myer, it met with indifferent reception and evoked hostility in its early stages. When the stern actualities of war were realized, its evolution proceeded in the Federal army in face of corporation and departmental opposition, yet despite all adverse attacks it ultimately demonstrated its intrinsic merits. Denied a separate organization until the war neared its end, the corps suffered constantly from strife and dissension in Washington, its misfortunes culminating in the arbitrary removal of its first two chiefs. Thus its very existence was threatened. Nevertheless, the gallant, efficient services of its patriotic men and officers in the face of the foe were of such striking military value as to gain the confidence and win the commendation of the most distinguished generals.

Major Myer began work in 1861, at Georgetown, District of Columbia, with small details from the volunteers, though the

CONFEDERATE SIGNALMEN IN '61

The Confederate signal service was first in the field. Beauregard's report acknowledges the aid rendered his army at Bull Run by Captain (afterwards General) E. P. Alexander, a former pupil of Major A. J. Myer. McDowell was then without signalmen, and so could not communicate regularly with Washington. While Major Myer was establishing a Federal signal training-school at Red Hill, such towers were rising along the already beleaguered Confederate coast. This one at Charleston, South Carolina, is swarming with young Confederate volunteers gazing out to sea in anticipation of the advent of the foe. They had not long to wait. During nearly four years the Union fleet locked them in their harbor. For all that time Fort Sumter and its neighbors defied the Union power.

corps eventually numbered about three hundred officers and twenty-five hundred men. Authorized as a separate corps by the act of Congress, approved March 3, 1863, its organization was not completed until August, 1864. The outcome was an embodiment of the army aphorism that "one campaign in Washington is worth two in the field." More than two thousand signalmen served at the front, of whom only nine were commissioned in the new corps, while seventeen were appointed from civil life. As a result of degradation in rank, eleven detailed officers declined commissions or resigned after acceptance. Colonel Myer, the inventor and organizer of the service, had his commission vacated in July, 1864, and his successor, Colonel Nicodemus, was summarily dismissed six months later, the command then devolving on Colonel B. F. Fisher, who was never confirmed by the Senate. That a corps so harassed should constantly distinguish itself in the field is one of the many marvels of patriotism displayed by the American soldier.

Signal messages were sent by means of flags, torches, or lights, by combinations of three separate motions. The flag (or torch) was initially held upright: "one" was indicated by waving the flag to the left and returning it from the ground to the upright position; "two" by a similar motion to the right, and "three" by a wave (or dip) to the front. Where a letter was composed of several figures, the motions were made in rapid succession without any pause. Letters were separated by a very brief pause, and words or sentences were distinguished by one or more dip motions to the front.

SIGNAL ALPHABET, AS USED LATE IN THE WAR

A— 11	G—1122	M—2112	S— 121	Y— 222
B—1221	H— 211	N— 22	T— 1	Z—1111
C— 212	I— 2	O— 12	U— 221	&—2222
D— 111	J—2211	P—2121	V—2111	tion—2221
E— 21	K—1212	Q—2122	W—2212	ing—1121
F—1112	L— 112	R— 122	X—1211	ed—1222

GENERAL MORELL'S LOOKOUT TOWARD THE CONFEDERATE LINES—1861

When General McClellan was rapidly organizing his army from the mass of troops, distinguished only by regimental numerals, into brigades, divisions, and corps, in the fall and winter of 1861, General George W. Morell was placed in command of the first brigade of the Army of the Potomac and stationed at the extreme front of Minor's Hill, Virginia, just south of Washington. The city was distraught with apprehension, and the lookout, or tower, in the foreground was erected especially for the purpose of observations toward the Confederate lines, then in the direction of Manassas. At the particular moment when this picture was taken, the lookout has undoubtedly shouted some observation to General Morell, who stands with his finger pointing toward the south, the Confederate position. That the army has not yet advanced is made evident by the fact that a lady is present, dressed in the fashion of the day.

NUMERALS

1—12221 — Wait a moment.
2—21112 — Are you ready?
3—11211 — I am ready.
4—11121 — Use short pole and small flag.
5—11112 — Use long pole and large flag.
6—21111 — Work faster.
7—22111 — Did you understand?
8—22221 — Use white flag.
9—22122 — Use black flag.
0—11111 — Use red flag.

CODE SIGNALS

3 = " End of word." 33 = " End of sentence." 333 = " End of message." 121212 = " Error." 11, 11, 11, 3 = " Message received (or understood)." 11, 11, 11, 3 = " Cease signaling." Constant and unbroken waving = " Attention, look for signals."

To hasten work there were many abbreviations, such as: A = " After "; B = " Before "; C = " Can "; Imy = " Immediately "; N = " Not "; Q = " Quiet "; R = " Are "; U = " You " and Y = " Why."

When using Coston signals there were more than twenty combinations of colored lights which permitted an extended system of prearranged signals. White rockets (or bombs) = one; red = two, and green = three. White flags with a square red center were most frequently employed for signaling purposes, though when snow was on the ground a black flag was used, and with varying backgrounds the red flag with a white center could be seen at greater distances than the white.

To secure secrecy all important messages were enciphered by means of a cipher disk. Two concentric disks, of unequal size and revolving on a central pivot, were divided along their outer edges into thirty equal compartments. The inner and smaller disk contained in its compartments letters, terminations, and word-pauses, while the outer, larger disk contained

[316]

AT YORKTOWN

Skilled Union signal parties were available for the Peninsular campaign of 1862, where they rendered invaluable service to McClellan. Work strictly for the army was supplemented by placing signal officers with the navy, and thus ensuring that coöperation so vitally essential to success. The victory of Franklin's command at West Point, after the evacuation of Yorktown, was largely due to the efficiency of the Signal Corps. Vigorously attacked by an unknown force, Franklin ordered his signal officer to call up the fleet just appearing down the river. A keen-sighted signal officer was alert on the gunboat, and in a few minutes Franklin's request that the woods be shelled was thoroughly carried out. This photograph shows the location of Union Battery No. 1 on the left, in the peachorchard, at Yorktown, and the York River lies at hand, to the right of the house.

A LOOKOUT ON THE ROOF OF FARENHOLT'S HOUSE, YORKTOWN

SIGNAL CORPS HEADQUARTERS IN AUGUST, 1862

ARMY AND NAVY

These quarters were established near Harrison's Landing, Virginia, in July, 1862, after the "Seven Days" battles during McClellan's retreat. Colonel (then Lieutenant) Benjamin F. Fisher, of the Signal Corps, then in command, opened a local station on the famous Berkely mansion. The Signal Corps had proved indispensable to the success of McClellan in changing his base from York River to James River. When the vigorous Confederate attack at Malvern Hill threatened the rout of the army, McClellan was aboard the gunboat *Galena*, whose army signal officer informed him of the situation through messages flagged from the shore. Through information from the signal officers directing the fire of the fleet, he was aided in repelling the advances of the Confederates. The messages ran like this: "Fire one mile to the right. Fire low into the woods near the shore."

groups of signal numbers to be sent. Sometimes this arrangement was changed and letters were on the outer disks and the numbers on the inner. By the use of prearranged keys, and through their frequent interchange, the secrecy of messages thus enciphered was almost absolutely ensured.

In every important campaign and on every bloody ground, the red flags of the Signal Corps flaunted defiantly at the forefront, speeding stirring orders of advance, conveying warnings of impending danger, and sending sullen suggestions of defeat. They were seen on the advanced lines of Yorktown, Petersburg, and Richmond, in the saps and trenches at Charleston, Vicksburg, and Port Hudson, at the fierce battles of Chickamauga and Chancellorsville, before the fort-crowned crest of Fredericksburg, amid the frightful carnage of Antietam, on Kenesaw Mountain deciding the fate of Allatoona, in Sherman's march to the sea, and with Grant's victorious army at Appomattox and Richmond. They spoke silently to Du Pont along the dunes and sounds of the Carolinas, sent word to Porter clearing the central Mississippi River, and aided Farragut when forcing the passage of Mobile Bay.

Did a non-combatant corps ever before suffer such disproportionate casualties—killed, wounded, and captured? Sense of duty, necessity of exposure to fire, and importance of mission were conditions incompatible with personal safety—and the Signal Corps paid the price. While many found their fate in Confederate prisons, the extreme danger of signal work, when conjoined with stubborn adherence to outposts of duty, is forcefully evidenced by the fact that the killed of the Signal Corps were one hundred and fifty per cent. of the wounded, as against the usual ratio of twenty per cent.

The Confederates were first in the field, for Beauregard's report acknowledges the aid rendered his army at Bull Run by Captain E. P. Alexander, a former pupil of Myer. McDowell was then without signalmen, and so could neither communicate regularly with Washington nor receive word of the

OCTOBER, 1862—WHERE THE CONFEDERATE INVASION OF MARYLAND WAS DISCOVERED

The signal officer is on outlook duty near the Point of Rocks station, in Maryland. This station was opened and operated by First-Lieutenant John H. Fralick for purposes of observation. It completely dominated Pleasant Valley. On the twelfth of the month Fra'ick had detected and reported General J. E. B. Stuart's raiding cavalry crossing the Potomac on their way back from Maryland and Pennsylvania. The Confederate cavalry leader had crossed the Potomac at Williamsport on the 10th of October, ridden completely around the rear of the Army of the Potomac, and eluded the vigorous pursuit of General Pleasonton and his Union cavalry. Within twenty hours he had marched sixty-five miles and kept up his artillery. Lieutenant-Colonel Edwin R. Biles, with the Ninety-ninth Pennsylvania, opposed Stuart's crossing at Monocacy Ford, but was unable to detain him. This was one of the combination of events which finally cost McClellan the command of the Army of the Potomac. Lee's invasion of Maryland in 1862 would have been a complete surprise, except for the watchful vigilance of Lieutenant Miner of the Signal Corps, who occupied Sugar Loaf, the highest point in Maryland. From this lofty station were visible the more important fords of the Potomac, with their approaches on both sides of the river. Miner detected the Confederate advance-guard, then the wagon-train movements, and finally the objective points of their march. Although unprotected, he held his station to the last and was finally captured by the Southern troops.

SIGNAL OFFICER PIERCE

RECEIVING A MESSAGE FROM

GENERAL McCLELLAN

AT THE ELK MOUNTAIN STATION

AFTER THE BATTLE OF ANTIETAM

Elk Mountain is in the South Mountain Range of the Blue Ridge; its summit here shown commanded a view of almost the entire Antietam battlefield during September 17th, 1862, the bloodiest single day of the Civil War. The Elk Mountain Signal Station was operated after the battle by Lieutenants Pierce and Jerome. As the photograph above was taken, the former officer was receiving a dispatch from General McClellan, presumably requesting further information in regard to some reported movement of General Lee. The Union loss in this terrific battle was twelve thousand five hundred, and the Confederate loss over ten thousand. The correspondent of a Richmond paper, describing his part as an eye-witness of the engagement, wrote on the succeeding day: "Their signal stations on the Blue Ridge commanded a view of every movement. We could not make a maneuver in front or rear that was not instantly revealed by keen lookouts; and as soon as the intelligence could be communicated to their batteries below, shot and shell were launched against the moving columns. It was this information, conveyed by the little flags upon the mountain-top, that no doubt enabled the enemy to concentrate his force against our weakest points and counteract the effect of whatever similar movements may have been attempted by us." Captain Joseph Gloskoski, who had received commendation for bravery at Gaines' Mill, sent many important messages to Burnside as a result of the telescopic reconnoitering of Lieutenants N. H. Camp and C. Herzog. It was the message received from this station, "Look well to your left," which enabled Burnside to guard his left against A. P. Hill's advance from Harper's Ferry.

vitally important despatch from Patterson at Harper's Ferry telling of Johnston's departure to reenforce Beauregard at Manassas, which should have obviated the battle. Major Myer was quick, however, to establish a signal training-school at Red Hill, Georgetown, District of Columbia.

In view of modern knowledge and practice, it seems almost incredible to note that the Secretary of War disapproved, in 1861, the recommendation made by Major Myer, signal officer of the army, for an appropriation for field-telegraph lines. While efforts to obtain, operate, and improve such lines were measurably successful on the part of the army, they were strenuously opposed by the civilian telegraph corporations so potent at the War Department.

Active protests proved unavailing and injurious. Colonel Myer's circular, in 1863, describing the systematic attempts of the civilian organization to deprive the Signal Corps of such lines " as an interference with a part of the Signal Corps' legitimate duties," caused him to be placed on waiting orders, while all field-trains were ordered to be turned over to the civilian force. It may be added that both organizations in the field cooperated with a degree of harmony and good-fellowship that was often lacking in Washington.

Skilled parties were thus available for the Peninsula campaign of 1862, where McClellan utilized them, strictly army work being supplemented by placing signal officers with the navy, and thus ensuring that cooperation vitally essential to success. Not only was military information efficiently collected and distributed, but at critical junctures McClellan was able to control the fire-direction of both the field-artillery of the army and the heavy guns of the navy.

At Yorktown, coigns of vantage were occupied in high trees and on lofty towers, whence messages were sent to and fro, especially those containing information of the position and movements of the foe, which were discerned by high-power telescopes—an important duty not always known or

SIGNAL CORPS RECONNOITERING AT FREDERICKSBURG, VIRGINIA

From December 11 to 13, 1862, four signal stations were engaged in observing and reporting the operations of the Confederates on the south side of the Rappahannock River at Fredericksburg. The flag station at headquarters kept General Burnside in constant touch with the Federal attacking force on the right, under Couch and Hooker, through their signalmen in the courthouse steeple. This is prominent in the center of the lower photograph. One station near a field hospital came under a fire that killed about twenty men and wounded many others nearby. Finally the surgeons requested a suspension of flagging, that the lives of the wounded might be spared.

FREDERICKSBURG—THE COURTHOUSE STEEPLE IN THE CENTER CONTAINED FEDERAL SIGNALMEN

appreciated. Often their work drew the Confederate artillery and sharpshooters' fire, of unpleasant accuracy. The saving of Franklin's command at West Point, after the evacuation of Yorktown, was in large part due to the efficiency of the Signal Corps.

Valuable as was the work before Richmond, under fire, in reconnoitering and in cooperation with the military telegraph service, it proved to be indispensable to the success of McClellan in changing his base from York River to James River —its importance culminating at Malvern Hill. It will be recalled that the Seven Days' Battles ended with the bloody struggle on the banks of the James, where the use of the Signal Corps enabled McClellan to transform impending defeat into successful defense. When the vigorous Confederate attack at Malvern Hill threatened the flank of the army, McClellan was aboard the United States steamship *Galena,* whose army signal officer informed him of the situation through messages flagged from the army. McClellan was thus enabled not only to give general orders to the army then in action, but also to direct the fire of the fleet, which had moved up the James for cooperation, most efficiently.

Lee's invasion of Maryland in 1862 would have been a complete surprise, except for the watchful vigilance of an officer of the Signal Corps, Lieutenant Miner, who occupied Sugar Loaf, the highest point in Maryland. From this lofty station were visible the more important fords of the Potomac, with their approaches on both sides of the river. Miner detected the Confederate advance guard, the train movements, and noted the objective points of their march. Notifying Washington of the invasion, although unprotected he held his station to the last and was finally captured by the Southern troops. The reoccupancy of Sugar Loaf a week later enabled McClellan to establish a network of stations, whose activities contributed to the victory of South Mountain.

As Elk Mountain dominated the valley of the Antietam,

[324]

After the surrender of Vicksburg, July 4, 1863, the Signal Corps of Grant's army was under the command of Lieutenant John W. Deford, a recently exchanged prisoner of war. Its location was on the southern continuation of Cherry Street near the A. & V. railway. From the balcony of the house are hanging two red flags with square white centers, indicating the headquarters of the Signal Corps. Many times before the fall were orders flashed by night by means of waving torches to commands widely separated; and in the daytime the signal-men standing drew on themselves the attention of the Confederate sharpshooters. A message begun by one signal-man was often finished by another who picked up the flag his fallen companion had dropped. The tower at Jacksonville, Florida, over a hundred feet high, kept in communication with the signal tower at Yellow Bluff, at the mouth of the St. John's River. Note the two men with the Signal Corps flag on its summit. Just below them is an enclosure to which they could retire when the efforts of the Confederate sharpshooters became too threatening.

HEADQUARTERS OF THE UNION SIGNAL
CORPS AT VICKSBURG
1864

SIGNAL STATIONS

FROM

THE MISSISSIPPI

TO

THE ATLANTIC

TOWER AT JACKSONVILLE

EVIDENCE OF THE

SIGNAL—MAN'S ACTIVITY

THROUGHOUT

THE

THEATER OF WAR

LOOKOUT MOUNTAIN—THE ANTICIPATED SIGNALS

After Grant arrived and occupied Chattanooga, Bragg retired up the Cumberland Mountains and took up two strong positions—one upon the top of Lookout Mountain, overlooking Chattanooga from the south, and the other on Missionary Ridge, a somewhat lower elevation to the east. His object was to hold the passes of the mountain against any advance upon his base at Dalton, Georgia, at which point supplies arrived from Atlanta. Grant, about the middle of November, 1863, advanced with 80,000 men for the purpose of dislodging the Confederates from these positions. At the very summit of Lookout Mountain, "The Hawk's Nest" of the Cherokees, the Confederates had established a signal station from which every movement of the Federal Army was flashed to the Confederate headquarters on Missionary Ridge. The Federals had possessed themselves of this signal code, and could read all of Bragg's messages. Hence an attempt to surprise Hooker when he advanced, on November 23d, failed.

it was occupied only to find that the dense woods on its summit cut off all view. However, energetic action soon cleared a vista, known to the soldiers as "McClellan's Gap," through which systematic telescopic search revealed all extended movements of the foe. The busy ax furnished material for a rude log structure, from the summit of which messages of great importance, on which were based the general disposition of the Federal troops, were sent.

At Fredericksburg flag-work and telescopic reconnoitering were supplemented by the establishment of a field-telegraph line connecting army headquarters with Franklin's Grand Division on the extreme left. The flag station at headquarters kept Burnside in constant touch with the Federal attacking force on the right, under Couch and Hooker, through their signalmen in the court-house steeple. One station near a field-hospital was under a fire, which killed about twenty men and wounded many others near by, until the surgeons asked suspension of flagging to save the lives of the wounded.

A most important part of the Signal Corps' duty was the interception and translation of messages interchanged between the Confederate signalmen. Perhaps the most notable of such achievements occurred in the Shenandoah valley, in 1864. On Massanutten, or Three Top Mountain, was a signal station which kept Early in touch with Lee's army to the southeastward, near Richmond, and which the Federals had under close watch. Late in the evening of October 15th, a keen-eyed lieutenant noted that "Three Top" was swinging his signal torch with an unwonted persistency that betokened a message of urgency. The time seemed interminable to the Union officer until the message began, which he read with suppressed excitement as follows: "To Lieutenant-General Early. Be ready to move as soon as my forces join you, and we will crush Sheridan. Longstreet, Lieutenant-General."

Sheridan was then at Front Royal, en route to Washington. The message was handed to General Wright, in

THE SIGNAL CORPS
AT GETTYSBURG

In the battle of Gettysburg the Confederates established their chief signal station in the cupola of the Lutheran Seminary, which commanded an extended field of operations. From here came much of Lee's information about the battle which surged and thundered to and fro until the gigantic wave of Pickett's charge was dashed to pieces against the immovable rock of Meade's defense on the third culminating day. The

HEADQUARTERS, CONFEDERATE SIGNAL CORPS
AT GETTYSBURG, PENNSYLVANIA

Union Signal Corps was equally active in gathering information and transmitting orders. Altogether, for perhaps the first time in military history, the generals-in-chief of two large armies were kept in constant communication during active operations with their corps and division commanders. It was the Union Signal Corps with its deceptive flags that enabled General Warren to hold alone the strangely neglected eminence of Little Round Top, the key to the Federal left, until troops could be sent to occupy it.

SIGNAL CORPS OFFICERS, HEADQUARTERS ARMY OF THE POTOMAC, OCTOBER, 1863

Among these officers is General (then Captain) Charles E. Davis (leaning on peach-tree), and Captain P. A. Taylor, Captain Fountain Wilson, Lieutenant A. B. Capron (afterwards Member of Congress), and Lieutenant G. J. Clarke, all members of the Signal Corps.

temporary command, at once, and was forwarded by him to Sheridan at midnight. The importance of this information is apparent, yet Early took the Union army completely by surprise three days later, at daybreak of October 19th, although the tide of morning defeat was turned to evening victory under the inspiration of Sheridan's matchless personality.

In the battles at Gettysburg the Confederates established their chief signal station in the cupola of the Lutheran seminary, which commanded an extended field of operations. The Union Signal Corps was extremely active in gathering information and transmitting orders, and for perhaps the first time in military history the commanding general of a large army was kept in communication during active operations with his corps and division commanders.

The most important Union signal station, on the second day of this titanic struggle, was at Little Round Top on the Federal left flank, which commanded a view of the country occupied by the right of Lee's army. Heavy was the price paid for flag-work at this point, where the men were exposed to the fierce shrapnel of artillery and the deadly bullet of Confederate sharpshooters in Devil's Den. On or beside this signal station, on a bare rock about ten feet square, seven men were killed or seriously wounded. With rash gallantry, Captain James A. Hall held his ground, and on July 2d, at the most critical phase of the struggle signaled to Meade's headquarters, "A heavy column of enemy's infantry, about ten thousand, is moving from opposite our extreme left toward our right."

General Warren had hastened by Meade's order to Little Round Top to investigate. He says: "There were no troops on it [Little Round Top] and it was used as a signal station. I saw that this was the key of the whole position, and that our troops in the woods in front of it could not see the ground in front of them, so that the enemy could come upon them unawares." A shot was fired into these woods by Warren's

SIGNALING ORDERS FROM GENERAL MEADE'S HEADQUARTERS, JUST BEFORE THE WILDERNESS

In April, 1864, General Meade's headquarters lay north of the Rapidan. The Signal Corps was kept busy transmitting the orders preliminary to the Wilderness campaign, which was to begin May 5th. The headquarters are below the brow of the hill. A most important part of the Signal Corps' duty was the interception and translation of messages interchanged between the Confederate signal-men. A veteran of Sheridan's army tells of his impressions as follows: "On the evening of the 18th of October, 1864, the soldiers of Sheridan's army lay in their lines at Cedar Creek. Our attention was suddenly directed to the ridge of Massanutten, or Three Top Mountain, the slope of which covered the left wing of the army—the Eighth Corps. A lively series of signals was being flashed out from the peak, and it was evident that messages were being sent both eastward and westward of the ridge. I can recall now the feeling with which we looked up at those flashes going over our heads, knowing that they must be Confederate messages. It was only later that we learned that a keen-eyed Union officer had been able to read the message: 'To Lieutenant-General Early. Be ready to move as soon as my forces join you, and we will crush Sheridan. Longstreet, Lieutenant-General.' The sturdiness of Sheridan's veterans and the fresh spirit put into the hearts of the men by the return of Sheridan himself from 'Winchester, twenty miles away,' a ride rendered immortal by Read's poem, proved too much at last for the pluck and persistency of Early's worn-out troops."

orders. He continues: "This motion revealed to me the enemy's line of battle, already formed and far outflanking our troops. . . . The discovery was intensely thrilling and almost appalling." After narrating how he asked Meade for troops, Warren continues, "While I was still alone with the signal officer, the musket balls began to fly around us, and he was about to fold up his flags and withdraw, but remained, at my request, and kept them waving in defiance." This action saved the day for the Federals, as Warren declares.

The system around Vicksburg was such as to keep Grant fully informed of the efforts of the Confederates to disturb his communications in the rear, and also ensured the fullest coöperation between the Mississippi flotilla and his army. Judicious in praise, Grant's commendation of his signal officer speaks best for the service. Messages were constantly exchanged with the fleet, the final one of the siege being flagged as follows on the morning of July 4th: " 4.30 A. M. 4: 1863. Admiral Porter: The enemy has accepted in the main my terms of capitulation and will surrender the city, works and garrison at 10 A. M. . . . U. S. Grant, Major-General, Commanding."

The fleets of Farragut and Porter, while keeping the Mississippi open, carried signal officers to enable them to communicate with the army, their high masts and lofty trees enabling signals to be exchanged great distances. Doubtless the loftiest perch thus used during the war was that on the United States steamship *Richmond,* one of Farragut's fleet at Port Hudson. The *Richmond* was completely disabled by the central Confederate batteries while attempting to run past Port Hudson, her signal officer, working, meanwhile, in the maintop. As the running of the batteries was thus found to be too dangerous, the vessel dropped back and the signal officer suggested that he occupy the very tip of the highest mast for his working perch, which was fitted up, one hundred and sixty feet above the water. From this great height it was barely possible to signal over the highland occupied by the foe, and thus maintain

"CROW'S NEST"—SIGNAL TOWER TO THE RIGHT
OF BERMUDA HUNDRED

AT HEADQUARTERS OF 14TH N. Y. HEAVY
ARTILLERY NEAR PETERSBURG

THE PEEBLE'S FARM SIGNAL TOWER
NEAR PETERSBURG

THE SIGNAL TOWER
NEAR POINT OF ROCKS

uninterrupted communication and essential cooperation between the fleets of the central and lower Mississippi.

The most dramatic use of the Signal Corps was connected with the successful defense of Allatoona, Sherman's reserve depot in which were stored three millions of rations, practically undefended, as it was a distance in the rear of the army. Realizing the utmost importance of the railroad north of Marietta and of the supplies to Sherman, Hood threw Stewart's corps in the rear of the Union army, and French's division of about sixty-five hundred men was detached to capture Allatoona. With the Confederates intervening and telegraph lines destroyed, all would have been lost but for the Signal Corps station on Kenesaw Mountain. Corse was at Rome, thirty-six miles beyond Allatoona. From Vining's Station, the message was flagged over the heads of the foe to Allatoona by way of Kenesaw, and thence telegraphed to Corse, as follows: " General Corse: Sherman directs that you move forward and join Smith's division with your entire command, using cars if to be had, and burn provisions rather than lose them. General Vandever." At the same time a message was sent to Allatoona: " Sherman is moving with force. Hold out." And again: " Hold on. General Sherman says he is working hard for you."

Sherman was at Kenesaw all day, October 5th, having learned of the arrival of Corse that morning, and anxiously watched the progress of the battle. That afternoon came a despatch from Allatoona, sent during the engagement: " We are all right so far. General Corse is wounded." Next morning Dayton, Sherman's assistant adjutant-general, asked how Corse was and he answered, " I am short a cheekbone and one ear, but am able to whip all h—l yet." That the fight was desperate is shown by Corse's losses, seven hundred and five killed and wounded, and two hundred captured, out of an effective force of about fifteen hundred.

An unusual application of signal stores was made at the

COLONEL BENJAMIN F. FISHER AND HIS ASSISTANTS AT SIGNAL CORPS HEAD-
QUARTERS, WASHINGTON

Although authorized as a separate corps by the Act of Congress approved March 3, 1863, the Signal Corps did not complete its organization until August, 1864. More than two thousand signal-men served at the front, of whom only nine were commissioned in the new corps, while seventeen officers were appointed from civil life. Colonel A. J. Myer, the inventor and organizer of the service, had his commission vacated in July, 1864. On December 26th of that year Colonel Benjamin F. Fisher was placed in command of the Signal Corps, but his appointment was never confirmed by the Senate. Note the curious wording of the sign by the door: "Office of the Signal Officer of the Army," as if there were but one. That a corps so harassed should constantly distinguish itself in the field is one of the many marvels of American patriotism.

SIGNALING FROM FORT McALLISTER, GEORGIA—THE END OF THE MARCH
TO THE SEA

General Sherman's flag message with Hazen's soldierly answer upon their arrival at Savannah, December 13, 1864, has become historic. Sherman's message was an order for Hazen's Division of the Fifteenth Army Corps to make an assault upon the fort. Hazen's terse answer was: "I am ready and will assault at once." The fort was carried at the first rush. A flag station was immediately established on the parapet. It wigwagged to Dahlgren's expectant fleet the news that Sherman had completed the famous march to the sea with his army in excellent condition. Only a week later General Hardee evacuated Savannah with his troops.

HOW SHERMAN WAS WELCOMED UPON HIS ARRIVAL AT THE SEA

This photograph shows a party of Admiral John A. Dahlgren's signal-men on board ship receiving a message from the Georgia shore. The two flagmen are standing at attention, ready to send Dahlgren's answering message, and the officer with the telescope is prepared to read the signals from the shore. Thus Sherman's message from the parapet of Fort McAllister was read. Commander C. P. R. Rodgers and Admiral Dupont had been prompt to recognize the value of the Army Signal Corps system and to introduce it in the navy. This concert between the North's gigantic armies on shore and her powerful South Atlantic fleet was bound to crush the Confederacy sooner or later. Without food for her decimated armies she could not last.

siege of Knoxville, when Longstreet attacked at dawn. Sending up a signal by Roman candles to indicate the point of attack, the signal officer followed it by discharging the candles toward the advancing Confederates, which not only disconcerted some of them, but made visible the approaching lines and made possible more accurate fire on the part of the Union artillery.

While at Missionary Ridge, the following message was flagged at a critical point: "Sherman: Thomas has carried the hill and lot in his immediate front. Now is your time to attack with vigor. Do so. Grant." Other signal work of value intervened between Missionary Ridge and Allatoona, so that the Signal Corps was placed even more to the front in the Atlanta campaign and during the march to the sea.

The Confederates had changed their cipher key, but Sherman's indefatigable officers ascertained the new key from intercepted messages, thus giving the general much important information.

Several stations for observation were established in high trees, some more than a hundred feet from the ground, from which were noted the movements of the various commands, of wagon trains, and railroad cars. Hood's gallant sortie from Atlanta was detected at its very start, and despite the severity of the fight, during which one flagman was killed, messages were sent throughout the battle—even over the heads of the foe.

Of importance, though devoid of danger, among the final messages on arrival at Savannah was one ordering, by flag, the immediate assault on Fort McAllister by Hazen, with the soldierly answer, "I am ready and will assault at once," and the other announcing to the expectant fleet that Sherman had completed the famous march to the sea with his army in excellent condition.

In the approaches and siege of Petersburg, the work of the Signal Corps was almost entirely telescopic reconnoitering.

SIGNALING

BY

THE SEA

THE WHITE FLAG

WITH

THE RED CENTER

This station was established by Lieutenant E. J. Keenan on the roof of the mansion of a planter at the extreme northern point of Hilton Head Island, Port Royal Bay. Through this station were exchanged many messages between General W. T. Sherman and Admiral S. F. Dupont. Sherman had been forced by Savannah's stubborn resistance to prepare for siege operations against the city, and perfect coöperation between the army and navy became imperative. The signal station adjoining the one portrayed above was erected on the house formerly owned by John C. Calhoun, lying within sight of Fort Pulaski, at the mouth of the Savannah River. Late in December, General Hardee and his Confederate troops evacuated the city. Sherman was enabled to make President Lincoln a present of one of the last of the Southern strongholds.

FROM SHORE TO SHIP—HILTON HEAD SIGNAL STATION

While an occasional high tree was used for a perch, yet the country was so heavily timbered that signal towers were necessary. There were nearly a dozen lines of communication and a hundred separate stations. The most notable towers were Cobb's Hill, one hundred and twenty-five feet; Crow's Nest, one hundred and twenty-six feet, and Peebles Farm, one hundred and forty-five feet, which commanded views of Petersburg, its approaches, railways, the camps and fortifications. Cobb's Hill, on the Appomattox, was particularly irritating and caused the construction of an advance Confederate earthwork a mile distant, from which fully two hundred and fifty shot and shell were fired against the tower in a single day—with slight damage, however. Similar futile efforts were made to destroy Crow's Nest.

At General Meade's headquarters a signal party had a unique experience—fortunately not fatal though thrilling in the extreme. A signal platform was built in a tree where, from a height of seventy-five feet the Confederate right flank position could be seen far to the rear. Whenever important movements were in progress this station naturally drew a heavy fire, to prevent signal work. As the men were charged to hold fast at all hazards, descending only after two successive shots at them, they became accustomed in time to sharpshooting, but the shriek of shell was more nerve-racking. On one occasion several shots whistled harmlessly by, and then came a violent shock which nearly dislodged platform, men, and instruments. A solid shot, partly spent, striking fairly, had buried itself in the tree half-way between the platform and the ground.

When Petersburg fell, field flag-work began again, and the first Union messages from Richmond were sent from the roof of the Confederate Capitol. In the field the final order of importance flagged by the corps was as follows: " Farmville, April 7, 1865. General Meade: Order Fifth Corps to follow the Twenty-fourth at 6 A. M. up the Lynchburg road.

STRIKING THE SIGNAL CORPS FLAG FOR THE LAST TIME—AUGUST, 1865

THE SIGNAL CAMP OF INSTRUCTION ON RED HILL

In this camp all signal parties were trained before taking the field. In the center is the signal tower, from which messages could be sent to all stations in Virginia not more than twenty miles distant. The farthest camps were reached from the Crow's Nest; nearer ones from the base of the tower. Here General A. J. Myer, then a civilian, appeared after the muster out of his old comrades to witness the dissolution of the corps which owed its inception, organization, and efficiency to his inventive genius and administrative ability.

[I—22]

The Second and Sixth to follow the enemy north of the river. U. S. Grant, Lieutenant-General."

It must not be inferred that all distinguished signal work was confined to the Union army, for the Confederates were first in the field, and ever after held their own. Captain (afterward General) E. P. Alexander, a former pupil in the Union army under Myer, was the first signal officer of an army, that of Northern Virginia. He greatly distinguished himself in the first battle of Bull Run, where he worked for several hours under fire, communicating to his commanding general the movements of opposing forces, for which he was highly commended. At a critical moment he detected a hostile advance, and saved a Confederate division from being flanked by a signal message, "Look out for your left. Your position is turned."

Alexander's assignment as chief of artillery left the corps under Captain (later Colonel) William Norris. Attached to the Adjutant-General's Department, under the act of April 19, 1862, the corps consisted of one major, ten each of captains, first and second lieutenants, and twenty sergeants, the field-force being supplemented by details from the line of the army. Signaling, telegraphy, and secret-service work were all done by the corps, which proved to be a potent factor in the efficient operations of the various armies.

It was at Island No. 10; it was active with Early in the Valley; it was with Kirby Smith in the Trans-Mississippi, and aided Sidney Johnston at Shiloh. It kept pace with wondrous "Stonewall" Jackson in the Valley, withdrew defiantly with Johnston toward Atlanta, and followed impetuous Hood in the Nashville campaign. It served ably in the trenches of beleaguered Vicksburg, and clung fast to the dismantled battlements of Fort Sumter. Jackson clamored for it until Lee gave a corps to him, Jackson saying, "The enemy's signals give him a great advantage over me."

TELEGRAPHING
FOR THE ARMIES

"NO ORDERS EVER HAD TO BE GIVEN TO ESTABLISH
THE TELEGRAPH." THUS WROTE GENERAL GRANT
IN HIS MEMOIRS. "THE MOMENT TROOPS WERE
IN POSITION TO GO INTO CAMP, THE MEN WOULD
PUT UP THEIR WIRES." GRANT PAYS A GLOWING
TRIBUTE TO "THE ORGANIZATION AND DISCIPLINE
OF THIS BODY OF BRAVE AND INTELLIGENT MEN."

THE MILITARY-TELEGRAPH SERVICE

By A. W. Greely
Major-General, United States Army

[The Editors express their grateful acknowledgment to David Homer Bates, of the United States Military-Telegraph Corps, manager of the War Department Telegraph Office and cipher-operator, 1861–1866, and author of "Lincoln in the Telegraph Office," etc., for valued personal assistance in the preparation of the photographic descriptions, and for many of the incidents described in the following pages, which are recorded in fuller detail in his book.]

THE exigencies and experiences of the Civil War demonstrated, among other theorems, the vast utility and indispensable importance of the electric telegraph, both as an administrative agent and as a tactical factor in military operations. In addition to the utilization of existing commercial systems, there were built and operated more than fifteen thousand miles of lines for military purposes only.

Serving under the anomalous status of quartermaster's employees, often under conditions of personal danger, and with no definite official standing, the operators of the military-telegraph service performed work of most vital import to the army in particular and to the country in general. They fully merited the gratitude of the Nation for their efficiency, fidelity, and patriotism, yet their services have never been practically recognized by the Government or appreciated by the people.

For instance, during the war there occurred in the line of duty more than three hundred casualties among the operators —from disease, death in battle, wounds, or capture. Scores of these unfortunate victims left families dependent upon charity, as the United States neither extended aid to their destitute families nor admitted needy survivors to a pensionable status.

AT THE TELEGRAPHERS' TENT, YORKTOWN— MAY, 1862

These operators with their friends at dinner look quite contented, with their coffee in tin cups, their hard-tack, and the bountiful appearing kettle at their feet. Yet their lot, as McClellan's army advanced toward Richmond and later, was to be far from enviable. "The telegraph service," writes General A. W. Greely, "had neither definite personnel nor corps organization. It was simply a civilian bureau attached to the quartermaster's department, in which a few of its favored members received commissions. The men who performed the dangerous work in the field were mere employees—mostly underpaid and often treated with scant consideration. During the war there occurred in the line of duty more than three hundred casualties among the operators—by disease, killed in battle, wounded, or made prisoners. Scores of these unfortunate victims left families dependent on charity, for the Government of the United States neither extended aid to their destitute families nor admitted needy survivors to a pensionable status."

The Military Telegraph ❖ ❖ ❖ ❖ ❖

The telegraph service had neither definite personnel nor corps organization. It was simply a civilian bureau attached to the Quartermaster's Department, in which a few of its favored members received commissions. The men who performed the dangerous work in the field were mere employees—mostly underpaid, and often treated with scant consideration. The inherent defects of such a nondescript organization made it impossible for it to adjust and adapt itself to the varying demands and imperative needs of great and independent armies such as were employed in the Civil War.

Moreover, the chief, Colonel Anson Stager, was stationed in Cleveland, Ohio, while an active subordinate, Major Thomas T. Eckert, was associated with the great war secretary, who held the service in his iron grasp. Not only were its commissioned officers free from other authority than that of the Secretary of War, but operators, engaged in active campaigning thousands of miles from Washington, were independent of the generals under whom they were serving. As will appear later, operators suffered from the natural impatience of military commanders, who resented the abnormal relations which inevitably led to distrust and contention. While such irritations and distrusts were rarely justified, none the less they proved detrimental to the best interests of the United States.

On the one hand, the operators were ordered to report to, and obey only, the corporation representatives who dominated the War Department, while on the other their lot was cast with military associates, who frequently regarded them with a certain contempt or hostility. Thus, the life of the field-operator was hard, indeed, and it is to the lasting credit of the men, as a class, that their intelligence and patriotism were equal to the situation and won final confidence.

Emergent conditions in 1861 caused the seizure of the commercial systems around Washington, and Assistant Secretary of War Thomas A. Scott was made general manager of all such lines. He secured the cooperation of E. S. Sanford,

TELEGRAPHERS AFTER GETTYSBURG

The efficient-looking man leaning against the tent-pole in the rear is A. H. Caldwell, chief cipher operator for McClellan, Burnside, Hooker, Meade, and Grant.   To him, just at the time this photograph was made, Lincoln addressed the famous despatch sent to Simon Cameron at Gettysburg. After being deciphered by Caldwell and delivered, the message ran: "I would give much to be relieved of the impression that Meade, Couch, Smith, and all, since the battle of Gettysburg, have striven only to get the enemy over the river without another fight.   Please tell me if you know who was the one corps commander who was for fighting, in the council of war on Sunday night."   It was customary for cipher messages to be addressed to and signed by the cipher operators.   All of the group are mere boys, yet they coolly kept open their telegraph lines, sending important orders, while under fire and amid the utmost confusion.

of the American Telegraph Company, who imposed much-needed restrictions as to cipher messages, information, and so forth on all operators. The scope of the work was much increased by an act of Congress, in 1862, authorizing the seizure of any or all lines, in connection with which Sanford was appointed censor.

Through Andrew Carnegie was obtained the force which opened the War Department Telegraph Office, which speedily attained national importance by its remarkable work, and with which the memory of Abraham Lincoln must be inseparably associated. It was fortunate for the success of the telegraphic policy of the Government that it was entrusted to men of such administrative ability as Colonel Anson Stager, E. S. Sanford, and Major Thomas T. Eckert. The selection of operators for the War Office was surprisingly fortunate, including, as it did, three cipher-operators—D. H. Bates, A. B. Chandler, and C. A. Tinker—of high character, rare skill, and unusual discretion.

The military exigencies brought Sanford as censor and Eckert as assistant general manager, who otherwise performed their difficult duties with great efficiency; it must be added that at times they were inclined to display a striking disregard of proprieties and most unwarrantedly to enlarge the scope of their already extended authority. An interesting instance of the conflict of telegraphic and military authority was shown when Sanford mutilated McClellan's passionate despatch to Stanton, dated Savage's Station, June 29, 1862, in the midst of the Seven Days' Battles.*

Eckert also withheld from President Lincoln the despatch announcing the Federal defeat at Ball's Bluff. The suppression by Eckert of Grant's order for the removal of Thomas

---

* By cutting out of the message the last two sentences, reading: "If I save this army now, I tell you plainly that I owe no thanks to you or to any other person in Washington. You have done your best to sacrifice this army."

QUARTERS OF TELEGRAPHERS AND PHOTOGRAPHERS AT ARMY OF THE POTOMAC HEADQUARTERS,
BRANDY STATION, APRIL, 1864

It was probably lack of military status that caused these pioneer corps in science to bunk together here. The photographers were under the protection of the secret service, and the telegraphers performed a similar function in the field of "military information."

THE TELEGRAPHER'S BOMB–PROOF BEFORE SUMTER

It is a comfort to contemplate the solidity of the bomb-proof where dwelt this telegraph operator; he carried no insurance for his family such as a regular soldier can look forward to in the possibility of a pension. This photograph was taken in 1863, while General Quincy A. Gillmore was covering the marshes before Charleston with breaching batteries, in the attempt to silence the Confederate forts. These replied with vigor, however, and the telegrapher needed all the protection possible while he kept the general in touch with his forts.

finds support only in the splendid victory of that great soldier at Nashville, and that only under the maxim that the end justifies the means. Eckert's narrow escape from summary dismissal by Stanton shows that, equally with the President and the commanding general, the war secretary was sometimes treated disrespectfully by his own subordinates.

One phase of life in the telegraph-room of the War Department—it is surprising that the White House had no telegraph office during the war—was Lincoln's daily visit thereto, and the long hours spent by him in the cipher-room, whose quiet seclusion made it a favorite retreat both for rest and also for important work requiring undisturbed thought and undivided attention.

There Lincoln turned over with methodical exactness and anxious expectation the office-file of recent messages. There he awaited patiently the translation of ciphers which forecasted promising plans for coming campaigns, told tales of unexpected defeat, recited the story of victorious battles, conveyed impossible demands, or suggested inexpedient policies. Masking anxiety by quaint phrases, impassively accepting criticism, harmonizing conflicting conditions, he patiently pondered over situations—both political and military—swayed in his solutions only by considerations of public good. For in this room were held conferences of vital national interest, with cabinet officers, generals, congressmen, and others. But his greatest task done here was that which required many days, during which was written the original draft of the memorable proclamation of emancipation.

Especially important was the technical work of Bates, Chandler, and Tinker enciphering and deciphering important messages to and from the great contending armies, which was done by code. Stager devised the first cipher, which was so improved by the cipher-operators that it remained untranslatable by the Confederates to the end of the war. An example of the method in general use, given by Plum in his "History of

TELEGRAPH CONSTRUCTION CORPS—STRINGING WIRE IN THE FIELD

This corps was composed of about one hundred and fifty men, with an outfit of wagons, tents, pack-mules, and paraphernalia. During the first two years of the war the common wire was used; but when Grant set out in his Wilderness campaign, a flexible insulated wire was substituted. The large wire was wound on reels and placed in wagons, which drove along the route where the line was to be erected. The men followed, putting up the wire as rapidly as it was unreeled. So expert were the linemen that the work seldom became disarranged. The first lines were constructed around Washington and to Alexandria, Virginia, in May. On the Peninsula the next year, the telegraph followed the troops in all directions. During the Fredericksburg and Chancellorsville campaigns it proved an unfailing means of communication between the army and Washington. As it was intended only for temporary use, the poles were not required to be very substantial, and could usually be found in the wooded Virginia country near any proposed route. The immense labor required in such construction led to the adoption of insulated wire, which could be strung very quickly. A coil of the latter was placed on a mule's back and the animal led straight forward without halting. While the wire unreeled, two men followed and hung up the line on the fences and bushes, where it would not be run over. When the telegraph extended through a section unoccupied by Federal forces in strength, cavalry patrols watched it, frequently holding the inhabitants responsible for its safety.

the Military Telegraph," is Lincoln's despatch to ex-Secretary Cameron when with Meade south of Gettysburg. As will be seen, messages were addressed to and signed by the cipher-operators. The message written out for sending is as follows:

Washington, D. C.	July	15th	18	60	3	for
Sigh	man	Cammer	on	period	I	would
give	much	to be	relieved	of the	impression	that
Meade	comma	Couch	comma	Smith	and	all
comma	since	the	battle	of	get	ties
burg	comma	have	striven	only	to	get
the enemy	over	the river	without	another	fight	period
please	tell	me	if	you	know	who
was	the	one	corps	commander	who	was
for	fighting	comma	in the	council	of	war
on	Sunday	night	signature	A. Lincoln	Bless	him

In the message as sent the first word (blonde) indicated the number of columns and lines in which the message was to be arranged, and the route for reading. Arbitrary words indicated names and persons, and certain blind (or useless) words were added, which can be easily detected. The message was sent as follows:

"WASHINGTON, D. C., July 15, 1863.
" A. H. Caldwell, Cipher-operator, General Meade's Head-
quarters:
" Blonde bless of who no optic to get an impression 1 madison-square Brown cammer Toby ax the have turnip me Harry bitch rustle silk adrian counsel locust you another only of children serenade flea Knox county for wood that awl ties get hound who was war him suicide on for was please village large bat Bunyan give sigh incubus heavy Norris on trammeled cat knit striven without if Madrid quail upright martyr Stewart man much bear since ass skeleton tell the oppressing Tyler monkey.
" BATES."

Brilliant and conspicuous service was rendered by the cipher-operators of the War Department in translating Con-

ONE OF GRANT'S FIELD–TELEGRAPH STATIONS IN 1864

This photograph, taken at Wilcox Landing, near City Point, gives an excellent idea of the difficulties under which telegraphing was done at the front or on the march.   With a tent-fly for shelter and a hard-tack box for a table, the resourceful operator mounted his "relay," tested his wire, and brought the commanding general into direct communication with separated brigades or divisions.   The U. S. Military Telegraph Corps, through its Superintendent of Construction, Dennis Doren, kept Meade and both wings of his army in communication from the crossing of the Rapidan in May, 1864, till the siege of Petersburg.   Over this field-line Grant received daily reports from four separate armies, numbering a quarter of a million men, and replied with daily directions for their operations over an area of seven hundred and fifty thousand square miles.   Though every corps of Meade's army moved daily, Doren kept them in touch with headquarters. The field-line was built of seven twisted, rubber-coated wires which were hastily strung on trees or fences.

federate cipher messages which fell into Union hands. A notable incident in the field was the translation of General Joseph E. Johnston's cipher message to Pemberton, captured by Grant before Vicksburg and forwarded to Washington. More important were the two cipher despatches from the Secretary of War at Richmond, in December, 1863, which led to a cabinet meeting and culminated in the arrest of Confederate conspirators in New York city, and to the capture of contraband shipments of arms and ammunition. Other intercepted and translated ciphers revealed plans of Confederate agents for raiding Northern towns near the border. Most important of all were the cipher messages disclosing the plot for the wholesale incendiarism of leading hotels in New York, which barely failed of success on November 25, 1864.

Beneficial and desirable as were the civil cooperation and management of the telegraph service in Washington, its forced extension to armies in the field was a mistaken policy. Patterson, in the Valley of Virginia, was five days without word from the War Department, and when he sent a despatch, July 20th, that Johnston had started to reenforce Beauregard with 35,200 men, this vital message was not sent to McDowell with whom touch was kept by a service half-telegraphic and half-courier.

The necessity of efficient field-telegraphs at once impressed military commanders. In the West, Fremont immediately acted, and in August, 1861, ordered the formation of a telegraph battalion of three companies along lines in accord with modern military practice. Major Myer had already made similar suggestions in Washington, without success. While the commercial companies placed their personnel and material freely at the Government's disposal, they viewed with marked disfavor any military organization, and their recommendations were potent with Secretary of War Cameron. Fremont was ordered to disband his battalion, and a purely civil bureau was substituted, though legal authority and funds were equally lack-

A TELEGRAPH BATTERY–WAGON NEAR PETERSBURG, JUNE, 1864

The operator in this photograph is receiving a telegraphic message, writing at his little table in the wagon as the machine clicks off the dots and dashes. Each battery-wagon was equipped with such an operator's table and attached instruments. A portable battery of one hundred cells furnished the electric current. No feature of the Army of the Potomac contributed more to its success than the field telegraph. Guided by its young chief, A. H. Caldwell, its lines bound the corps together like a perfect nervous system, and kept the great controlling head in touch with all its parts. Not until Grant cut loose from Washington and started from Brandy Station for Richmond was its full power tested. Two operators and a few orderlies accompanied each wagon, and the army crossed the Rapidan with the telegraph line going up at the rate of two miles an hour. At no time after that did any corps lose direct communication with the commanding general. At Spotsylvania the Second Corps, at sundown, swung round from the extreme right in the rear of the main body to the left. Ewell saw the movement, and advanced toward the exposed position; but the telegraph signaled the danger, and troops on the double-quick covered the gap before the alert Confederate general could assault the Union lines.

ing. Efforts to transfer quartermaster's funds and property to this bureau were successfully resisted, owing to the manifest illegality of such action.

Indirect methods were then adopted, and Stager was commissioned as a captain in the Quartermaster's Department, and his operators given the status of employees. He was appointed general manager of United States telegraph lines, November 25, 1861, and six days later, through some unknown influence, the Secretary of War reported (incorrectly, be it known), "that under an appropriation for that purpose at the last session of Congress, a telegraph bureau was established." Stager was later made a colonel, Eckert a major, and a few others captains, and so eligible for pensions, but the men in lesser positions remained employees, non-pensionable and subject to draft.

Repeated efforts by petitions and recommendations for giving a military status were made by the men in the field later in the war. The Secretary of War disapproved, saying that such a course would place them under the orders of superior officers, which he was most anxious to avoid.

With corporation influence and corps rivalries so rampant in Washington, there existed a spirit of patriotic solidarity in the face of the foe in the field that ensured hearty cooperation and efficient service. While the operators began with a sense of individual independence that caused them often to resent any control by commanding officers, from which they were free under the secretary's orders, yet their common sense speedily led them to comply with every request from commanders that was not absolutely incompatible with loyalty to their chief.

Especially in the public eye was the work connected with the operations in the armies which covered Washington and attacked Richmond, where McClellan first used the telegraph for tactical purposes. Illustrative of the courage and resourcefulness of operators was the action of Jesse Bunnell, attached to General Porter's headquarters. Finding himself on the fight-

HEADQUARTERS FIELD–TELEGRAPH PARTY AT PETERSBURG, VIRGINIA, JUNE 22, 1864

A battery-wagon in "action"; the operator has opened his office and is working his instrument.   Important despatches were sent in cipher which only a chosen few operators could read.   The latter were frequently under fire but calmly sat at their instruments, with the shells flying thick about them, and performed their duty with a faithfulness that won them an enviable reputation.   At the Petersburg mine fiasco, in the vicinity of where this photograph was taken, an operator sat close at hand with an instrument and kept General Meade informed of the progress of affairs.   The triumph of the field telegraph exceeded the most sanguine expectations.   From the opening of Grant's campaign in the Wilderness to the close of the war, an aggregate of over two hundred miles of wire was put up and taken down from day to day; yet its efficiency as a constant means of communication between the several commands was not interfered with.   The Army of the Potomac was the first great military body to demonstrate the advantages of the field telegraph for conducting military operations.   The later campaigns of all civilized nations benefited much by these experiments.   The field telegraph was in constant use during the Russian-Japanese War.   **Wireless stations are now an integral part of the United States army organization.**

ing line, with the Federal troops hard pressed, Bunnell, without orders, cut the wire and opened communication with McClellan's headquarters. Superior Confederate forces were then threatening defeat to the invaders, but this battle-office enabled McClellan to keep in touch with the situation and ensure Porter's position by sending the commands of French, Meagher, and Slocum to his relief. Operator Nichols opened an emergency office at Savage's Station on Sumner's request, maintaining it under fire as long as it was needed.

One of the great feats of the war was the transfer, under the supervision of Thomas A. Scott, of two Federal army corps from Virginia to Tennessee, consequent on the Chickamauga disaster to the Union arms. By this phenomenal transfer, which would have been impossible without the military telegraph, twenty-three thousand soldiers, with provisions and baggage, were transported a distance of 1,233 miles in eleven and a half days, from Bristoe Station, Virginia, to Chattanooga, Tennessee. The troops had completed half their journey before the news of the proposed movement reached Richmond.

While most valuable elsewhere, the military telegraph was absolutely essential to successful operations in the valleys of the Cumberland and of the Tennessee, where very long lines of communication obtained, with consequent great distances between its separate armies. Apart from train-despatching, which was absolutely essential to transporting army supplies for hundreds of thousands of men over a single-track railway of several hundred of miles in length, an enormous number of messages for the control and cooperation of separate armies and detached commands were sent over the wires. Skill and patience were necessary for efficient telegraph work, especially when lines were frequently destroyed by Confederate incursions or through hostile inhabitants of the country.

Of great importance and of intense interest are many of the cipher despatches sent over these lines. Few, however, ex-

MEN WHO WORKED THE WIRES BEFORE PETERSBURG

These photographs of August, 1864, show some of the men who were operating their telegraph instruments in the midst of the cannonading and sharpshooting before Petersburg. Nerve-racking were the sounds and uncomfortably dangerous the situation, yet the operators held their posts. Amidst the terrible confusion of the night assault, the last despairing attempt of the Confederates to break through the encircling Federal forces, hurried orders and urgent appeals were sent. At dawn of March 25, 1865, General Gordon carried Fort Stedman with desperate gallantry and cut the wire to City Point. The Federals speedily sent the message of disaster: "The enemy has broken our right, taken Stedman, and are moving on City Point." Assuming command, General Parke ordered a counter-attack and recaptured the fort. The City Point wire was promptly restored and Meade, controlling the whole army by telegraph, made a combined and successful attack by several corps, capturing the entrenched picket-line of the Confederates.

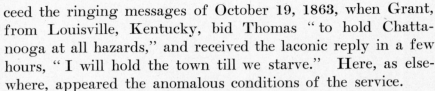

ceed the ringing messages of October 19, 1863, when Grant, from Louisville, Kentucky, bid Thomas " to hold Chattanooga at all hazards," and received the laconic reply in a few hours, " I will hold the town till we starve." Here, as elsewhere, appeared the anomalous conditions of the service.

While telegraph duties were performed with efficiency, troubles were often precipitated by divided authority. When Superintendent Stager ordered a civilian, who was engaged in building lines, out of Halleck's department, the general ordered him back, saying, " There must be one good head of telegraph lines in my department, not two, and that head must be under me." Though Stager protested to Secretary of War Stanton, the latter thought it best to yield in that case.

When General Grant found it expedient to appoint an aide as general manager of lines in his army, the civilian chief, J. C. Van Duzer, reported it to Stager, who had Grant called to account by the War Department. Grant promptly put Van Duzer under close confinement in the guardhouse, and later sent him out of the department, under guard. As an outcome, the operators planned a strike, which Grant quelled by telegraphic orders to confine closely every man resigning or guilty of contumacious conduct. Stager's efforts to dominate Grant failed through Stanton's fear that pressure would cause Grant to ask for relief from his command.

Stager's administration culminated in an order by his assistant, dated Cleveland, November 4, 1862, strictly requiring the operators to retain " the original copy of every telegram sent by any military or other Government officer . . . and mailed to the War Department." Grant answered, " Colonel Stager has no authority to demand the original of military despatches, and cannot have them." The order was never enforced, at least with Grant.

If similar experiences did not change the policy in Washington, it produced better conditions in the field and ensured harmonious cooperation. Of Van Duzer, it is to be said that

FRIENDS OF LINCOLN IN HIS LAST DAYS—MILITARY TELEGRAPH OPERATORS AT
CITY POINT, 1864

When Lincoln went to City Point at the request of General Grant, March 23, 1865, Grant directed his cipher operator to report to the President and keep him in touch by telegraph with the army in its advance on Richmond and with the War Department at Washington. For the last two or three weeks of his life Lincoln virtually lived in the telegraph office in company with the men in this photograph. He and Samuel H. Beckwith, Grant's cipher operator, were almost inseparable and the wires were kept busy with despatches to and from the President. Beckwith's tent adjoined the larger tent of Colonel Bowers, which Lincoln made his headquarters, and where he received the translations of his numerous cipher despatches.

he later returned to the army and performed conspicuous service. At the battle of Chattanooga, he installed and operated lines on or near the firing-line during the two fateful days, November 24–25, 1863, often under heavy fire. Always sharing the dangers of his men, Van Duzer, through his coolness and activity under fire, has been mentioned as the only fighting officer of the Federal telegraph service.

Other than telegraphic espionage, the most dangerous service was the repair of lines, which often was done under fire and more frequently in a guerilla-infested country. Many men were captured or shot from ambush while thus engaged. Two of Clowry's men in Arkansas were not only murdered, but were frightfully mutilated. In Tennessee, conditions were sometimes so bad that no lineman would venture out save under heavy escort. Three repair men were killed on the Fort Donelson line alone. W. R. Plum, in his "Military Telegraph," says that "about one in twelve of the operators engaged in the service were killed, wounded, captured, or died in the service from exposure."

Telegraphic duties at military headquarters yielded little in brilliancy and interest compared to those of desperate daring associated with tapping the opponent's wires. At times, offices were seized so quickly as to prevent telegraphic warnings. General Mitchel captured two large Confederate railway trains by sending false messages from the Huntsville, Alabama, office, and General Seymour similarly seized a train near Jacksonville, Florida.

While scouting, Operator William Forster obtained valuable despatches by tapping the line along the Charleston-Savannah railway for two days. Discovered, he was pursued by bloodhounds into a swamp, where he was captured up to his armpits in mire. Later, the telegrapher died in prison.

In 1863, General Rosecrans deemed it most important to learn whether Bragg was detaching troops to reenforce the garrison at Vicksburg or for other purposes. The only cer-

MILITARY TELEGRAPH OPERATORS AT CITY POINT, AUGUST, 1864

The men in this photograph, from left to right, are Dennis Doren, Superintendent of Construction; A. H. Caldwell, who was for four years cipher clerk at the headquarters of the Army of the Potomac; James A. Murray, who as wire-tapper of Confederate telegraph lines accompanied Kilpatrick in his raid toward Richmond and down the Peninsula in February, 1864, when the Union cavalry leader made his desperate attempt to liberate the Union prisoners in Libby prison. The fourth is J. H. Emerick, who was complimented for distinguished services in reporting Pleasonton's cavalry operations in 1863, and became cipher operator in Richmond in 1865. Through Emerick's foresight and activity the Union telegraph lines were carried into Richmond the night after its capture. Samuel H. Beckwith was the faithful cipher operator who accompanied Lincoln from City Point on his visit to Richmond April 4, 1865. In his account of this visit, published in "Lincoln in the Telegraph Office," by David Homer Bates, he tells how the President immediately repaired to his accustomed desk in Colonel Bowers' tent, next to the telegraph office, upon his return to City Point. Beckwith found a number of cipher messages for the President awaiting translation, doubtless in regard to Grant's closing in about the exhausted forces of Lee.

tain method seemed to be by tapping the wires along the Chattanooga railroad, near Knoxville, Tennessee. For this most dangerous duty, two daring members of the telegraph service volunteered—F. S. Van Valkenbergh and Patrick Mullarkey. The latter afterward was captured by Morgan, in Ohio. With four Tennesseeans, they entered the hostile country and, selecting a wooded eminence, tapped the line fifteen miles from Knoxville, and for a week listened to all passing despatches. Twice escaping detection, they heard a message going over the wire which ordered the scouring of the district to capture Union spies. They at once decamped, barely in time to escape the patrol. Hunted by cavalry, attacked by guerillas, approached by Confederate spies, they found aid from Union mountaineers, to whom they owed their safety. Struggling on, with capture and death in daily prospect, they finally fell in with Union pickets—being then half starved, clothed in rags, and with naked, bleeding feet. They had been thirty-three days within the Confederate lines, and their stirring adventures make a story rarely equaled in thrilling interest.

Confederate wires were often tapped during Sherman's march to the sea, a warning of General Wheeler's coming raid being thus obtained. Operator Lonergan copied important despatches from Hardee, in Savannah, giving Bragg's movements in the rear of Sherman, with reports on cavalry and rations.

Wiretapping was also practised by the Confederates, who usually worked in a sympathetic community. Despite their daring skill the net results were often small, owing to the Union system of enciphering all important messages. Their most audacious and persistent telegraphic scout was Ellsworth, Morgan's operator, whose skill, courage, and resourcefulness contributed largely to the success of his daring commander. Ellsworth was an expert in obtaining despatches, and especially in disseminating misleading information by bogus messages.

In the East, an interloper from Lee's army tapped the

WAR SERVICE OVER—MILITARY TELEGRAPH OPERATORS IN RICHMOND, JUNE, 1865

"The cipher operators with the various armies were men of rare skill, unswerving integrity, and unfailing loyalty," General Greeley pronounces from personal knowledge. Caldwell, as chief operator, accompanied the Army of the Potomac on every march and in every siege, contributing also to the efficiency of the field telegraphers. Beckwith remained Grant's cipher operator to the end of the war. He it was who tapped a wire and reported the hiding-place of Wilkes Booth. The youngest boy operator, O'Brien, began by refusing a princely bribe to forge a telegraphic reprieve, and later won distinction with Butler on the James and with Schofield in North Carolina. W. R. Plum, who wrote a "History of the Military Telegraph in the Civil War," also rendered efficient service as chief operator to Thomas, and at Atlanta. The members of the group are, from left to right: 1, Dennis Doren, Superintendent of Construction; 2, L. D. McCandless; 3, Charles Bart; 4, Thomas Morrison; 5, James B. Norris; 6, James Caldwell; 7, A. Harper Caldwell, chief cipher operator, and in charge; 8, Maynard A. Huyck; 9, Dennis Palmer; 10, J. H. Emerick; 11, James H. Nichols. Those surviving in June, 1911, were Morrison, Norris, and Nichols.

wire between the War Department and Burnside's headquarters at Aquia Creek, and remained undetected for probably several days. With fraternal frankness, the Union operators advised him to leave.

The most prolonged and successful wiretapping was that by C. A. Gaston, Lee's confidential operator. Gaston entered the Union lines near City Point, while Richmond and Petersburg were besieged, with several men to keep watch for him, and for six weeks he remained undisturbed in the woods, reading all messages which passed over Grant's wire. Though unable to read the ciphers, he gained much from the despatches in plain text. One message reported that 2,586 beeves were to be landed at Coggins' Point on a certain day. This information enabled Wade Hampton to make a timely raid and capture the entire herd.

It seems astounding that Grant, Sherman, Thomas, and Meade, commanding armies of hundreds of thousands and working out the destiny of the Republic, should have been debarred from the control of their own ciphers and the keys thereto. Yet, in 1864, the Secretary of War issued an order forbidding commanding generals to interfere with even their own cipher-operators and absolutely restricting the use of cipher-books to civilian " telegraph experts, approved and appointed by the Secretary of War." One mortifying experience with a despatch untranslatable for lack of facilities constrained Grant to order his cipher-operator, Beckwith, to reveal the key to Colonel Comstock, his aide, which was done under protest. Stager at once dismissed Beckwith, but on Grant's request and insistence of his own responsibility, Beckwith was restored.

The cipher-operators with the various armies were men of rare skill, unswerving integrity, and unfailing loyalty. Caldwell, as chief operator, accompanied the Army of the Potomac on every march and in every siege, contributing also to the efficiency of the field-telegraphs. Beckwith was Grant's cipher-

A TELEGRAPH OFFICE IN THE TRENCHES

In this photograph are more of the "minute men" who helped the Northern leaders to draw the coils closer about Petersburg with their wonderful system of instantaneous intercommunication. They brought the commanding generals actually within seconds of each other, though miles of fortifications might intervene. There has evidently been a lull in affairs, and they have been dining at their ease. Two of them in the background are toasting each other, it may be for the last time. The mortality among those men who risked their lives, with no hope or possibility of such distinction and recognition as come to the soldier who wins promotion, was exceedingly high.

operator to the end of the war, and was the man who tapped a wire and reported the hiding-place of Wilkes Booth. Another operator, Richard O'Brien, in 1863 refused a princely bribe to forge a telegraphic reprieve, and later won distinction with Butler on the James and with Schofield in North Carolina. W. R. Plum, who wrote " History of the Military Telegraph in the Civil War," also rendered efficient service as chief operator to Thomas, and at Atlanta. It is regrettable that such men were denied the glory and benefits of a military service, which they actually, though not officially, gave.

The bitter contest, which lasted several years, over field-telegraphs ended in March, 1864, when the Signal Corps transferred its field-trains to the civilian bureau. In Sherman's advance on Atlanta, Van Duzer distinguished himself by bringing up the field-line from the rear nearly every night. At Big Shanty, Georgia, the whole battle-front was covered by working field-lines which enabled Sherman to communicate at all times with his fighting and reserve commands. Hamley considers the constant use of field-telegraphs in the flanking operations by Sherman in Georgia as showing the overwhelming value of the service. This duty was often done under fire and other dangerous conditions.

In Virginia, in 1864–65, Major Eckert made great and successful efforts to provide Meade's army with ample facilities. A well-equipped train of thirty or more battery-wagons, wire-reels, and construction carts were brought together under Doren, a skilled builder and energetic man. While offices were occasionally located in battery-wagons, they were usually under tent-flies next to the headquarters of Meade or Grant. Through the efforts of Doren and Caldwell, all important commands were kept within control of either Meade or Grant—even during engagements. Operators were often under fire, and at Spotsylvania Court House telegraphers, telegraph-cable, and battery-wagons were temporarily within the Confederate lines. From these trains was sent the ringing des-

THE TELEGRAPH CONSTRUCTION TRAIN, IN RICHMOND AT LAST

This train, under the direction of Mr. A. Harper Caldwell, Chief Operator of the Army of the Potomac, was used in the construction of field-telegraph lines during the Wilderness campaign and in operations before Petersburg. After the capture of Richmond it was used by Superintendent Dennis Doren to restore the important telegraph routes of which that city was the center. In Virginia in 1864-5, Major Eckert made great and successful efforts to provide Meade's army with ample facilities. A well-equipped train of thirty or more battery wagons, wire-reels, and construction carts was brought together under the skilful and energetic Doren.

patch from the Wilderness, by which Grant inspired the North, " I propose to fight it out on this line if it takes all summer."

During siege operations at Petersburg, a system of lines connected the various headquarters, depots, entrenchments, and even some picket lines. Cannonading and sharpshooting were so insistent that operators were often driven to bomb-proof offices—especially during artillery duels and impending assaults. Nerve-racking were the sounds and uncomfortably dangerous the situations, yet the operators held their posts. Under the terrible conditions of a night assault, the last despairing attempt to break through the encircling Federal forces at Petersburg, hurried orders and urgent appeals were sent. At dawn of March 25, 1865, General Gordon carried Fort Stedman with desperate gallantry, and cut the wire to City Point. The Federals speedily sent the message of disaster, " The enemy has broken our right, taken Stedman, and are moving on City Point." Assuming command, General Parke ordered a counter-attack and recaptured the fort. Promptly the City Point wire was restored, and Meade, controlling the whole army by telegraph, made a combined attack by several corps, capturing the entrenched picket line of the Confederates.

First of all of the great commanders, Grant used the military telegraph both for grand tactics and for strategy in its broadest sense. From his headquarters with Meade's army in Virginia, May, 1864, he daily gave orders and received reports regarding the operations of Meade in Virginia, Sherman in Georgia, Sigel in West Virginia, and Butler on the James River. Later he kept under direct control military forces exceeding half a million of soldiers, operating over a territory of eight hundred thousand square miles in area. Through concerted action and timely movements, Grant prevented the re-enforcement of Lee's army and so shortened the war. Sherman said, " The value of the telegraph cannot be exaggerated, as illustrated by the perfect accord of action of the armies of Virginia and Georgia."

PART II
MILITARY INFORMATION

ARMY
BALLOONS

OBSERVING THE BATTLE OF FAIR OAKS, MAY, 1862
PROFESSOR LOWE IN HIS BALLOON

THE BALLOONS WITH THE ARMY OF THE POTOMAC

By T. S. C. Lowe

A personal reminiscence by Professor T. S. C. Lowe, who introduced and made balloon observations on the Peninsula for the Union army

IT was through the midnight observations with one of my war-balloons that I was enabled to discover that the fortifications at Yorktown were being evacuated, and at my request General Heintzelman made a trip with me that he might confirm the truth of my discovery. The entire great fortress was ablaze with bonfires, and the greatest activity prevailed, which was not visible except from the balloon. At first the general was puzzled on seeing more wagons entering the forts than were going out, but when I called his attention to the fact that the ingoing wagons were light and moved rapidly (the wheels being visible as they passed each camp-fire), while the outgoing wagons were heavily loaded and moved slowly, there was no longer any doubt as to the object of the Confederates. General Heintzelman then accompanied me to General McClellan's headquarters for a consultation, while I, with orderlies, aroused other quietly sleeping corps commanders in time to put our whole army in motion in the very early hours of the morning, so that we were enabled to overtake the Confederate army at Williamsburg, an easy day's march beyond Yorktown on the road to Richmond.

Firing the day before had started early in the morning and continued until dark, every gun in the fortification being turned on the balloon, and then the next morning they were still pointing upward in the hope of preventing us in some way from further annoying the Confederates by watching their

CONFEDERATE BATTERY AT YORKTOWN WHICH FIRED UPON THE FEDERAL BALLOONIST AND UPON
WHICH "BALLOON BRYAN" LOOKED DOWN

Captain John Randolph Bryan, aide-de-camp to General J. B. Magruder, then commanding the Army of the Peninsula near Yorktown, Virginia, made three balloon trips in all above the wonderful panorama of the Chesapeake Bay, the York and the James Rivers,
Old Point Comfort and Hampton, the fleets lying in both the York and the James, and the two opposing armies facing each other
across the Peninsula. General Johnston complimented him upon the detailed information which he secured in this fashion, braving
the shells and shrapnel of the Union batteries, and his fellow-soldiers nicknamed the young aeronaut "Balloon Bryan." On his final
trip, made just before Williamsburg, May 5, 1862, the rope which held him to the earth entangled a soldier. It was cut. The balloon
bounded two miles into the air. First it drifted out over the Union lines, then was blown back toward the Confederate lines near
Yorktown. The Confederates, seeing it coming from that direction, promptly opened fire. Finally it skimmed the surface of the
York River, its guide-rope splashing in the water, and landed in an orchard. On this trip the balloon made a half-moon circuit of
about fifteen miles, about four miles of which was over the York River. The information which Captain Bryan was able to give
General Johnston as to the roads upon which the Federals were moving enabled him to prepare for an attack the following morning.

movements. The last shot, fired after dark, came into General Heintzelman's camp and completely destroyed his telegraph tent and instruments, the operator having just gone out to deliver a despatch. The general and I were sitting together, discussing the probable reasons for the unusual effort to destroy the balloon, when we were both covered with what appeared to be tons of earth, which a great 12-inch shell had thrown up. Fortunately, it did not explode. I suggested that the next morning we should move the balloon so as to draw the foe's fire in another direction, but the general said that he could stand it if I could. Besides, he would like to have me near by, as he enjoyed going up occasionally himself. He told me that, while I saw a grand spectacle by watching the discharge of all those great guns that were paying their entire compliments to a single man, it was nothing as compared with the sight I would look down upon the next day when our great mortar batteries would open their siege-guns on the fortifications, which General McClellan expected to do.

I could see readily that I could be of no service at Williamsburg, both armies being hidden in a great forest. Therefore, General McClellan at the close of the battle sent orders to me to proceed with my outfit, including all the balloons, gas-generators, the balloon-inflating boat, gunboat, and tug up the Pamunkey River, until I reached White House and the bridge crossing the historic river, and join the army which would be there as soon as myself.

This I did, starting early the next morning, passing by the great cotton-bale fortifications on the York River, and soon into the little winding but easily navigated stream of the Pamunkey. Every now and then I would let the balloon go up to view the surrounding country, and over the bridge beyond the Pamunkey River valley, I saw the rear of the retreating Confederates, which showed me that our army had not gotten along as fast as it was expected, and I could occasionally see a few scouts on horseback on the hills beyond. I saw my helpless

Professor T. S. C. Lowe appears here standing by his father in camp before the battle of Fair Oaks, explaining by means of an engineers' map the service he proposed to render the Union army. Below is the balloon from which General George Stoneman, McClellan's cavalry leader on the Peninsula, and Professor Lowe were able to look into the windows of Richmond. In this balloon also Professor Lowe was telegraphing, reporting, and sketching during the battle of May 31–June 1st, and it was from his night observations at this time that came knowledge on which McClellan acted in saving his army. On arriving in sight of Richmond, Lowe took observations to ascertain the best location for crossing the Chickahominy River and sketched the place where the

PROFESSOR LOWE AND HIS FATHER

"Grapevine" or Sumner Bridge was afterward built across that stream. His main station and personal camp lay on Gaines' Hill, four miles from Mechanicsville, overlooking the bridge where the army was to cross. Desperate efforts were made by the Confederates at Mechanicsville to destroy the observation balloon in order to conceal their movements. At one point they masked twelve of their best rifled cannon; while Professor Lowe was taking an early morning observation, the whole twelve guns were simultaneously discharged at short range, some of the shells passing through the rigging of the balloon and nearly all bursting not more than two hundred feet beyond it. Professor Lowe immediately changed his base of operations, and escaped the imminent danger.

AT "BALLOON CAMP," GAINES' HILL, WHILE THE TWO ARMIES WAITED

condition without my gunboat, the *Cœur de Lion,* which had served me for the past year so well on the Potomac, Chesapeake, and York, and which I had sent to Commodore Wilkes to aid him in the bombardment of Fort Darling, on the James River, thinking I would have no further use for it. Therefore, all I had was the balloon-boat and the steam-tug and one hundred and fifty men with muskets, a large number of wagons and gas-generators for three independent balloon outfits. My balloon-boat was almost a facsimile of our first little *Monitor* and about its size, and with the flag which I kept at the stern it had the appearance of an armed craft, which I think is all that saved me and my command, for the *Monitor* was what the Confederates dreaded at that time more than anything else.

After General Stoneman had left me at White House, I soon had a gas-generating apparatus beside a little pool of water, and from it extracted hydrogen enough in an hour to take both the general and myself to an altitude that enabled us to look into the windows of the city of Richmond and view its surroundings, and we saw what was left of the troops that had left Yorktown encamped about the city.

While my illness at Malvern Hill prevented me from reporting to headquarters until the army reached Antietam, those in charge of transportation in Washington took all my wagons and horses and left my command without transportation. Consequently I could render no service there, but the moment General McClellan saw me he expressed his regret that I had been so ill, and that he did not have the benefit of my services; for if he had he could have gotten the proper information, he could have prevented a great amount of stores and artillery from recrossing the Potomac and thus depleted the Confederate army that much more. I explained to him why he had been deprived of my services, which did not surprise him, because he stated that everything had been done to annoy him, but that he must still perform his duty regardless of

SAVING "A MILLION DOLLARS A MINUTE" IN 1862

This is a photograph of a feat that would be noteworthy in the twentieth century, and in 1862 was revolutionary—actually being performed on the field of battle. At Fair Oaks, May 31, 1862, the lifting force of the balloon *Constitution* proved too weak to carry up the telegraph apparatus, its wires, and cables to a height sufficient to overlook the forests and hills. "I was at my wit's end," writes Professor Lowe, "as to how I could best save an hour's time—the most precious and important hour of all my experience in the army. As I saw the two armies coming nearer and nearer together, there was no time to be lost. It flashed through my mind that if I could only get the gas which was in the smaller balloon *Constitution* into the balloon *Intrepid*, which was then half filled, I would save an hour's time, and to us that hour's time would be worth a million dollars a minute." By the ingenious use of a 10-inch camp kettle with the bottom cut out, a connection was made and the gas in the *Constitution* was transferred to the *Intrepid*.

annoyances. When I asked him if I should accompany him across the river in pursuit of Lee, he replied that he would see that I had my supply trains immediately, but that the troops after so long a march were nearly all barefoot, and in no condition to proceed until they had been properly shod and clothed.

Without the time and knowledge gained by the midnight observations referred to at the beginning of this chapter, there would have been no battle of Williamsburg, and McClellan would have lost the opportunity of gaining a victory, the importance of which has never been properly appreciated. The Confederates would have gotten away with all their stores and ammunition without injury. It was also my night observations that gave the primary knowledge which saved the Federal army at the battle of Fair Oaks.

On arriving in sight of Richmond, I took observations to ascertain the best location for crossing the Chickahominy River. The one selected was where the Grapevine, or Sumner, Bridge was afterward built across that stream. Mechanicsville was the point nearest to Richmond, being only about four miles from the capital, but there we would have had to face the gathering army of the Confederacy, at the only point properly provided with trenches and earthworks. Here I established one of my aeronautic stations, where I could better estimate the increase of the Confederate army and observe their various movements. My main station and personal camp was on Gaines' Hill, overlooking the bridge where our army was to cross.

When this bridge was completed, about half of our army crossed over on the Richmond side of the river, the remainder delaying for a while to protect our transportation supplies and railway facilities. In the mean time, the Confederate camp in and about Richmond grew larger every day.

My night-and-day observations convinced me that with the great army then assembled in and about Richmond we were too late to gain a victory, which a short time before was within our grasp. In the mean time, desperate efforts were made by

PROFESSOR LOWE IN HIS BALLOON AT A CRITICAL MOMENT

As soon as Professor Lowe's balloon soars above the top of the trees the Confederate batteries will open upon him, and for the next few moments shells and bullets from the shrapnels will be bursting and whistling about his ears. Then he will pass out of the danger-zone to an altitude beyond the reach of the Confederate artillery. After the evacuation of Yorktown, May 4, 1862, Professor Lowe, who had been making daily observations from his balloon, followed McClellan's divisions, which was to meet Longstreet next day at Williamsburg. On reaching the fortifications of the abandoned city, Lowe directed the men who were towing the still inflated balloon in which he was riding to scale the corner of the fort nearest to his old camp, where the last gun had been fired the night before. This fort had devoted a great deal of effort to attempting to damage the too inquisitive balloon, and a short time previously one of the best Confederate guns had burst, owing to over-charging and too great an elevation to reach the high altitude. The balloonist had witnessed the explosion and a number of gunners had been killed and wounded within his sight. His present visit was in order to touch and examine the pieces and bid farewell to what he then looked upon as a departed friend. This is indicated as the same gun on page 371.

the Confederates to destroy my balloon at Mechanicsville, in order to prevent my observing their movements.

At one point they masked twelve of their best rifle-cannon, and while taking an early morning observation, all the twelve guns were simultaneously discharged at short range, some of the shells passing through the rigging of the balloon and nearly all bursting not more than two hundred feet beyond me, showing that through spies they had gotten my base of operations and range perfectly. I changed my base, and they never came so near destroying the balloon or capturing me after that.

I felt that it was important to take thorough observations that very night at that point, which I did. The great camps about Richmond were ablaze with fires. I had then experience enough to know what this meant, that they were cooking rations preparatory to moving. I knew that this movement must be against that portion of the army then across the river. At daylight the next morning, May 31st, I took another observation, continuing the same until the sun lighted up the roads. The atmosphere was perfectly clear. I knew exactly where to look for their line of march, and soon discovered one, then two, and then three columns of troops with artillery and ammunition wagons moving toward the position occupied by General Heintzelman's command.

All this information was conveyed to the commanding general, who, on hearing my report that the force at both ends of the bridge was too slim to finish it that morning, immediately sent more men to work on it.

I used the balloon *Washington* at Mechanicsville for observations, until the Confederate army was within four or five miles of our lines. I then telegraphed my assistants to inflate the large balloon, *Intrepid,* in case anything should happen to either of the other two. This order was quickly carried out, and I then took a six-mile ride on horseback to my camp on Gaines' Hill, and made another observation from the balloon

THE PHOTOGRAPH THE BALLOONIST RECOGNIZED FORTY-EIGHT YEARS AFTER

"When I saw the photograph showing my inflation of the balloon *Intrepid* to reconnoiter the battle of Fair Oaks," wrote Professor T. S. C. Lowe in the *American Review of Reviews* for February, 1911, "it surprised me very much indeed.   Any one examining the picture will see my hand at the extreme right, resting on the network, where I was measuring the amount of gas already in the balloon, preparatory to completing the inflation from gas in the smaller balloon in order that I might ascent to a greater height.   This I did within a space of five minutes, saving a whole hour at the most vital point of the battle."   A close examination of this photograph will reveal Professor Lowe's hand resting on the network of the balloon, although his body is not in the photograph.   It truly is remarkable that Professor Lowe should have seen and recognized, nearly half a century afterward, this photograph taken at one of the most critical moments of his life.

Constitution. I found it necessary to double the altitude usually sufficient for observations in order to overlook forests and hills, and thus better to observe the movements of both our army and that of the Confederates.

To carry my telegraph apparatus, wires, and cables to this higher elevation, the lifting force of the *Constitution* proved to be too weak. It was then that I was put to my wits' end as to how I could best save an hour's time, which was the most important and precious hour of all my experience in the army. As I saw the two armies coming nearer and nearer together, there was no time to be lost. It flashed through my mind that if I could only get the gas that was in the smaller balloon, *Constitution,* into the *Intrepid,* which was then half filled, I would save an hour's time, and to us that hour's time would be worth a million dollars a minute. But how was I to rig up the proper connection between the balloons? To do this within the space of time necessary puzzled me until I glanced down and saw a 10-inch camp-kettle, which instantly gave me the key to the situation. I ordered the bottom cut out of the kettle, the *Intrepid* disconnected with the gas-generating apparatus, and the *Constitution* brought down the hill. In the course of five or six minutes connection was made between both balloons and the gas in the *Constitution* was transferred into the *Intrepid.*

I immediately took a high-altitude observation as rapidly as possible, wrote my most important despatch to the commanding general on my way down, and I dictated it to my expert telegraph operator. Then with the telegraph cable and instruments, I ascended to the height desired and remained there almost constantly during the battle, keeping the wires hot with information.

The Confederate skirmish line soon came in contact with our outposts, and I saw their whole well-laid plan. They had massed the bulk of their artillery and troops, not only with the intention of cutting off our ammunition supplies, but of

[380]

COMPLETING A DESPATCH AT FAIR OAKS BEFORE THE ASCENSION
DURING THE BATTLE OF FAIR OAKS
MAY 31, 1862

It was during the American Civil War that war information was first telegraphed from the sky. This photograph shows Professor Lowe during the battle of Fair Oaks, completing a despatch just before ascending with telegraph apparatus and wire. "It was one of the greatest strains upon my nerves that I have ever experienced," he writes in regard to this ascension, "to observe for many hours an almost drawn battle, while the Union forces were waiting to complete the bridge to connect their separated army. This fortunately was accomplished, and our first troops under Sumner's command were able to cross at four o'clock in the afternoon, followed by wagons of ammunition for those who needed it. Earlier in the day many brigades and regiments had entirely exhausted their ammunition. Brave Heintzelman rode along the line giving orders for the men to shout in order to deceive the Confederates as to their real situation. When Sumner's troops swung into line, I could hear a real shout, which sounded entirely different from the former response."

preventing the main portion of the army from crossing the bridge to join Heintzelman.

As I reported the movements and maneuvers of the Confederates, I could see, in a very few moments, that our army was maneuvering to offset their plans.

At about twelve o'clock, the whole lines of both armies were in deadly conflict. Ours not only held its line firmly, but repulsed the foe at all his weaker points.

It was one of the greatest strains upon my nerves that I ever have experienced, to observe for many hours a fierce battle, while waiting for the bridge connecting the two armies to be completed. This fortunately was accomplished and our first reenforcements, under Sumner, were able to cross at four o'clock in the afternoon, followed by ammunition wagons.

It was at that time that the first and only Confederate balloon was used during the war. This balloon, which I afterward captured, was described by General Longstreet as follows:*

It may be of interest at the outset to relate an incident which illustrates the pinched condition of the Confederacy even as early as 1862.

The Federals had been using balloons in examining our positions, and we watched with envious eyes their beautiful observations as they floated high up in the air, well out of range of our guns. While we were longing for the balloons that poverty denied us, a genius arose for the occasion and suggested that we send out and gather silk dresses in the Confederacy and make a balloon. It was done, and we soon had a great patchwork ship of many varied hues which was ready for use in the Seven Days' campaign.

We had no gas except in Richmond, and it was the custom to inflate the balloon there, tie it securely to an engine, and run it down the York River Railroad to any point at which we desired to send it up. One day it was on a steamer down on the James River, when the tide went out and left the vessel and balloon high and dry on a bar. The Federals gathered it in, and with it the last silk dress in the Confederacy. This capture was the meanest trick of the war and one that I have never yet forgiven.

*Battles and Leaders of the Civil War. (New York.)

[382]

ONE OF THE BOY SOLDIERS

CHARLES F. MOSBY, A CONFEDERATE DRUMMER-BOY
WHO ENLISTED AT THE AGE OF THIRTEEN AND SERVED
FROM '61 TO '65 THROUGHOUT THE WAR, FIRST WITH
THE "ELLIOTT GRAYS" OF THE SIXTH VIRGINIA INFAN-
TRY AND LATER WITH HENDERSON'S HEAVY ARTILLERY.